T0211785

Lecture Notes in Computer Science 14415

Founding Editors

Gerhard Goos
Juris Hartmanis

Editorial Board Members

The series Lecture Notes in Computer Science (LNCS), including its subseries Lecture Notes in Artificial Intelligence (LNAI) and Lecture Notes in Bioinformatics (LNBI), has established itself as a medium for the publication of new developments in computer science and information technology research, teaching, and education.

LNCS enjoys close cooperation with the computer science R & D community, the series counts many renowned academics among its volume editors and paper authors, and collaborates with prestigious societies. Its mission is to serve this international community by providing an invaluable service, mainly focused on the publication of conference and workshop proceedings and postproceedings. LNCS commenced publication in 1973.

Paolo Arcaini · Tao Yue · Erik M. Fredericks
Editors

Search-Based Software Engineering

15th International Symposium, SSBSE 2023
San Francisco, CA, USA, December 8, 2023
Proceedings

 Springer

Editors
Paolo Arcaini (iD)
National Institute of Informatics
Tokyo, Japan

Tao Yue (iD)
Beihang University
Beijing, China

Erik M. Fredericks (iD)
Grand Valley State University
Allendale, MI, USA

ISSN 0302-9743   ISSN 1611-3349 (electronic)
Lecture Notes in Computer Science
ISBN 978-3-031-48795-8   ISBN 978-3-031-48796-5 (eBook)
https://doi.org/10.1007/978-3-031-48796-5

This Springer imprint is published by the registered company Springer Nature Switzerland AG
The registered company address is: Gewerbestrasse 11, 6330 Cham, Switzerland

Paper in this product is recyclable.

Preface

Message from the General Chair

We are very excited to bring you the proceedings of the 15th edition of the International Symposium on Search-Based Software Engineering (SSBSE 2023). SSBSE is a premier event for all who are interested in the intersection of search optimization and difficult software engineering problems spanning numerous domains. This year SSBSE was held as a hybrid event; physically located in San Francisco, California, USA and remote for those that were unable to attend in person. We continue to be co-located with ESEC/FSE and are grateful for their support of our symposium.

Thank you to Tao Yue and Paolo Arcaini for putting together an exciting research track program; without your constant feedback and support planning this event would have been extremely difficult! I would also like to thank the track chairs for their hard work supporting SSBSE as well: Rebecca Moussa and Thomas Vogel (Hot Off the Press track), Gregory Gay and Max Hort (RENE/NIER track), and Bobby Bruce, José Miguel Rojas, and Vali Tawosi (Challenge track). I would also like to thank Alexander Lalejini for his work on the SSBSE website and Emeralda Sesari for her work on publicizing our event. Many thanks to our multiple Program Committees as well for their tireless work on reviewing papers and suggesting improvements and to our Steering Committee for continuing to oversee and support this event.

Very special thanks to our sponsor, Grand Valley State University. I would also like to thank Satish Chandra from Google for his support as the general chair of ESEC/FSE 2023, as well as Federica Sarro at University College London as a point of contact in the Steering Committee for continuing support whenever an issue arose that I did not have an answer for.

I enjoyed seeing you all at SSBSE 2023 and hope you enjoyed the program!

December 2023   Erik Fredericks

Message from the Program Chairs

Speaking for the SSBSE 2023 Program Committee, we are delighted to introduce the proceedings of the 15th International Symposium on Search-Based Software Engineering. Search-Based Software Engineering (SBSE) focuses on formulating various optimization problems in software engineering as search problems and then addressing them with search techniques, intending to automate complex software engineering tasks. A wide class of software engineering challenges can be formulated into SBSE problems, including test optimization, design and code refactoring, software/system development process optimization, and many more, which have been addressed with various search techniques. The community continuously advances the field by identifying, formulating, and solving new challenges such as searching for critical driving scenarios for testing autonomous vehicles, optimizing the energy consumption of software applications, and automating hyperparameter tuning of machine learning models.

SSBSE 2023 upheld the longstanding tradition of SSBSE by gathering the SBSE community yearly to share and discuss advancements in the field. This year, we welcomed submissions showcasing innovative contributions across all SBSE domains. Specifically, we received 13 submissions to the main Research track, four to the Replications and Negative Results (RENE)/New Ideas and Emerging Results (NIER) track, six to the SBSE Challenge track, and two to the Hot Off the Press (HOP) track. Each valid submission to the Research track were double-blind reviewed by at least three PC members and, eventually, six papers were accepted. For the RENE/NIER track, three papers were accepted. For the SBSE Challenge track, five papers were accepted. The HOP track accepted two papers.

December 2023

Paolo Arcaini
Tao Yue

Organization

General Chair

Erik Fredericks — Grand Valley State University, USA

Research Track Chairs

Paolo Arcaini — National Institute of Informatics, Japan
Tao Yue — Beihang University, China

Hot Off the Press Track Chairs

Rebecca Moussa — University College London, UK
Thomas Vogel — Humboldt-Universtität zu Berlin, Germany

RENE/NIER Track Chairs

Gregory Gay — Chalmers—University of Gothenburg, Sweden
Max Hort — Simula Research Laboratory, Norway

Challenge Track Chairs

Bobby Bruce — University of California at Davis, USA
José Miguel Rojas — University of Sheffield, UK
Vali Tawosi — J. P. Morgan AI Research, UK

Publicity Chair

Emeralda Sesari — University of Groningen, The Netherlands

Web Chair

Alexander Lalejini   Grand Valley State University, USA

Steering Committee

Shaukat Ali   Simula Research Laboratory and Oslo
                                     Metropolitan University, Norway
Andrea Arcuri   Kristiania University College and Oslo
                                     Metropolitan University, Norway
Giovani Guizzo   University College London, UK
Gordon Fraser   University of Passau, Germany
Phil McMinn   University of Sheffield, UK
Justyna Petke   University College London, UK
Federica Sarro   University College London, UK
Silva Regina Vergilio   Federal University of Paraná, Brazil
Shin Yoo   KAIST, Republic of Korea

Research Track Committee

Paolo Arcaini (Chair)   National Institute of Informatics, Japan
Tao Yue (Chair)   Beihang University, China
Shaukat Ali   Simula Research Laboratory and Oslo
                                     Metropolitan University, Norway
Andrea Arcuri   Kristiania University College and Oslo
                                     Metropolitan University, Norway
Aitor Arrieta   Mondragon University, Spain
Marcio Barros   Universidade Federal do Estado do Rio de
                                     Janeiro, Brazil
Matteo Biagiola   Università della Svizzera Italiana, Italy
Betty H. C. Cheng   Michigan State University, USA
Pouria Derakhshanfar   JetBrains Research, The Netherlands
Xavier Devroey   University of Namur, Belgium
Thiago Ferreira   University of Michigan - Flint, USA
Gordon Fraser   University of Passau, Germany
Alessio Gambi   IMC University of Applied Sciences Krems,
                                     Austria
Gregory Gay   Chalmers—University of Gothenburg, Sweden
Lars Grunske   Humboldt-Universität zu Berlin, Germany
Hadi Hemmati   York University, Canada

Fuyuki Ishikawa	National Institute of Informatics, Japan
Fitsum Kifetew	Fondazione Bruno Kessler, Italy
Thelma Elita Colanzi Lopez	State University of Maringá, Brazil .
Phil McMinn	University of Sheffield, UK
Inmaculada Medina-Bulo	Universidad de Cádiz, Spain
Leandro Minku	University of Birmingham, UK
Manuel Núñez	Universidad Complutense de Madrid, Spain
Annibale Panichella	Delft University of Technology, The Netherlands
Vincenzo Riccio	University of Udine, Italy
José Miguel Rojas	University of Sheffield, UK
Federica Sarro	University College London, UK
Jeongju Sohn	University of Luxembourg, Luxembourg
Valerio Terragni	University of Auckland, New Zealand
Silva Regina Vergilio	Federal University of Paraná, Brazil
Thomas Vogel	Humboldt-Universtität zu Berlin, Germany
Man Zhang	Kristiania University College, Norway

RENE/NIER Track Committee

Gregory Gay (Chair)	Chalmers—University of Gothenburg, Sweden
Max Hort (Chair)	Simula Research Laboratory, Norway
Gabin An	KAIST, Republic of Korea
Marcio Barros	UNIRIO, Brazil
Carlos Cetina	San Jorge University, Spain
Michael C. Gerten	Iowa State University, USA
Emanuele Iannone	University of Salerno, Italy
Bruno Lima	University of Porto and INESC TEC, Portugal
Ruchika Malhotra	Delhi Technological University, India
Pasqualina Potena	RISE Research Institutes of Sweden AB, Sweden
José Raúl Romero	University of Cordoba, Spain
Jeongju Sohn	University of Luxembourg, Luxembourg
Andrea Stocco	Technical University of Munich & fortiss, Germany
Fiorella Zampetti	University of Sannio, Italy

Challenge Track Committee

Bobby Bruce (Chair)	University of California at Davis, USA
José Miguel Rojas (Chair)	University of Sheffield, UK

Vali Tawosi (Chair)   J. P. Morgan AI Research, UK
Wesley Assunção   North Carolina State University, USA
Kate M. Bowers   Oakland University, USA
José Campos   University of Porto, Portugal
Tao Chen   University of Birmingham, UK
Thelma Elita   State University of Maringá, Brazil
Colanzi Lopez   .
Gregory Kapfhammer   Allegheny College, USA
Stephan Lukasczyk   University of Passau, Germany
Inmaculada Medina-Bulo   Universidad de Cádiz, Spain
Rebecca Moussa   University College London, UK
Sebastian Schweikl   University of Passau, Germany

Keynotes

Search-Based Software Engineering for Learning-Enabled Self-Adaptive Systems

Betty H. C. Cheng

Michigan State University, USA

Abstract. Trustworthy artificial intelligence (Trusted AI) is essential when autonomous, safety-critical systems use learning-enabled components (LECs) in uncertain environments. When reliant on deep learning, these learning-enabled systems (LES) must address the reliability, interpretability, and robustness (collectively, the assurance) of learning models. Three types of uncertainty most significantly affect assurance. First, uncertainty about the physical environment can cause suboptimal, and sometimes catastrophic, results as the system struggles to adapt to unanticipated or poorly understood environmental conditions. For example, when lane markings are occluded (either on the camera and/or the physical lanes), lane management functionality can be critically compromised. Second, uncertainty in the cyber environment can create unexpected and adverse consequences, including not only performance impacts (network load, real-time responses, etc.) but also potential threats or overt (cybersecurity) attacks. Third, uncertainty can exist with the components themselves and affect how they interact upon reconfiguration. Left unchecked, this may cause unexpected and unwanted feature interactions. While learning-enabled technologies have made great strides in addressing uncertainty, challenges remain in addressing the assurance of such systems when encountering uncertainty not addressed in training data. Furthermore, we need to consider LESs as first-class software-based systems that should be rigorously developed, verified, and maintained (i.e., software engineered). In addition to developing specific strategies to address these concerns, appropriate software architectures are needed to coordinate LECs and ensure they deliver acceptable behavior even under uncertain conditions. To this end, this presentation overviews a number of our multi-disciplinary research projects involving industrial collaborators, which collectively support a search-based software engineering, model-based approach to address Trusted AI and provide assurance for learning-enabled systems (i.e., SBSE4LES). In addition to sharing lessons learned from more than two decades of research addressing assurance for (learning-enabled) self-adaptive systems operating under a range of uncertainty, near-term and longer-term research challenges for addressing assurance of LESs will be overviewed.

SSBSE Summary of .NET/C# Instrumentation for Search-Based Software Testing

Amid Golmohammadi[1] , Man Zhang[1] , and Andrea Arcuri[1,2]

[1] Kristiania University College, Norway, Norway
{amid.golmohammadi,man.zhang,andrea.arcuri}@kristiania.no
[2] Oslo Metropolitan University, Norway

Abstract. C# is a widely used programming language. However, to the best of our knowledge, there is no documented work on enabling Search-Based Software Testing methods for C# and .NET applications. This paper introduces a white-box testing approach and an open-source tool for C# applications that collects code coverage information in real-time via .NET bytecode instrumentation. The method improves the search's direction by using *Branch Distance* heuristics. The tool was evaluated on three .NET RESTful APIs after being integrated into the EvoMaster test generator. Results show that our strategy achieves significantly higher code coverage than grey-box testing tools.

Keywords: .NET instrumentation · SBST · REST APIs

Summary

This paper provides a summary of [3].

We have used the `Mono.Cecil` library to implement instrumentation for .NET programs, allowing analysis and modification of CIL code. This works offline with .NET libraries compiled as DLLs. Integration with SBST techniques is essential for generating tests. Our experiments leverage EVOMASTER [2], which produces system-level tests for RESTful APIs. EVOMASTER has two main components: a core process and a driver, facilitating instrumentation and interaction through RESTful APIs. This instrumentation takes place via a .NET Core console application. To utilize EVOMASTER, we created a C# driver mirroring the existing JVM driver's endpoints. The core, written in Kotlin, was adapted to include C# output, enabling the generation of test cases as HTTP call sequences based on xUnit.

.NET programs consist of assemblies with classes containing methods. EVOMASTER is designed to optimize test case creation, maximizing coverage of these methods' targets. For tracking coverage, `EnteringStatement` and `CompletedStatement` probes are inserted before and after each statement. These probes, essentially calls to

This project has received funding from the European Research Council (ERC) under the European Union's Horizon 2020 research and innovation programme (grant agreement No 864972).

static methods in a console application developed to support the instrumentation, use parameters like class name and line number to uniquely identify statements. Coverage is measured heuristically between 0 (not covered) and 1 (fully covered). While `EnteringStatement` marks a statement's start, its error-free execution is confirmed by `CompletedStatement`. Inserting these probes presents challenges, especially with control-altering instructions such as jump or exit instructions (i.e., `br`, `throw`, `rethrow`, `endfinally`, `leave` and `ret`).

During the search, calculating branch distances for both numeric and string values are vital as they can provide gradient to the search algorithm to solve constraints. Numeric branch instructions are categorized into three types: *one-arg jump*, *two-arg compare*, and *two-arg jump*. One-arg jumps decide control flow based on a single value, while two-arg compare instructions compare two values and push the result (i.e., either 0 or 1) back on the evaluation stack, and two-arg jumps combine both. Calculating numeric branch distance involves challenges like duplication of values on the stack, using bytecode method replacements, and detecting specific data types. For string branch distances, boolean-returning operators and methods within `System.String` class are identified and replaced with probes to calculate the distance while retaining original functionality. The entire process ensures better test coverage and represents an intricate part of understanding how a system's control flow works, enhancing overall software reliability.

Our team assessed the efficacy of our approach by integrating bytecode instrumentation and branch distance-based heuristics into EVOMASTER, calling it EVOMASTER.NET. Utilizing default settings, we contrasted it with a grey-box testing approach on three .NET REST APIs (i.e., `rest-ncs`, `rest-scs`, and `menu-api`) from *EMB* repository [1]. The findings revealed substantial improvements in the numerical and string problems (i.e., `rest-ncs` and `rest-scs`, respectively) up to 98% and 86% line coverage respectively compared to the grey-box approach, but equivalent results for the `menu-api`. The enhanced performance illustrates our method's ability to resolve the majority of numeric and string branches. However, for the `menu-api`, which involves working with a database, the performance was not enhanced, signifying the necessity for SQL database-specific adaptations.

References

1. Arcuri, A., et al.: EMB: a curated corpus of web/enterprise applications and library support for software testing research. IEEE (2023)
2. Arcuri, A., Galeotti, J.P., Marculescu, B., Zhang, M.: EvoMaster: a search-based system test generation tool. J. Open Source Softw. **6**(57), 2153 (2021)
3. Golmohammadi, A., Zhang, M., Arcuri, A.: .NET/C# instrumentation for search-based software testing. Softw. Qual. J. 1–27 (2023)

Contents

Research Track

Generating Android Tests Using Novelty Search 3
  Michael Auer, Michael Pusl, and Gordon Fraser

Expound: A Black-Box Approach for Generating Diversity-Driven Adversarial
Examples 19
  Kenneth H. Chan and Betty H. C. Cheng

Developer Views on Software Carbon Footprint and Its Potential for Automated
Reduction 35
  Haozhou Lyu, Gregory Gay, and Maiko Sakamoto

Search-Based Mock Generation of External Web Service Interactions 52
  Susruthan Seran, Man Zhang, and Andrea Arcuri

Exploring Genetic Improvement of the Carbon Footprint of Web Pages 67
  Haozhou Lyu, Gregory Gay, and Maiko Sakamoto

A Novel Mutation Operator for Search-Based Test Case Selection 84
  Aitor Arrieta and Miren Illarramendi

RENE/NIER Track

Multi-objective Black-Box Test Case Prioritization Based
on Wordnet Distances 101
  Imara van Dinten, Andy Zaidman, and Annibale Panichella

On the Impact of Tool Evolution and Case Study Size on SBSE Experiments:
A Replicated Study with EvoMaster 108
  Amid Golmohammadi, Man Zhang, and Andrea Arcuri

Search-Based Optimisation of LLM Learning Shots for Story Point Estimation 123
  Vali Tawosi, Salwa Alamir, and Xiaomo Liu

Challenge Track

StableYolo: Optimizing Image Generation for Large Language Models 133
  *Harel Berger, Aidan Dakhama, Zishuo Ding, Karine Even-Mendoza,
  David Kelly, Hector Menendez, Rebecca Moussa, and Federica Sarro*

Improving the Readability of Generated Tests Using GPT-4 and ChatGPT Code
Interpreter 140
  Gregory Gay

Evaluating Explanations for Software Patches Generated by Large Language
Models 147
  *Dominik Sobania, Alina Geiger, James Callan, Alexander Brownlee,
  Carol Hanna, Rebecca Moussa, Mar Zamorano López, Justyna Petke,
  and Federica Sarro*

Enhancing Genetic Improvement Mutations Using Large Language Models 153
  *Alexander E. I. Brownlee, James Callan, Karine Even-Mendoza, Alina Geiger,
  Carol Hanna, Justyna Petke, Federica Sarro, and Dominik Sobania*

SearchGEM5: Towards Reliable Gem5 with Search Based Software Testing
and Large Language Models 160
  *Aidan Dakhama, Karine Even-Mendoza, W.B. Langdon, Hector Menendez,
  and Justyna Petke*

Author Index 167

Research Track

Generating Android Tests Using Novelty Search

Michael Auer[(✉)], Michael Pusl, and Gordon Fraser

University of Passau, Passau, Germany
{M.Auer,Gordon.Fraser}@uni-passau.de

Abstract. Search-based approaches have become a standard technique in automated Android testing. However, deceptive fitness landscapes make it difficult to find optimal solutions in a reasonable time. An alternative to classical search algorithms is offered by novelty search algorithms, which replace classical coverage-based fitness functions with a fitness function that rewards chromosomes based on how different, i.e., *novel*, they are compared to prior solutions. An open question is how to best quantify novelty for Android tests. In this paper, we therefore study two alternative approaches: First, we use a k-nearest neighbours (kNN) approach to determine the novelty in terms of coverage; second, we quantify the novelty of a chromosome based on the second-order uncertainty derived from subjective logic. We integrated both approaches into the open source Android test generator MATE and study its performance on 108 complex apps. Our experiments suggest that novelty search represents a promising alternative but requires further research to fully unleash its power: While both novelty search variants outperform a random-based exploration, they cannot yet compete with the state-of-the-art many-objective search algorithm MIO.

Keywords: Android · Novelty Search · Subjective Logic · Automated Test Generation

1 Introduction

The rapid growth of Android apps in the last decade makes it necessary to test such apps in an automated manner. Many different testing approaches have been proposed, and search-based algorithms [16,17,24] have become a prominent category of Android testing techniques. However, the deceptive fitness landscapes of Android apps often hinder classical coverage-based fitness functions in finding optimal solutions in a reasonable time [4]. In such cases, novelty search [14] has been shown to be beneficial in other domains [15,18,20].

Novelty search algorithms replace classical fitness functions with a measurement of how novel a solution's behaviour is compared to prior solutions. In order to apply novelty search for Android testing, in this paper we explore two alternative approaches to quantify novelty: A classical approach lies in a k-nearest neighbours (kNN) distance metric [14] on the current population and an optional archive comprising the most novel chromosomes over time [10], where distance

P. Arcaini et al. (Eds.): SSBSE 2023, LNCS 14415, pp. 3–18, 2024.
https://doi.org/10.1007/978-3-031-48796-5_1

can for example be based on code coverage. We introduce an alternative app-roach that uses subjective logic [12] to quantify novelty: We model the interplay between the different GUI states of an Android application with a subjective opinion state machine (SOSM) [29], which associates with each outgoing tran-sition not only a probability based on the execution frequency but also further probabilities that describe, among other things, the uncertainty and disbelief of the former probability. This information together with a dedicated multiplica-tion operator for subjective opinions allows us to reason about the probability of a test case executing a particular sequence of actions.

In order to study these two approaches we implemented them into the open source Android test generator MATE [9], and evaluate it on a set of 108 complex apps, measuring its usefulness in terms of coverage and unique crashes compared to a random-based exploration as well as to the state-of-the-art many-objective search algorithm MIO [2]. Thus, the contributions of this paper are as follows:

- We propose a novelty search algorithm with two alternative novelty functions for automated Android test generation.
- We empirically evaluate the effects of both variants in terms of coverage and the number of unique crashes using a set of 108 complex apps.

Our results demonstrate a clear improvement over purely random exploration, thus confirming novelty search to be a viable strategy for testing Android apps. On the other hand, the state-of-the-art many-objective search algorithm MIO achieves higher coverage, suggesting that further improvements of the novelty search algorithm that makes use of the proposed novelty functions is necessary.

2   Background

2.1   Automated Android Testing

A basic approach to automatically test Android apps is to send random input actions. This approach has been shown to be effective, and often serves as a basis for further testing strategies [13], and is also applied as a form of fuzzing with the intent to find crashes, which may benefit from sending valid and invalid test data [13]. Search-based testing (e.g., [1,9,16,17]) extends random approaches by including (1) fitness functions that evaluate how close test executions are to reaching a testing objective (e.g., code coverage), and (2) search algorithms that make use of the fitness function to guide the generation and evolution of tests towards reaching the objective. Since deriving classical coverage-based fitness functions for Android apps is challenging, a recent trend lies in applying reinforcement learning techniques such as Q-Learning [26], SARSA [22], or Deep Learning [21], which aim to learn how to explore apps. Android test generators are often complemented with finite state machine (FSM) models, where states may describe activities or GUI states, and edges refer to actions that trigger the respective transition from one state to another. In this paper, we use this type of model to build a subjective opinion state machine (SOSM) model.

2.2   Search-Based Android Testing

Search-based test generation typically uses genetic algorithms (GAs), in which a multi-set (called *population*) of candidate solutions (called *chromosomes* or *individuals*) is iteratively subjected to *selection, mutation* and *crossover* [8]. A fitness value, which describes how close the chromosome is to an optimal solution of the optimisation problem, is assigned to each newly generated chromosome. The fitness values are used during selection to decide which chromosomes in the population are used to generate the next population. GAs are a great tool for solving certain optimisation problems but often the fitness landscape contains local optima or plateaus that inhibit the search. Some search algorithms for test generation, e.g., MIO [2], try to counter this problem by promoting a diverse set of chromosomes early in the search and switching to a focused search later on. For extremely deceptive fitness landscapes, however, this approach might still not be sufficient, thus affecting the achieved coverage. In other search domains novelty search has been proposed to overcome this problem.

2.3   Novelty Search

Novelty Search (NS) is an adaption of GAs that tries to alleviate this problem by not relying on a fitness function to guide the search. Instead, the optimisation goal is to discover novel parts of the search space. That way, NS can explore different parts of a search space without being distracted by a deceptive fitness landscape, but might also explore parts of the search space that are entirely irrelevant with respect to reaching an optimal solution. NS is implemented by replacing the fitness function of a GA by a *novelty function* that computes how novel the behaviour of a chromosome is compared to a reference set of chromosomes. This reference set can be the population of the last generation, but also the combination of the last generation and an archive containing the most novel chromosomes over time [10]. The novelty function is typically implemented by using a k nearest neighbour (kNN) approach where a distance metric, e.g., cosine distance, is used to quantify how close two chromosomes are with respect to one or more objectives. The novelty is then computed as the averaged distance to the k closest neighbours [4]. There are also NS variants that try to combine novelty with fitness [10] or apply multiobjectivisation [19], i.e., constructing pareto fronts as in NSGA-II [5], when dealing with multiple conflicting objectives. A sketch of a novelty search algorithm is illustrated in Algorithm 1.

2.4   Subjective Logic

Subjective logic is a formalism for reasoning about uncertainties of subjective opinions. For instance, the probability that a certain event happens might be based on a low number of observations, thus the uncertainty about the specified probability is high, while with an increasing number of observations we can be more certain that the assigned probability is reasonable. There are different types

---

Algorithm 1. Sketch of a Novelty Search Algorithm.

Require: Population size populationSize $\in \mathbb{N}$
Require: Archive limit archiveLimit $\in \mathbb{N}$
Require: Nearest neighbours nearestNeighbours $\in \mathbb{N}$
  archive := *createArchive(archiveLimit)*
  population := *createInitialPopulation(populationSize)*
  while Terminal condition not met **do**
    newPopulation := $\varnothing$
    while |*newPopulation*| < *populationSize* **do**
      parent1, parent2 := *select(population)*
      offspring := *crossover(parent1, parent2)*
      offspring := *mutate(offspring)*
      offspring.novelty := *novelty(offspring, population, archive, nearestNeighbours)*
      newPopulation := *newPopulation* $\cup$ *{offspring}*
    end while
    archive := *updateArchive(newPopulation, archive)*
    population := *newPopulation*
  end while
  return *population*

---

of subjective opinions but we restrict ourselves to binomial and multinomial opinions in the following. A binomial opinion has two possible outcomes to which a belief, disbelief and uncertainty mass as well as an a-priori probability can be assigned, while a multinomial opinion can have multiple outcomes and the probability assignment is seamlessly extended. We can retrieve a binomial opinion from a multinomial opinion by applying a process called coarsening [29]. Furthermore, traditional logic operators can be applied to combine multiple subjective opinions, e.g., one can multiply binomial opinions. This kind of multiplication allows us to reason about the uncertainty attributed to a test case executing a particular sequence of actions with individual subjective opinions. For a detailed explanation of subjective logic we refer to the book of Jøsang [12].

3 Novelty Search for Android Testing

In the following we first describe the common parts of both novelty search algorithms, and then the specific details of the kNN-based and SOSM-based novelty search algorithms. In both cases a chromosome is a test case with a limited sequence of actions. Each test case records which (screen) states it has visited during action execution. Novelty search can use classical selection algorithms such as rank selection, and we use a traditional single-point crossover function with the restriction that the cutpoint is derived such that the resulting action sequence is executable according to the underlying GUI model. If no such sequence exists, crossover returns the parent chromosomes unmodified.

3.1   kNN-based Novelty Search

The kNN-based novelty search follows largely the sketch outlined in Algorithm 1: First, an initial population is generated that is evolved over time by applying crossover and mutation with pre-defined probabilities. In addition to the current population an archive of limited size consisting of the most novel chromosomes is maintained. Chromosomes are inserted into the archive if their novelty is greater than some pre-defined threshold [4]. This ensures that the archive is not polluted with arbitrary (less novel) chromosomes. Since the archive is limited in size, we employ a replacement strategy that removes the least novel chromosome if a new chromosome with a higher novelty is inserted into a full archive.

Novelty Function. The novelty of a chromosome is computed by averaging the distance to the k nearest neighbours in the current population and the archive. The distance is computed by constructing a coverage vector for each chromosome and then applying the cosine distance metric for each pair of chromosomes. A coverage vector simply describes for a pre-defined number of objectives, e.g., the lines or branches of the AUT, which objectives have been covered in the form of a binary vector. For the very first chromosome of the initial population, we assign a novelty of 1.0 since there are no other chromosomes to compare to and the very first chromosome is novel by construction. Since the cosine distance is bounded to $[0, 1]$, the resulting novelty after taking the average distance to the k nearest neighbours is also in $[0, 1]$, where we aim to maximise novelty.

Mutation Function. We employ a cutpoint mutation that keeps actions from an input chromosome up to a randomly chosen cutpoint, and then chooses arbitrary actions up to a specified limit.

3.2   SOSM-Based Novelty Search

Our SOSM-based novelty search algorithm follows essentially a classical novelty search algorithm as outlined in Algorithm 1 with the exception that the archive is replaced by a SOSM model and the kNN-based novelty function is substituted by a subjective opinion driven novelty function. This means that the call for updating the archive is replaced by updating the SOSM model.

Subjective Opinion State Machine (SOSM). A SOSM is an extension of a finite state machine (FSM) that records how often each transition is traversed and uses this information to compute with which probability each transition in a particular state is taken. Depending on the number of observations and a user supplied certainty threshold (i.e., a positive number that describes how often a state needs to be traversed that the computed probabilities are deemed certain), the computed probabilities are subject to a higher or lower degree of uncertainty, thus a SOSM makes use of subjective logic to quantify the trustworthiness of the computed probabilities. This formalism not only allows us to compute an uncertainty (a subjective opinion) for a single transition but enables us to associate an uncertainty to a complete path by applying a subjective logic multiplication operator [29]. A SOSM can be directly derived from a set of traces (observations) and we refer the interested reader to Walkinshaw et al. [29] for a formal definition of a SOSM, the inference algorithm, the coarsening of a binomial opinion from a multinomial opinion and the multiplication operator for binomial opinions.

We can directly map SOSMs to the Android domain: A state refers to a screen state while a transition represents an action that can be taken in a particular state as in a traditional FSM. A trace is then a sequence of triples (*source, action, target*) that describe a transition from a source to a target state with a given action. To each state a multinomial opinion is assigned that describes the uncertainty along each outgoing transition. By applying coarsening [29] we can retrieve a binomial opinion that can be multiplied with further binomial opinions along a path to compute a subjective opinion from which the uncertainty for that particular path can be derived. The SOSM model is updated with traces collected from the current population at the end of each generation. This in turn updates the multinomial opinions associated with each state.

Example. The example in Fig. 1 shows an artificial screen state on the left, and on the right the corresponding state in the SOSM along with the applicable actions and the associated uncertainties. This SOSM state is essentially a multinomial opinion, and by applying coarsening we can derive the uncertainty for a particular action. Assuming that filling out the first and second name in the given screen state leads to the same screen state again, we can compute the uncertainty for that particular action sequence by basically multiplying the uncertainties with the help of the multiplication operator for binomial opinions. This procedure can be iteratively applied to compute a subjective opinion over the action sequence of a test case and then derive its uncertainty. The shown uncertainties in Fig. 1 are dependent on the number of observations (traces). If the number of observations is increased the uncertainty will naturally decrease and vice versa. While a first-order probability simply describes how often a particular action has been executed in a particular state, the uncertainty describes how much trustworthiness can be attributed to the computed probability. For instance, if we have only observed the actions first name and second name a single time and there are no traces for the remaining actions, the first order probability would be equally distributed among this two actions and all remaining actions would have a probability of zero. This sounds very unrealistic and since the number of observations is very low, a very high uncertainty would be assigned to the probabilities of both actions to counteract this scenario.

Mutation Function. We probabilistically choose the cutpoint based on a rank selection over the uncertainties described through a chromosome's trace. The mutated chromosome consists of the original actions up to the cutpoint and is then filled with actions according to the SOSM model. Here we perform another

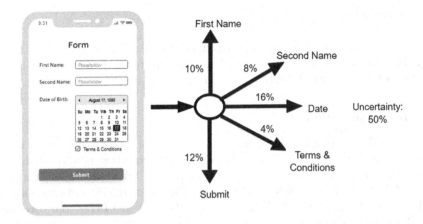

Fig. 1. An example app screen and the associated uncertainties for each outgoing transition.

rank selection over the disbelief values associated to the applicable actions in the current state. The former rank selection ensures that we re-visit states with a high uncertainty, i.e., a quite novel area in the search space, while the latter favours actions that have been executed in the current state rarely.

Novelty Function. The novelty of a chromosome is bounded in $[0, 1]$ with the objective to being maximised. If a chromosome visits during the action execution a new state according to the SOSM model, a novelty of 1.0 is assigned. This favours the exploration of new states. Otherwise, the novelty of a chromosome is computed with the help of the following formula:

$$\text{novelty}(\text{chromosome}) = \text{noveltyWeight} \times \text{novelty'} + (1 - \text{noveltyWeight}) \times \text{coverage}$$

This means a linear combination of novelty and coverage controlled by a weight that either favours novelty or coverage. The coverage here refers to the line coverage of the chromosome but can be any coverage in general. The novelty itself is computed as follows:

$$\text{novelty'}(\text{chromosome}) = \text{uncertainty} + \text{disbelief} \times \text{disbeliefWeight}.$$

The uncertainty and disbelief are computed with the help of the trace of the chromosome and the SOSM model, while the disbelief weight is a value in $[0, 1]$ that controls how much emphasis should be put on the disbelief. The uncertainty and disbelief are based on the subjective opinion derived from multiplying the coarsened binomial opinions described by the trace. We only multiply a subsequence of binomial opinions such that uncertainty is maximised. For a formal description of how binomial opinions are coarsened and the multiplication of binomial opinions we refer to Walkinshaw et al. [29].

4   Evaluation

We aim to answer the following research question:
RQ: How do the novelty search algorithms compare to random exploration and the state-of-the-art search-based approach MIO?

4.1   Implementation

We extended the open source Android test generator MATE [9] with a kNN-based and SOSM-based novelty search strategy. All experiments were conducted on a compute cluster, where each node is equipped with two Intel Xeon E5-2620v4 CPUs (16 cores) with 2.10 GHz and 256 GB of RAM, and runs Debian GNU/Linux 11 with Java 11. We limited executions of MATE to four cores and 60 GB of RAM, where the emulator (Pixel XL) runs a x86 image with API level 25 (Android 7.1.1) and is limited to 4 GB of RAM with a heap size of 576 MB.

4.2   Parameter Tuning

In order to determine reasonable values for the parameters arising in novelty search, we conducted a tuning study on a data set of 10 apps used in prior research [3]. In order to determine the best configurations for both novelty search algorithms, we performed a micro-tuning on the core parameters of both algorithms. The remaining parameters, e.g., the population size, were chosen based on preliminary results and suggestions of previous studies. Table 1 lists the possible values for all parameters. In particular, we fixed the population size (denoted as n) to a value of five instead of 10 or 20 in order to avoid the degeneration to a random search as the test execution in Android is costly [3] and the number of produced generations would be very low in the chosen time frame of one hour. For the classical kNN-based novelty search we evaluated in total six different configurations by varying the number of the nearest neighbours k and the archive size limit l according to Table 1, while for the SOSM-based novelty search we examined in total 12 configurations by trying out different values for the certainty threshold c, the disbelief weight d and whether to linearly combine coverage with novelty ($nw = 0.5$) or not ($nw = 1.0$). This yields in total 18 configurations, which we executed using MATE for each of the 10 tuning apps 10 times for one hour in order to reduce the effects caused through randomness.

To determine the best configuration for each novelty search algorithm, we applied the following tournament ranking for the configurations of each algorithm in separation: For each pair of configurations (c_1, c_2) we statistically compare the two configurations for each of the apps in terms of activity and line coverage as well as the number of unique crashes using a Wilcoxon-Mann-Whitney U test with a 95% confidence level. If a statistical difference is observed in any coverage metric or the number of unique crashes, we use the Vargha-Delaney $\hat{A}_{12}$ effect size [27] to determine which of the two configurations is better, and the *score* for this configuration and the particular coverage metric or the number of unique crashes is increased by one. At the end, the configuration with the highest combined score (sum) is the overall best configuration. We consider two crashes as identical if (1) their exception types match, and (2) they share the same stack trace. We do not compare the exception messages, as they often vary in terms of object references or user inputs included.

Table 1. The parameters used for both novelty search algorithms.

Parameter	Value
Initial population	Random
Selection	Rank selection
Crossover	Single point crossover
Population size n	5
Probability mutation	0.3 [24]
Probability crossover	0.7 [24]
Nearest neighbours k	3/5
Archive limit l	5/10/20
Novelty threshold	0.0
Fitness	kNN-based cosine distance on basic blocks
Mutation	Cut point mutation
Certainty threshold c	5/10/20
Disbelief weight d	0.0/1.0
Novelty weight nw	0.5/1.0
Fitness	Uncertainty + disbelief
Mutation	Uncertainty-based cut point mutation

The top section contains the parameters and its values shared by both novelty search algorithms, while the middle part is specific for the kNN-based novelty search and the last section describes the core parameters for the SOSM-based novelty search.

For space reasons we only list for each novelty search algorithm the best configuration and refer to the replication package for detailed data. The best SOSM-based novelty search variant (denoted as *NS_SOSM* from now) is configured with a certainty threshold c of 20.0, a disbelief weight d of 1.0 and a novelty weight nw of 1.0, while the best kNN-based novelty search variant denoted as *NS* from now onwards is configured with an archive limit l of 5 and the number of nearest neighbours k is set to 5. We can observe from the tournament ranking scores of the 12 SOSM-based novelty search variants that most configurations disregarding coverage in the novelty function perform better than their counterparts including coverage. In contrast, the kNN-based novelty search variants are best configured with a small archive limit.

4.3 Study Subjects

To empirically answer the stated research question, we sampled a data set consisting of 108 apps from FDroid. We initially downloaded 1000 random APKs and then excluded apps matching any of the following reasons: (i) The app represents a game (35); (ii) the APK is not suitable for the x86 architecture or API level 25 to allow running all apps on the same emulator (13); (iii) the APK could not be re-built after being instrumented (382); (iv) the app crashed / behaved unexpected after being re-signed (8); (v) MATE has troubles to interact with the app (8); (vi) the app appeared already in the TUNING dataset (5). This resulted in 547 apps. However, since preliminary results showed no differences between the algorithms on many apps of this set of apps, we examined the reasons for this. First, many of the apps are too simple and second, a non-negligible number of apps requires some sort of authentication to reach the main application logic, which MATE currently cannot handle. Thus, we further removed apps that (1) have less than five activities and (2) require some kind of authentication. This process resulted in 108 complex apps, which we used for our experiments.

4.4 Experiment Procedure

Using the best configuration for each novelty search algorithm, we evaluated how those configurations compare to a random exploration and MIO in terms of activity and line coverage as well as the number of unique crashes. We ran MATE for one hour per app on the EVALUATION dataset and repeated each run 10 times for statistical analysis. We applied a Wilcoxon-Mann-Whitney U test with a 95% confidence level in combination with the Vargha-Delaney $\hat{A}_{12}$ effect size to assess on how many apps there is a statistical difference between any two algorithms. We configured MIO according to the author's suggestions [2], i.e., we set the mutation rate to 1, the probability for sampling a random chromosome to 0.5, the start of the focused search to half of the search budget and the archive size for each testing target to 10. We employ the same cutpoint mutation function as used in the kNN-based novelty search algorithm and the fitness function considers the basic blocks as testing targets. Moreover, all algorithms were configured with a maximum test case length of 100 actions.

4.5 Threats to Validity

Threats to external validity may arise from our sample of subject apps, and results may not generalise beyond the tested apps. To counteract selection bias, we picked the 547 apps for the evaluation study randomly. There may also be some implicit bias, e.g., the apps on *F-Droid* might be simpler than those on *Google PlayStore*. We also stuck to one specific emulator configuration and API level, but results may differ on other versions. *Threats to internal validity* may arise from bugs in MATE or our analysis scripts. To mitigate this risk, we manually reviewed the results, and tested and reviewed all code. To reduce the risk of favouring one algorithm over the other, we used the same default parameters wherever applicable, e.g., the maximum number of actions per test case was fixed to 100 actions. *Threats to construct validity* may result from our choice of metrics, in particular activity and line coverage. However, these are the de facto standard metrics in Android testing and represent a reasonable combination of a fine as well as coarse-grained coverage metric. The classification of unique crashes has also been used in previous studies, and reporting unique crashes is a standard metric in Android testing.

4.6 Comparison of Novelty Search vs. Random vs. MIO

Figure 2 shows the coverage and crash distributions for the four configurations *MIO*, *NS*, *NS_SOSM* and *Random*. Regarding activity coverage, the configuration *MIO* achieves a median of 66.84% closely followed by *NS* with 66.67%, while *NS_SOSM* achieves 64.69% and *Random* only 60.00%. A similar picture can be drawn regarding line coverage: *MIO* yields 43.46% followed by *NS_SOSM* with 41.11% and *NS* with 41.08% while *Random* only achieves 38.33%. Looking at the number of unique crashes shows that *MIO* achieves a median of 0.9 followed by *NS* with 0.65, while *NS_SOSM* and *Random* only achieve a median of 0.6.

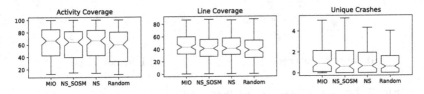

Fig. 2. Activity, line coverage and unique crashes of the EVALUATION dataset.

This at a first glance conveys the impression that *MIO* performs better than both novelty search algorithms, which in turn perform better than *Random*. To reinforce this observation Fig. 3 shows the Vargha-Delaney $\hat{A}_{12}$ effect sizes between any pair of algorithm for both activity and line coverage. Recall that an effect size $\hat{A}_{12} > 0.5$ implies that the first algorithm is better than the second and vice versa. We can observe that *MIO* yields in comparison to any algorithm an effect size $\hat{A}_{12} >= 0.5$, thus promoting its strong position, while *Random* achieves an effect size clearly lower than 0.5 in any direct comparison, thus strengthening the impression that *Random* is outperformed by the remaining three algorithms. The comparison between *NS* and *NS_SOSM* shows that *NS* performs slightly better for both coverage criteria. We omit the plot of the number of unique crashes since the median effect size is 0.5 between any pair of algorithms, indicating that any differences regarding crashes are not practically significant.

Apart from the effect size distributions we also examined for how many apps there is a statistical significance between any two algorithms using a Wilcoxon-Mann-Whitney U test with a 95% confidence level. *MIO* performs regarding activity coverage in 34 cases better than *Random*, in 10 cases better than *NS* and in 24 cases better than *NS_SOSM*, while for line coverage there is a statistical difference in favour of *MIO* in 56, 28 and 46 cases, respectively. In contrast, *NS* performs better than *NS_SOSM* in 14 (activity coverage) and 24 (line coverage) cases, respectively, and in comparison to *Random* in 28 and 43 cases, respectively. Similarly, *NS_SOSM* outperforms *Random* in 14 and 30 cases, respectively. The results are similar regarding the number of crashes. We refer the interested reader to the replication package for a detailed analysis.

Summary (*RQ*): Both novelty search algorithms perform better than random exploration in terms of coverage and crashes but are behind MIO.

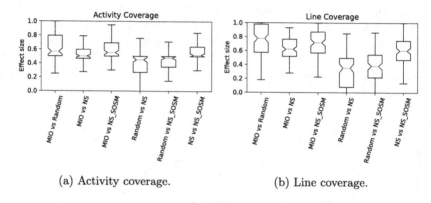

(a) Activity coverage.   (b) Line coverage.

Fig. 3. Effect size distributions between the different configurations.

4.7   Discussion

The previous results show that *MIO* performs better than both novelty search algorithms and better than random exploration, which means that both novelty search variants can be used as baselines in future work. Many previous studies in the Android testing domain demonstrated that random exploration often performs as good as a more systematic approach. We believe that novelty search in Android testing represents a viable alternative and this work lays the foundation.

Our original hypothesis was that the SOSM-based novelty search should perform better than the kNN-based novelty search variant since the combination of uncertainty and disbelief nicely favours test cases that visit new states and executes rarely executed actions in these states. However, as the novelty over time plot for the 108 apps illustrates in Fig. 4a, the SOSM-based novelty is quite constant after some time, effectively guiding the search in no concrete direction. In contrast, the novelty of the kNN-based novelty search variant behaves more natural, i.e., decreasing over time but remaining greater than zero. This means that the search still finds novel chromosomes but less likely as in the beginning.

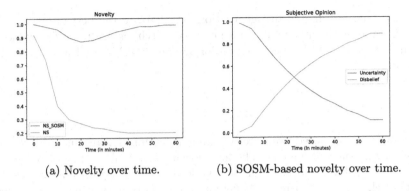

(a) Novelty over time.   (b) SOSM-based novelty over time.

Fig. 4. Novelty over time.

To better understand why the SOSM-based novelty is quite steady we decompose it into uncertainty and disbelief as Fig. 4b illustrates. Recall from the definition of the SOSM-based novelty function that the novelty value is a linear combination of both uncertainty and disbelief. While the uncertainty decreases over time the disbelief steadily increases, thus dominating the computed novelty value and rewarding each chromosome as highly novel. Since the configurations disregarding the disbelief at all performed worse than those putting emphasis on the disbelief, we thought that a configuration balancing the emphasis on disbelief more evenly in comparison to uncertainty should perform better. However, preliminary experiments could not verify this assumption. We believe that future work needs to address this issue in more detail and may find alternative combination possibilities of uncertainty and disbelief. Another assumption is that *MIO* performs better than both novelty search variants since it includes the option to sample a new random chromosome, while the chromosomes in both novelty search algorithms are crafted through a mix of crossover and mutation, thus not having the same level of freedom. We believe that a more sophisticated exploration strategy can boost the performance of both novelty search algorithms.

5   Related Work

Novelty search was introduced by Lehman and Stanley [14], and since then applied in many different domains [15,18,20]. In the literature we can find many different novelty search variants such as progressive minimal criteria novelty search [11], which considers also the fitness value to guide the search, or even variants requiring neither an archive nor a kNN-based novelty function [23]. Recently, a novelty search algorithm incorporating deep reinforcement learning [25] or metamorphic testing [6] have been proposed. Further studies on a maze navigation task [10,19] showed that (1) certain parameters are domain or task specific and (2) novelty is better combined with fitness. In contrast, our findings showed that a pure novelty driven search algorithm performs better. Although novelty search has been practically applied for automatic bug repair (e.g., [28]), and automated test generation (e.g., [4]), to the best of our knowledge this paper is the first to introduce novelty search for Android. The work by Walkinshaw et al. [29] laid the foundation for our SOSM-based novelty search algorithm.

6   Conclusions

In this study we proposed two novelty search algorithms for automated test generation in the Android domain. The first novelty search algorithm makes use of a classical kNN-based novelty function while the second algorithm assesses the novelty of chromosomes using disbelief and uncertainty measuring using subjective logic. Our experiments demonstrate that both novelty search variants can compete with a random-based exploration in terms of coverage and crashes. However, the state-of-the-art many-objective search algorithm MIO achieves higher coverage, suggesting that further research is required.

In particular, although we laid the foundation for using novelty search in the automated Android testing domain, we believe that there are several open points that need to be addressed in future work: Our hypothesis is that a more sophisticated underlying genetic algorithm can boost the performance. One may sample chromosomes not only from the current population but also purely at random as MIO does or use the SOSM model to derive novel chromosomes. In our view the SOSM-based novelty search algorithm underperformed although the underlying idea of assessing the novelty of a chromosome based on disbelief and uncertainty looks quite promising. This can have multiple reasons: First, the high disbelief over time may negatively impact the quality of the novelty function and more emphasis on the uncertainty might be applied. Second, similar to the SOSM-based mutation operator a dedicated crossover operator could be used to choose the crossover point such that the uncertainty at this state is maximised. Lastly, a longer search time may be required to observe positive effects of the SOSM-based novelty search, as the high disbelief values demonstrate that actions have been rarely or not executed at all in specific states.

To support reproduction of our experiments, we provide a replication package that contains all case studies, the tool implementation, and the raw results of our study. The replication package can be found at https://figshare.com/articles/dataset/replication-package-novelty-search-study_zip/23997864.

Acknowledgment. This work is supported by DFG project FR2955/4-1 "STUNT: Improving Software Testing Using Novelty".

References

1. Amalfitano, D., Amatucci, N., Fasolino, A.R., Tramontana, P.: AGRippin: a novel search based testing technique for android applications. In: Proceedings of DeMobile, pp. 5–12. ACM (2015)

2. Arcuri, A.: Many independent objective (MIO) algorithm for test suite generation. In: Menzies, T., Petke, J. (eds.) SSBSE 2017. LNCS, vol. 10452, pp. 3–17. Springer, Cham (2017). https://doi.org/10.1007/978-3-319-66299-2_1
3. Auer, M., Adler, F., Fraser, G.: Improving search-based android test generation using surrogate models. In: Papadakis, M., Vergilio, S.R. (eds.) SSBSE 2022. LNCS, vol. 13711, pp. 51–66. Springer, Cham (2022)
4. Boussaa, M., Barais, O., Sunyé, G., Baudry, B.: A novelty search approach for automatic test data generation. In: Procedings of SBST, pp. 40–43 (2015)
5. Deb, K., Pratap, A., Agarwal, S., Meyarivan, T.: A fast and elitist multiobjective genetic algorithm: NSGA-ii. IEEE TEC **6**(2), 182–197 (2002)
6. DeVries, B., Trefftz, C.: A novelty search and metamorphic testing approach to automatic test generation. In: Proceedings of SBST, pp. 8–11. IEEE (2021)
7. Doncieux, S., Laflaquière, A., Coninx, A.: Novelty search: A theoretical perspective. In: Proceedings of GECCO, p. 99–106. ACM (2019)
8. Eiben, A.E., Smith, J.E.: Introduction to Evolutionary Computing, 2nd edn. Springer, Heidelberg (2015). https://doi.org/10.1007/978-3-662-44874-8
9. Eler, M.M., Rojas, J.M., Ge, Y., Fraser, G.: Automated accessibility testing of mobile apps. In: ICST, pp. 116–126. IEEE (2018)
10. Gomes, J., Mariano, P., Christensen, A.L.: Devising effective novelty search algorithms: a comprehensive empirical study. In: Proceedings of GECCO, pp. 943–950. ACM (2015)
11. Gomes, J., Urbano, P., Christensen, A.L.: Progressive minimal criteria novelty search. In: Pavón, J., Duque-Méndez, N.D., Fuentes-Fernández, R. (eds.) IBERAMIA 2012. LNCS (LNAI), vol. 7637, pp. 281–290. Springer, Heidelberg (2012). https://doi.org/10.1007/978-3-642-34654-5_29
12. Jøsang, A.: Subjective Logic: A Formalism for Reasoning Under Uncertainty, 1st edn. Springer, Cham (2016). https://doi.org/10.1007/978-3-319-42337-1
13. Kong, P., Li, L., Gao, J., Liu, K., Bissyandé, T.F., Klein, J.: Automated testing of android apps: a systematic literature review. IEEE Trans. Reliab. **68**(1), 45–66 (2019)
14. Lehman, J., Stanley, K.O.: Exploiting open-endedness to solve problems through the search for novelty. In: IEEE Symposium on Artificial Life (2008)
15. Liapis, A., Yannakakis, G.N., Togelius, J.: Enhancements to constrained novelty search: two-population novelty search for generating game content. In: Proceedings of GECCO, pp. 343–350. ACM (2013)
16. Mahmood, R., Mirzaei, N., Malek, S.: Evodroid: segmented evolutionary testing of android apps. In: Proceedings of FSE, pp. 599–609. ACM (2014)
17. Mao, K., Harman, M., Jia, Y.: Sapienz: multi-objective automated testing for android applications. In: Proceedings of ISSTA, pp. 94–105. ACM (2016)
18. Mouret, J.B., Doncieux, S.: Encouraging behavioral diversity in evolutionary robotics: an empirical study. Evol. Comput. **20**(1), 91–133 (2012)
19. Mouret, J.B.: Novelty-based multiobjectivization. In: Doncieux, S., Bredèche, N., Mouret, J.B. (eds.) New Horizons in Evolutionary Robotics. Studies in Computational Intelligence, vol. 341, pp. 139–154. Springer, Heidelberg (2011). https://doi.org/10.1007/978-3-642-18272-3_10
20. Naredo, E., Trujillo, L.: Searching for novel clustering programs. In: Proceedings of GECCO, pp. 1093–1100. ACM (2013)
21. Romdhana, A., Merlo, A., Ceccato, M., Tonella, P.: Deep reinforcement learning for black-box testing of android apps. TOSEM **31**, 1–29 (2022)
22. Rummery, G., Niranjan, M.: On-line q-learning using connectionist systems. Technical report CUED/F-INFENG/TR 166 (1994)

23. Salehi, A., Coninx, A., Doncieux, S.: BR-NS: an archive-less approach to novelty search. In: Proceedings of GECCO, pp. 172–179. ACM (2021)
24. Sell, L., Auer, M., Frädrich, C., Gruber, M., Werli, P., Fraser, G.: An empirical evaluation of search algorithms for app testing. In: Gaston, C., Kosmatov, N., Le Gall, P. (eds.) ICTSS 2019. LNCS, vol. 11812, pp. 123–139. Springer, Cham (2019). https://doi.org/10.1007/978-3-030-31280-0_8
25. Shi, L., Li, S., Zheng, Q., Yao, M., Pan, G.: Efficient novelty search through deep reinforcement learning. IEEE Access **8**, 128809–128818 (2020)
26. Sutton, R.S., Barto, A.G.: Reinforcement Learning: An Introduction. A Bradford Book (2018)
27. Vargha, A., Delaney, H.D.: A critique and improvement of the CL common language effect size statistics of McGraw and Wong. J. Educ. Behav. Stat. **25**(2), 101–132 (2000)
28. Villanueva, O.M., Trujillo, L., Hernandez, D.E.: Novelty search for automatic bug repair. In: Proceedings of GECCO, pp. 1021–1028. ACM (2020)
29. Walkinshaw, N., Hierons, R.M.: Modelling second-order uncertainty in state machines. IEEE TSE **49**(5), 3261–3276 (2023)

Expound: A Black-Box Approach for Generating Diversity-Driven Adversarial Examples

Kenneth H. Chan[(✉)] and Betty H.C. Cheng

Department of Computer Science and Engineering, Michigan State University, 428 S Shaw Ln, East Lansing, MI 48824, USA
{chanken1,chengb}@msu.edu

Abstract. Deep neural networks (DNNs) have been increasingly used in safety-critical systems for decision-making (e.g., medical applications, autonomous vehicles, etc.). Early work with adversarial examples shows that they can hinder a DNN's ability to correctly process inputs. These techniques largely focused on identifying individual causes of failure, emphasizing that minimal perturbations can cause a DNN to fail. Recent research suggests that *diverse* adversarial examples, those that cause different erroneous model behaviors, can better assess the robustness of DNNs. These techniques, however, use white-box approaches to exhaustively search for diverse DNN misbehaviors. This paper proposes a black-box, model and data-agnostic approach to generate diverse sets of adversarial examples, where each set corresponds to one type of model misbehavior (e.g., misclassification of image to a specific label), thus termed a *failure category*. Furthermore, each failure category comprises a diverse set of perturbations, all of which produce the same type of model misbehavior. As such, this work provides both breadth and depth-based information for addressing robustness with respect to multiple categories of failures due to adversarial examples. We illustrate our approach by applying it to popular image classification datasets using different image classification models.

Keywords: Adversarial Example · Novelty Search · Machine Learning

1 Introduction

Due to their ability to learn abstract patterns and representations directly from data, an increasing number of autonomous systems are using machine learning, DNNs, and related technologies for decision making [8]. However, the existence of adversarial examples [19] suggests that they are prone to unexpected failures, such as uncertainty factors and minor perturbations possibly due to adversarial attacks. The *robustness* of DNNs describes their ability to correctly operate in the face of minor noise perturbations or uncertainty factors [2,28]. DNNs used in safety-critical autonomous systems (e.g., medical imaging, autonomous

© The Author(s), under exclusive license to Springer Nature Switzerland AG 2024
P. Arcaini et al. (Eds.): SSBSE 2023, LNCS 14415, pp. 19–34, 2024.
https://doi.org/10.1007/978-3-031-48796-5_2

vehicles [3,25], etc.) must be robust against minor data perturbations, as the failure of these systems may lead to potential injuries, financial damages, or loss of life. This paper introduces a black-box diversity-focused search framework to discover failure categories and enable the automated assessment of the severity of each failure category.

Recent state-of-the-art research has suggested the use of *diverse*[1] adversarial examples to address the inability of a DNN to generalize to previously unseen or unknown data deviations [1,21,27]. Traditional approaches to generate adversarial examples typically discover the "nearest" adversarial examples. In contrast, Rozsa *et al.* [21] promoted the use of adversarial examples that 1) have non-minimal perturbations and 2) that result in different model misbehaviors. Aghababaeyan *et al.* [1] showed that the robustness of a DNN model can be better assessed and improved using inputs that trigger different faults. Currently, state-of-the-art research identifies diverse adversarial examples by using white-box techniques to exhaustively search for perturbations, each of which triggers a unique given model misbehavior. However, white-box techniques require access to hidden model information and may not work if the gradient is obfuscated. Additionally, brute-force approaches do not scale as the number of model behaviors (e.g., number of class labels) in a dataset increases.

This paper introduces **EXP**loration and expl**O**itation **U**sing **N**ovelty search for **D**iversity (EXPOUND),[2] a black-box search-based approach to generate diverse adversarial examples to identify the failure categories for a DNN model. Our work contributes several key insights. As the space of possible perturbations for adversarial examples is large, our work leverages the *exploration and exploitation paradigm* [7] in order to strategically discover diverse adversarial examples for different failure categories. More specifically, EXPOUND first uses a coarse-grained *exploration* search to discover the categories of diverse erroneous behaviors for a DNN model, each of which is termed a *failure category*. Second, for each failure category, EXPOUND then applies a localized fine-grained *exploitation* search to identify a diverse secondary collection of adversarial examples, each of which leads to similar model misbehavior (i.e., different perturbations that lead to the same misclassification). Developers can then analyze the adversarial examples and focus their efforts to improve the model's performance against the most relevant adverse failure categories for their applications.

In order to generate diverse adversarial examples, EXPOUND uses novelty search [15] in two complementary ways. In contrast to traditional evolutionary search techniques, novelty search abandons the notion of objective fitness by promoting a diversity metric instead. Specifically, novelty search rewards individuals that are different from each other and produces an archive of diverse individuals. We developed two novelty-based techniques to support our objectives. First, KOBALOS[3] uses novelty search to *explore* the search space in order to *discover* the diverse set of possible failure categories for a DNN, where the

---

[1] This work uses the term *diversity* to describe different DNN model behaviors.

[2] One definition for *expound* is to explain systematically or in detail.

[3] Kobalos is a mischievous sprite in Greek mythology.

diversity metric is based on the diversity in the *output of the DNN model* (e.g., image classification label). KOBALOS *explores* and reduces the search space to diverse types of faults that are likely to induce a failure in the model. Next, TARAND[4] *exploits* the failure categories identified by KOBALOS. TARAND applies novelty search for each failure category, generating a *diverse set of faults* (e.g., perturbations) that cause the same type of model misbehavior. TARAND enables developers to assess the failure categories to determine which categories might be confidently misclassified. The breadth and depth-based approach to generate a diverse collection of image perturbations can better inform developers as to how a model's performance and robustness can be improved (e.g., select specific training data, robustness analysis, etc.). Figure 1 overviews the differences between image classification, existing black-box techniques for adversarial examples, and EXPOUND, where elements with hatched shading denote adversarial artifacts. Image classification algorithms seek to correctly label an object in an image (Fig. 1a). The objective of evolutionary search-based adversarial attacks, such as GenAttack [17] or EvoAttack [5], is to generate *one* adversarial example per execution (Fig. 1b) to establish the existence of adversarial examples. In contrast, EXPOUND identifies multiple failure categories, each of which comprises a number of distinct adversarial examples (Fig. 1c).

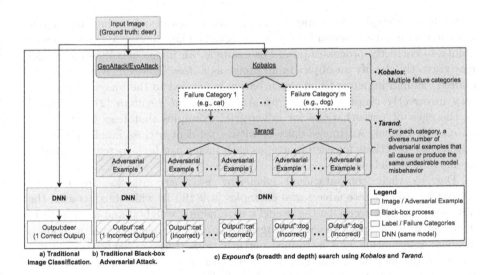

Fig. 1. Overview of image classification, adversarial example, and EXPOUND.

Preliminary results indicate that EXPOUND can discover adversarial examples that lead to different (undesirable) model behaviors that would otherwise not be discovered by existing evolutionary search-based approaches. We implemented the proposed two-phase framework and demonstrated the results on

---

[4] Tarand is a legendary creature with chameleon-like properties in Greek mythology.

existing image classification algorithms and benchmark datasets. To illustrate that our approach is model and data-agnostic, we used two different DNN architectures, ResNet-20 [10] and MobileNet-V2 [22], on two different benchmark datasets, CIFAR-10 [11] and German Traffic Sign Recognition Benchmark (GTSRB) dataset [23]. The remainder of the paper is organized as follows. Section 2 overviews background and related information for adversarial examples and novelty search. Section 3 describes the methodology for our proposed framework. Section 4 provides the implementation details and the results of a proof-of-concept validation experiment. Section 5 discusses related work. Section 6 concludes the paper and discusses future directions.

2   Background

This section overviews background information and enabling technologies used in this work. We describe adversarial examples and how they impact image classification algorithms. We also overview the key differences between traditional fitness-based evolutionary searches and novelty search.

2.1   Adversarial Examples

Adversarial examples are expected inputs for a machine learning model but modified with minor perturbations (i.e., noise). They hinder a DNN model's ability to correctly process inputs. For example, an image classification model may correctly classify an object in an image as a *deer*. However, when carefully crafted (human-imperceptible) perturbation is applied to the image, the model may incorrectly classify it as a *frog*. An *adversarial direction* [21] is defined as the class of perturbations for adversarial examples that lead to the same misclassified label. An image dataset with a total of n class labels has $n - 1$ adversarial directions for each image, as each image can be incorrectly classified as one of $n - 1$ labels.

Due to their computational efficiency, *white-box* attacks are popular approaches to generate adversarial examples [4,9,19]. In white-box attacks, the adversary has full access to the model's parameters, weights, and architecture. Traditional approaches for generating adversarial examples analyze a model's gradient information and introduce perturbations that are likely to induce a failure in the model. In practice, the model's hidden parameters are often proprietary (i.e., only the compiled model is available for public use). In contrast, black-box attacks assume that the adversary has no *a priori* knowledge of the model [24]. Instead, they may query the model with any valid input and obtain the model's output. The direction of perturbation must be inferred from the change in behavior caused by the perturbation during each query. Thus, black-box attacks are more realistic but more challenging to successfully generate adversarial examples when compared to white-box attacks [5,17].

2.2   Novelty Search

In contrast to traditional evolutionary techniques, whose objective is to seek solutions that optimize specific criteria, *novelty search* is an evolutionary search technique that focuses on the diversity of the evolved solutions. Traditional evolutionary algorithms focus on optimizing a fitness function (e.g., test case metrics, prediction confidence, etc.) and produce similar output(s). These algorithms are efficient and effective for simple problems, but are prone to be trapped in suboptimal regions [16]. Additionally, when there is no clear fitness metric or multiple solutions exist in different search regions/directions, fitness-based evolutionary search is no longer effective for such problem spaces. In order to explore the large search space and discover multiple interesting (unexpected) solutions, novelty search abandons the notion of fitness [15]. Specifically, novelty search promotes individuals in a population to be different than their neighbors. Example diversity criteria for novelty search include the diverse output labels of a DNN or diverse perturbation noise for adversarial examples. Finally, rather than searching for a single solution (i.e., one individual), novelty search produces and maintains an archive of the most diverse individuals by replacing similar individuals with least similar candidates in the archive during each generation.

3   Methodology

This section describes our EXPOUND framework, a two-phase search-based technique used to generate diverse archives of adversarial examples that result in different failure categories of the DNN model. Figure 2 shows a Data Flow Diagram (DFD) for EXPOUND, where circles indicate process bubbles, arrows indicate data flow between processes, and parallel lines indicate external data stores. EXPOUND takes a non-perturbed input image and the black-box image classification algorithm as inputs. First, a developer provides the evolutionary parameters (e.g., mutation rate, population size, etc.), operating context, and behavior specification for EXPOUND. The operating context defines the range of perturbations that EXPOUND can search to discover different model behaviors (i.e., the genome range). For example, a developer may define the operating context to generate adversarial examples with non-minimal perturbation, restricted to 10% of a pixel's maximum value. The behavior specification defines the possible range of behaviors exhibited by the model (i.e., the phenome range), such as image classification labels. Next, we describe the steps of EXPOUND in turn.

Step 1. Exploration. During the *exploration* phase, EXPOUND uses a coarse-grained novelty search to identify the broad adversarial directions when exposed to perturbations. For discussion purposes, we use the term *failure category* in this work to describe the diverse collection of adversarial examples that lead to the same adversarial direction. Specifically, different incorrect model outputs (e.g., misclassifying a *dog* as a *cat* versus a *dog* as a *deer*) are considered different failure categories, as the model incorrectly classified the image in different ways. For

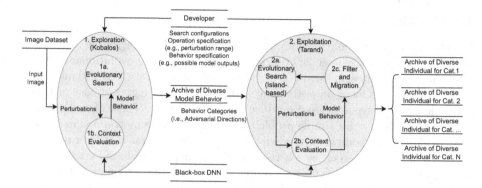

Fig. 2. EXPOUND's process to identify failure categories, each comprising diverse adversarial examples.

image classification problems, the number of potential failure categories increases based on the number of labels in the dataset. As such, it is computationally inefficient to exhaustively search every label to determine whether the model will misclassify an input image as the corresponding label when exposed to perturbations. Given an unperturbed input image and the DNN classifier, KOBALOS addresses this issue by exploring the search space and generating a collection of individuals that result in the most diverse model behaviors (i.e., most number of mutually exclusive class labels). The left portion of Fig. 3 provides a visual representation with colored regions denoting classification categories to illustrate KOBALOS's search on an input image of a *deer*. In this example, KOBALOS identifies two adversarial examples with different incorrect class labels, *dog* and *cat*, for the clean input image that has been exposed to perturbation. The bold arrows point towards incorrect class labels, indicating the failure categories identified by KOBALOS.

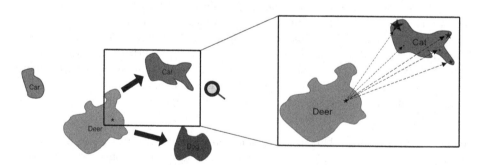

Fig. 3. High level interpretation of EXPOUND. Stars denote images. KOBALOS (left) discovers the failure categories while TARAND (right) exploits the information to discover diverse adversarial examples for each category identified.

Algorithm 1 shows the pseudo-code of KOBALOS to identify the broad failure categories using novelty search. KOBALOS largely follows a standard evolutionary algorithm approach in Step 1. First, a population of perturbation filters is randomly generated (i.e., filters are initialized with randomly sampled uniform noise). During each generation, individuals in the population are selected to reproduce, favoring those that result in phenome diversity. Specifically, the outputs of the DNN (i.e., vectors consisting of the label probabilities) are used as the phenomes. Parents create offspring using a single-point crossover operator and creep mutation operator. The creep mutation operator slightly increases or decreases the value of elements randomly sampled between a *mutation shift* variable with a *mutation rate* probability. Next, KOBALOS evaluates the individuals with the DNN to obtain the probability vectors (Step 1b in Fig. 2). Individuals are then ranked by computing a novelty score based on the *Euclidean distance* between phenomes with other individuals in the archive (line 13). Expression 1 shows the novelty score metric used in EXPOUND, computing the average distance between an individual (p) with the k-nearest neighbors in the archive (P).

$$\text{novelty}(\text{p}, \text{P}, k) = \text{mean}(\text{min-k}(\ \|\text{p} - \text{p}_i\|^2 \ \forall \text{p}_i \in \text{P} : \text{p}_i \neq \text{p}, k)) \qquad (1)$$

The archive of individuals (i.e., the output of KOBALOS) is then updated to maintain the most diverse individuals (i.e., those with different labels) discovered by replacing individuals with low novelty scores with individuals with higher scores (line 15). KOBALOS uses phenome diversity (i.e., classification output labels) to strategically explore the search space and identify the probable types of faults, instead of using a brute-force approach to explore all possible labels.

Algorithm 1: Pseudo-code for Kobalos and Tarand [13, 15].

```
 1  function NOVELTY-SEARCH(n_generations, image):
 2      archive ← ∅
 3      popl ← RANDOM-POPULATION()                // Initialize population with random noise.
 4      for ( n to n_generations ) {
 5          popl ← SELECTION(popl)                // Select genomes via tournament selection.
 6          popl ← RECOMBINATION(popl)            // Recombine via single-point crossover.
 7          popl ← MUTATION(popl)                       // Mutation via creep mutation.
 8          popl ← EVALUATE(popl)                   // Evaluate individuals using DNN.
 9          archive, popl ← COMMIT-TO-ARCHIVE(archive, popl)
10          popl ← FILTER(popl)                 // TARAND ONLY: filter and migrate individuals.
11      }
12      return archive
13  function COMMIT-TO-ARCHIVE(archive, popl):
14      scores ← RANK-INDIVIDUALS(archive, popl)          // Calc. novelty score (Eq.(1)).
15      archive ← TRIM(archive ∪ popl)          // Combine and truncate to desired size.
16      return archive, popl
```

Step 2. Exploitation. Once the failure categories have been identified in the exploration phase, EXPOUND uses TARAND for the *exploitation* phase in **Step 2**

to exploit the KOBALOS-discovered information. For each failure category identified in **Step 1**, TARAND uses novelty search to generate secondary archives of adversarial examples based on genome diversity (i.e., different combinations of noises that lead to the same misclassification). The archives of individuals (i.e., diverse types of faults) enable a more informed assessment of the types of perturbations within a given failure category. The right portion of Fig. 3 visually illustrates TARAND's search process to exploit the information identified by KOBALOS. Stars denote the original input image (i.e., deer) and adversarial examples generated by TARAND (e.g., an individual misclassified image). The relative size of individual stars contrast the respective confidence scores of the DNN for the image [21]. In this example, TARAND discovered a number of diverse adversarial examples that lead to the same *cat* misclassification. Adversarial examples discovered by TARAND in the archive have different types of perturbations, yet cause the same type of model misbehavior, denoted by thin dashed arrows. Understanding the nature and confidence scores for each failure category enables developers to focus their efforts to improve the robustness of the DNN (e.g., identify additional training data that addresses the misclassifications).

To discover a range of perturbations for each category of misclassification, TARAND maintains multiple islands of genomes. TARAND largely follows the same evolutionary process used by KOBALOS, but differs in the diversity metric. Specifically, KOBALOS optimizes a diversity metric based on the model's output (i.e., phenome defined in terms of image classification labels), while TARAND optimizes the diversity with respect to the perturbations that yield the same model output (i.e., genome). First, a population of perturbation filters are randomly generated using uniform sampling. During **Step 2a**, individuals are selected to evolve using single-point crossover and creep mutation operators based on their genome diversity. **Step 2b** evaluates the individuals in the population. The novelty score is computed using Expression 1, where P is based on the *genome* diversity of the population instead (i.e., TARAND promotes different perturbation filters). TARAND also includes an additional step, **Step 2c**, where individuals on an island that exhibit behavior different from other individuals on the same island are moved to the island with corresponding behavior (blue line 10 in Algorithm 1). For example, an adversarial example with the label *dog* on an island of *cats* will be filtered and migrated to the island containing *dogs*.

Misclassification Score. As novelty search promotes diversity, adversarial examples generated by TARAND can provide developers with insight on the boundaries of errors and confidence scores for the misclassifications in each failure category. For example, a developer may want to identify and prioritize categories that are confidently misclassified. Confidently misclassified inputs may pose a higher risk to safety-critical systems, as the system may mistakenly trust the model's output with higher weight based on the confidence score. Identifying confidently misclassified categories enables developers to include additional training data that may help the model distinguish between the two types of images. In this work, we first calculate and sort the archive of adversarial examples by confidence scores using the output of the model. We define the misclassification scores for each category using the average confidence score of the top 50% of sorted adversarial examples (i.e., archive[0.5 : 1].getConfidenceScores()), denoted by Expression (2). Specifically, categories that contain several confidently misclassified images will be assigned a higher score, close to 1.0.

$$\text{MisclassificationScore(archive)} = \text{mean(archive}[0.5 : 1].\text{getConfidenceScores())} \tag{2}$$

4   Validation Studies

This section demonstrates the EXPOUND framework using an empirical evaluation. We used two image classification DNNs with different architectures on two different image benchmark datasets to conduct our experiments. In order to assess whether EXPOUND can identify more failure categories for the DNN models, we compared KOBALOS with a Monte Carlo sampling method. Then, we compared the ability of TARAND and Monte Carlo sampling to generate archives of diverse adversarial examples for each failure category. This section addresses the following research questions:

RQ1: Can EXPOUND identify distinct failure categories using KOBALOS?
RQ2: Can EXPOUND identify more faults using TARAND for each failure category?

4.1   Experimental Setup

This section describes the experimental setup and evolutionary parameters used in our validation experiments. For our experiments, we used existing image classification algorithms implemented using the Pytorch deep learning research platform [18]. In order to illustrate that our approach is model and data-agnostic, we use two different benchmark datasets for our validation work. First, the CIFAR-10 benchmark dataset is commonly used for image classification algorithms [11], comprising ten evenly distributed categories. For the CIFAR-10 dataset, we used a ResNet-20 model with a base accuracy of 91.58% and a MobileNet-V2 model with a base accuracy of 91.52%. Second, we also use the GTSRB dataset [23]. Unlike the CIFAR-10 dataset, the GTSRB dataset consists of 43 classes of traffic signs with an uneven distribution of labels. For the GTSRB dataset, we used a ResNet-20 model with a base accuracy of 96.28% and a MobileNet-V2 model with a base accuracy of 90.77%.

In order to provide a baseline evaluation for our framework, we implemented a Monte Carlo sampling approach (i.e., randomly sample noise). Each approach generates an archive size based on the total number of labels in the dataset (i.e., 10 for CIFAR-10 and 43 for GTSRB). Table 1 shows the evolutionary parameters used in EXPOUND, where the parameters are based on empirical studies. The maximum perturbation for each approach is set to $[-0.1, +0.1]$ of the maximum pixel value. All experiments are conducted on a NVIDIA GeForce GTX 1080

GPU with an Intel Core i7-7700K CPU on Ubuntu 22.04. Finally, each experiment is repeated ten times using different seeds. We show the average value of the experiments, their standard deviations, and provide statistical analysis to ensure the feasibility of our approach. For the results, we verify their statistical significance using the Mann-Whitney U test.

Table 1. Configuration settings for EXPOUND

Parameter	CIFAR10		GTSRB	
	Value (Kobalos)	Value (Tarand)	Value (Kobalos)	Value (Tarand)
Archive Size	10	10	43	10
Population Size	10	10	10	43
Num Generations	100	500	100	500
Mutation Rate	0.15	0.15	0.15	0.15
Mutation Shift	0.2	0.2	0.2	0.2

4.2 Coarse-Grained Search for Distinct Failure Categories (RQ1)

To address our first research question, we evaluate KOBALOS's ability to discover distinct failure categories for DNN models by comparing the results with Monte Carlo sampling. We define our null and alternate hypotheses as follows:

$RQ1 - H_0$: KOBALOS does not identify more failure categories.
$RQ1 - H_1$: KOBALOS identifies more failure categories.

For each experiment and dataset, 30 randomly-sampled input images were used. For each image, a collection of 10 individuals is generated for the CIFAR-10 dataset while a collection of 43 individuals is generated for the GTSRB dataset, based on the number of possible labels for each dataset.

In order to ensure the feasibility of our approach, results are shown as the mean over ten trials to account for statistical variance. Table 2 shows the average number of unique labels identified by each approach when used to discover failure categories. The standard deviation is denoted in parenthesis, while the best performing technique is indicated in bold. The p-value for each experiment is shown in the last column. For each combination of DNN architectures and datasets, EXPOUND consistently discovered more failure categories than Monte Carlo sampling (on average 80% more for CIFAR-10 and 270% more for GTSRB). We found strong evidence ($p \leq 0.01$) to reject H_0 and support H_1. These results indicate EXPOUND can consistently discover more distinct failure categories.

Fig. 4 shows an example output of EXPOUND's exploration phase for an image randomly sampled in the CIFAR-10 dataset against the ResNet-20 model. The top image shows the clean input image and the model's correct classification output. Next, the collection of noise filters generated by KOBALOS (left) and

Table 2. Results for Monte Carlo sampling and EXPOUND's search for failure categories in the DNN's output. EXPOUND consistently identified more failure categories.

DNN and Dataset	Number of Average Unique Labels		p-value significance
	Monte Carlo	KOBALOS	
ResNet-20 - CIFAR-10	2.02 ($\sigma = 0.10$)	**3.62** ($\sigma = 0.17$)	< 0.01
MobileNet-V2 - CIFAR-10	1.83 ($\sigma = 0.09$)	**3.33** ($\sigma = 0.13$)	< 0.01
ResNet-20 - GTSRB	1.94 ($\sigma = 0.08$)	**7.11** ($\sigma = 0.19$)	< 0.01
MobileNet-V2 - GTSRB	1.73 ($\sigma = 0.09$)	**6.45** ($\sigma = 0.09$)	< 0.01

the corresponding adversarial examples (right) are shown in the second row. As indicated by the number of misclassifications, adversarial examples generated by KOBALOS induce different distinct misbehaviors in the model's output.

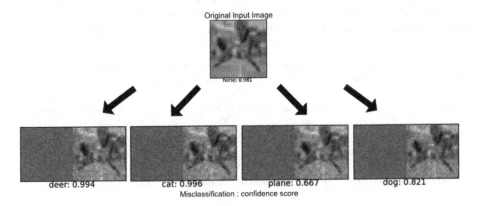

Fig. 4. Example output of KOBALOS on an input image of a *horse*. KOBALOS discovered four different incorrect model behaviors when exposed to perturbations.

4.3 Fine-Grained Search for Diverse Adversarial Examples (RQ2)

In this experiment, we demonstrate that TARAND can generate a diverse archive of adversarial examples for each failure category identified by KOBALOS. Specifically, we illustrate the ability of TARAND to exploit the information from KOBALOS and generate an archive of ten individuals for each category of misbehavior identified. For example, if six failure categories have been identified by KOBALOS, then TARAND attempts to generate six secondary archives of adversarial examples, one for each failure category. We compare the results of TARAND with Monte Carlo sampling. Monte Carlo sampling generates adversarial examples equal to the number of adversarial examples generated by TARAND. The adversarial examples generated by Monte Carlo sampling are then sorted into their corresponding failure categories. We define our null and alternate hypotheses to answer this question as follows:

$RQ2 - H_0$: TARAND does not identify more faults for each failure category.
$RQ2 - H_1$: TARAND identifies more faults for each failure category.

Table 3 shows the experimental results for the fine-grained exploitation search. The table shows how well a given technique under study is able to generate distinct and diverse adversarial examples, each resulting in similar misclassification labels. For example, a full archive (i.e., 100%) for an image from the CIFAR-10 dataset denotes that 10 adversarial examples were discovered for each failure category identified. The standard deviation is shown in parenthesis. The final column of the table shows the corresponding p-value using the Mann-Whitney U test. When applied to the same set of thirty images, TARAND is able to successfully generate a (relatively full) archive of adversarial examples for most failure categories. In contrast, Monte Carlo sampling consistently did not generate adversarial examples for the failure categories. For each experiment, we found strong evidence ($p \leq 0.01$) to reject H_0 and support H_1. The results indicate that TARAND can generate more and different perturbations for a given failure category, a new capability not offered by existing approaches.

Table 3. Comparing TARAND's generation of diverse archives of adversarial examples for the categories of misbehavior against Monte Carlo sampling.

DNN and Dataset	Percentage of Archives Filled		p-value significance
	Monte Carlo	TARAND	
ResNet-20 - CIFAR-10	26.36% ($\sigma = 2.69\%$)	**93.73%** ($\sigma = 1.35\%$)	< 0.01
MobileNet-V2 - CIFAR-10	33.43% ($\sigma = 1.09\%$)	**91.59%** ($\sigma = 1.20\%$)	< 0.01
ResNet-20 - GTSRB	14.48% ($\sigma = 1.05\%$)	**81.16%** ($\sigma = 1.09\%$)	< 0.01
MobileNet-V2 - GTSRB	11.12% ($\sigma = 0.95\%$)	**71.93%** ($\sigma = 1.43\%$)	< 0.01

The archives of adversarial examples generated by TARAND can be used to assess the model's robustness towards each of the incorrect labels identified by EXPOUND. Specifically, each archive of adversarial examples generated by TARAND promotes genome diversity that produces the same model behavior failure. Thus, we can identify relevant and confidently misclassified failure categories based on the confidence scores of the adversarial examples. We calculate the misclassification score based on Expression (2) defined in Sect. 3. Figure 5 shows a sample output of TARAND randomly sampled from the CIFAR-10 dataset. The ground truth for the clean input image is *truck*. Each row denotes a failure category identified by EXPOUND. Individual scores show the confidence scores for the diverse archive of adversarial examples generated by TARAND. Finally, the misclassification score of each category is computed and shown in parenthesis next to the class label. The failure categories are sorted based on the misclassification score, in descending order. As the results indicate, adversarial examples with the labels *bird* and *ship* are not commonly misclassified with high confidence scores (i.e., less than 0.7). However, the model confidently misclassifies adversarial examples as *frogs*. Thus, developers may use this information to include additional training samples that distinguish frogs from trucks.

Frog-(Score=0.78): [0.39, 0.40, 0.46, 0.50, 0.64, 0.67, 0.71, 0.81, 0.81, 0.90]
Cat-(Score=0.68): [0.31, 0.35, 0.43, 0.47, 0.48, 0.53, 0.59, 0.61, 0.71, 0.94]
Bird-(Score=0.65): [0.37, 0.39, 0.46, 0.49, 0.54, 0.56, 0.65, 0.67, 0.68, 0.69]
Ship-(Score=0.57): [0.32, 0.35, 0.38, 0.39, 0.47, 0.50, 0.52, 0.58, 0.58, 0.68]

Fig. 5. An analysis of adversarial examples generated with TARAND for an image of a *truck*. The (sorted) misclassification score is shown in parenthesis. The numbers in brackets show the confidence scores of individual adversarial examples.

4.4 Threats to Validity

The results in this paper show that a diverse collection of adversarial examples can be generated against DNNs using novelty search. The results of the experiment may vary with repeated executions, as novelty search and evolutionary search-based algorithms rely on randomness. To ensure the feasibility of our approach, a wide range of sample of input images were sampled from different datasets. Additionally, each experiment was repeated ten times with different randomly-generated seeds to ensure comparable results.

5 Related Work

Early work with adversarial examples was generated using white-box approaches [24]. These approaches leverage gradient information of the model to be attacked and introduce noise to hinder the model's capability. Szegedy *et al.* [19] first introduced adversarial examples generated using the L-BFGS algorithm. Carlini and Wagner [4] proposed a similar approach with a modified objective function and constraint, known as the C&W attack. Goodfellow *et al.* [9] introduced the Fast Gradient Sign Method (FGSM) that perturbs the target image based on the signed gradient at each step. However, these techniques are all white-box, where gradient information and other model parameters are assumed to be accessible.

A number of researchers have also explored black-box evolutionary search-based approaches to generate adversarial examples. Compared to white-box approaches, black-box approaches closely resemble a real attack scenario, where the development of the model is proprietary. Papernot *et al.* [20] demonstrated that white-box adversarial attacks can transfer to other models. In contrast, Alzantot *et al.* [17], Vidnerová *et al.* [26], Chen *et al.* [6] proposed various genetic algorithm approaches to generate adversarial examples against image classification algorithms. Chan and Cheng proposed EvoAttack [5] that showed adversarial attacks also apply to object detection algorithms, an important component for perception sensing in autonomous vehicles. However, these approaches generate adversarial examples that do not reveal diverse model behaviors.

Several existing work has explored the use of diversity for DNNs. Rozsa *et al.* [21] introduced the use of a diverse set of adversarial examples to evaluate and retrain models. However, their approach generates adversarial examples using a white-box approach and does not discover failure categories. Aghababaeyan *et al.*

[1] proposed the use of the geometric diversity metric to identify a diverse set of test cases from the original input dataset based on their similarity to other samples. Langford and Cheng [13,14] proposed several novelty search techniques to explore the effect of environmental uncertainties on DNNs. However, their approach does not address the robustness of the DNN against noise perturbation or adversarial examples. In their work, Enki [13] is used to generate environmental uncertainties against a DNN model applied over a dataset. The identified environmental uncertainties demonstrate the inability of the DNNs to process the occluded inputs, including those that prevent human classification. They also proposed Enlil [14], a novelty search framework to discover operating contexts that can lead to different categories of performance degradation. To the best of our knowledge, EXPOUND is the first black-box approach to explore the use of novelty search to generate diverse adversarial examples that can discover a number of distinct failure categories, providing both breadth and depth-based information about the types of perturbations that cause model misbehaviors.

6   Conclusion

This paper proposed EXPOUND, a novelty search-based framework to generate diverse adversarial examples. We showed that our two-phase framework first identifies failure categories for image classification algorithms that would otherwise not be discovered by existing approaches. Furthermore, EXPOUND then generates secondary archives of diverse adversarial examples for each failure category identified, enabling the assessment for the misclassification score of each category. We conducted a series of experiments to show that our approach can successfully generate adversarial examples against different datasets and models without access to model weights, architectures, and gradient information.

Future work will explore additional datasets and models for validation results. Additional studies may be performed to explore whether noise generated from EXPOUND transfers to other images. Future studies may also explore whether novelty search might be used to discover if "universal" adversarial perturbations exist and can be used to improve a DNN's robustness. Additional work may explore the ability of EXPOUND to generate diverse adversarial examples against models with defense mechanisms [12]. Finally, we will investigate whether EXPOUND can be applied to other types of machine learning algorithms, such as speech analysis, natural language processing, or object detection algorithms.

Acknowledgements. We greatly appreciate Michael Austin Langford's contributions on our preliminary work. We also greatly appreciate the insightful and detailed feedback from the reviewers. This work was supported in part by funding provided by Michigan State University, the BEACON Center, the Air Force Research Laboratory, and our industrial collaborators.

References

1. Aghababaeyan, Z., Abdellatif, M., Dadkhah, M., Briand, L.: DeepGD: a multi-objective black-box test selection approach for deep neural networks. arXiv (2023)
2. Arrieta, B., et al.: Explainable artificial intelligence (XAI): concepts, taxonomies, opportunities and challenges toward responsible AI. Inf. Fusion **58**, 82–115 (2020). https://doi.org/10.1016/j.inffus.2019.12.012
3. Cai, Z., Fan, Q., Feris, R.S., Vasconcelos, N.: A unified multi-scale deep convolutional neural network for fast object detection. In: Leibe, B., Matas, J., Sebe, N., Welling, M. (eds.) ECCV 2016. LNCS, vol. 9908, pp. 354–370. Springer, Cham (2016). https://doi.org/10.1007/978-3-319-46493-0_22
4. Carlini, N., Wagner, D.: Towards evaluating the robustness of neural networks. In: 2017 IEEE Symposium on Security and Privacy (SP), pp. 39–57. IEEE (2017)
5. Chan, K., Cheng, B.H.C.: EvoAttack: an evolutionary search-based adversarial attack for object detection models. In: Papadakis, M., Vergilio, S.R. (eds.) SSBSE 2022. LNCS, vol. 13711, pp. 83–97. Springer, Cham (2022). https://doi.org/10.1007/978-3-031-21251-2_6
6. Chen, J., et al.: POBA-GA: perturbation optimized black-box adversarial attacks via genetic algorithm. Comput. Secur. **85**, 89–106 (2019)
7. Črepinšek, M., Liu, S.H., Mernik, M.: Exploration and exploitation in evolutionary algorithms: a survey. ACM Comput. Surv. (CSUR) **45**(3), 1–33 (2013)
8. Gheibi, O., Weyns, D., Quin, F.: Applying machine learning in self-adaptive systems: a systematic literature review. ACM TAAS **15**(3), 1–37 (2021)
9. Goodfellow, I., Shlens, J., Szegedy, C.: Explaining and harnessing adversarial examples. In: International Conference on Learning Representations (2015)
10. He, K., et al.: Deep residual learning for image recognition. In: Proceedings of the IEEE Conference on Computer Vision and Pattern Recognition, pp. 770–778 (2016)
11. Krizhevsky, A., et al.: Learning multiple layers of features from tiny images (2009)
12. Kurakin, A., et al.: Adversarial attacks and defences competition. In: Escalera, S., Weimer, M. (eds.) The NIPS '17 Competition: Building Intelligent Systems. TSSCML, pp. 195–231. Springer, Cham (2018). https://doi.org/10.1007/978-3-319-94042-7_11
13. Langford, M.A., Cheng, B.H.C.: Enki: a diversity-driven approach to test and train robust learning-enabled systems. ACM TAAS **15**(2), 1–32 (2021)
14. Langford, M.A., Cheng, B.H.C.: "Know what you know": predicting behavior for learning-enabled systems when facing uncertainty. In: 2021 International Symposium on Software Engineering for Adaptive and Self-Managing Systems, pp. 78–89. IEEE (2021)
15. Lehman, J., Stanley, K.O.: Abandoning objectives: evolution through the search for novelty alone. Evol. Comput. **19**(2), 189–223 (2011)
16. Lehman, J., Stanley, K.O.: Novelty search and the problem with objectives. In: Riolo, R., Vladislavleva, E., Moore, J. (eds.) Genetic Programming Theory and Practice IX. Genetic and Evolutionary Computation, pp. 37–56. Springer, New York (2011). https://doi.org/10.1007/978-1-4614-1770-5_3
17. Alzantot et al.: GenAttack: practical black-box attacks with gradient-free optimization. In: Proceedings of the Genetic and Evolutionary Computation Conference, pp. 1111–1119 (2019)
18. Paszke, A., et al.: PyTorch: an imperative style, high-performance deep learning library. In: Wallach, H., et al. (eds.) Advances in Neural Information Processing Systems vol. 32, pp. 8024–8035. Curran Associates, Inc. (2019)

19. Szegedy et al.: Intriguing properties of neural networks. In: International Conference on Learning Representations (2014)
20. Papernot, N., McDaniel, P., Goodfellow, I.: Transferability in machine learning: from phenomena to black-box attacks using adversarial samples. arXiv (2016)
21. Rozsa, A., et al.: Adversarial diversity and hard positive generation. In: Proceedings of the IEEE Conference on Computer Vision and Pattern Recognition (2016)
22. Sandler, M., et al.: Mobilenetv 2: inverted residuals and linear bottlenecks. In: Proceedings of the IEEE Conference on Computer Vision and Pattern Recognition, pp. 4510–4520 (2018)
23. Stallkamp, J., et al.: The GTSRB: a multi-class classification competition. In: The 2011 International Joint Conference on Neural Networks, pp. 1453–1460. IEEE (2011)
24. Sun, L., et al.: A survey of practical adversarial example attacks. Cybersecurity **1**, 1–9 (2018)
25. Szegedy, C., Toshev, A., Erhan, D.: Deep neural networks for object detection. In: Advances in Neural Information Processing Systems, vol. 26 (2013)
26. Vidnerová, P., Neruda, R.: Vulnerability of classifiers to evolutionary generated adversarial examples. Neural Netw. **127**, 168–181 (2020)
27. Wallace, E., et al.: Trick me if you can: human-in-the-loop generation of adversarial examples for question answering. TACL **7**, 387–401 (2019)
28. Yu, F., et al.: Interpreting and evaluating neural network robustness (2019). https://doi.org/10.24963/ijcai.2019/583. (IJCAI 2019)

Developer Views on Software Carbon Footprint and Its Potential for Automated Reduction

Haozhou Lyu[1], Gregory Gay[1]([✉]) [iD], and Maiko Sakamoto[2]

[1] Chalmers and University of Gothenburg, Gothenburg, Sweden
haozhou@student.chalmers.se, greg@greggay.com
[2] University of Tokyo, Tokyo, Japan
m-sakamoto@k.u-tokyo.ac.jp

Abstract. Reducing software carbon footprint could contribute to efforts to avert climate change. Past research indicates that developers lack knowledge on energy consumption and carbon footprint, and existing reduction guidelines are difficult to apply. Therefore, we propose that automated reduction methods should be explored, e.g., through *genetic improvement*. However, such tools must be *voluntarily adopted and regularly used* to have an impact.

In this study, we have conducted interviews and a survey (a) to explore developers' existing opinions, knowledge, and practices with regard to carbon footprint and energy consumption, and (b), to identify the requirements that automated reduction tools must meet to ensure adoption. Our findings offer a foundation for future research on practices, guidelines, and automated tools that address software carbon footprint.

Keywords: Carbon Footprint · Energy Consumption · Sustainability · Genetic Improvement · Genetic Programming

1 Introduction

The carbon dioxide emitted through development and use of software may contribute to climate change. In 2015, data centers accounted for an estimated 3.00% of global energy consumption—double that of the United Kingdom and matching the airline industry [2]. Training a single neural network can emit as much carbon as the entire lifetime of five cars [8]. That carbon footprint *must be reduced*, but this is not a straight-forward task. There are sources of emissions at multiple stages of development, produced through development and use of software [18]. Further, while carbon footprint is largely a product of energy consumption, the *quantity*, *sources*, and *location* of consumption are important.

Researchers have begun to make recommendations on how to reduce carbon footprint (e.g., [10,19,22]). Such guidelines are highly important, but can be difficult to apply—especially after the code has been written. Further, it is not clear that developers have a clear understanding of carbon footprint, energy consumption, or how either can be reduced during development [12–14].

P. Arcaini et al. (Eds.): SSBSE 2023, LNCS 14415, pp. 35–51, 2024.
https://doi.org/10.1007/978-3-031-48796-5_3

Therefore, we are interested in exploring *automated* reduction of carbon footprint. There are multiple stages of development that could benefit from such reduction—e.g., design, implementation, or maintenance—and multiple practices or development artifacts that could be optimized—e.g., source code, processes, or design models. To ground this study, we focus on one example—where a tool would transform the existing source code of the project-under-development to reduce the carbon footprint caused by the usage of the software. This tool could take measurements, e.g., of energy consumption, data transfer, and other factors related to the carbon footprint—measured during test case execution—to assess the impact of the attempted transformations.

Such transformations should preserve semantic meaning while reducing the carbon footprint by, e.g., reducing energy consumption or controlling where energy is consumed. A promising technique to impose such changes is *genetic improvement* (GI) [3], where populations of program patches are scored according to qualities of interest, then evolved over many generations to maximize or minimize these scores. GI has been applied to reduce energy consumption (e.g., [3,6,10,11,20]), and other researchers have recently suggested the potential of GI with regard to carbon footprint reduction [7,15]. We, similarly, propose that such approaches could be extended, or new approaches could be developed, specifically to target carbon footprint.

The development of such tools could improve the sustainability of the IT industry. However, such tools *must be voluntarily adopted and regularly used by developers*. The goals of this study are (a) to explore developers' existing opinions, knowledge, and practices in this area, and (b), to identify the requirements that automated tools must meet to ensure voluntary adoption. We conducted a set of initial interviews, followed by a broader survey of software developers, and performed thematic and quantitative analyses of the collected data.

This study provides a foundation for future research by exploring requirements for automated carbon footprint reduction tools. We also offer insights to those interested in the existing opinions, knowledge, and practices of developers. To help enable future research, we also make a replication package available [9].

2 Background and Related Work

Carbon Footprint and Energy Consumption of Software: Carbon footprint is the total quantity of carbon dioxide emissions associated with an individual, product, or organization's activities. This can include direct (e.g., fuel consumed during production) or indirect emissions (e.g., energy consumption) [21].

Software is a source of carbon emissions. There are sources of both direct and indirect emission at multiple phases of development, including implementation, testing, delivery, usage, and maintenance [18]. In this research, our scope is primarily restricted to indirect emissions associated with energy consumption during software *usage*—i.e., when interactions take place with the software.

Within this scope, carbon footprint is affected both by the *quantity* of energy consumed and *where and how* that energy is produced or consumed, as some energy sources have a greater carbon footprint than others. Calculating and reducing software carbon footprint is not simple, as it is affected by energy usage on both the client-side (i.e., on consumer devices) and server-side (i.e., at data centers in disparate geographic areas), as well as on network transmissions between the two [1]. Automated approaches must consider not just energy quantity, but also aspects such as the location of computing elements.

Genetic Improvement: GI is the automated improvement of non-functional qualities (e.g., performance) of software through transformations to the source code [3]. Population of patches are produced and then judged using one or more fitness functions related to the qualities of interest. The patches that yield the best scores form a new population through mutation—where stochastic changes are introduced—or crossover—where aspects of "parent" patches combine to form new "children". Carbon footprint can be considered a quality, improved through appropriate program transformations and fitness functions.

Related Work: Researchers have found that most programmers are largely unaware of energy consumption, lack knowledge on the causes or how to measure consumption, and rarely address energy issues [12–14]. Some developers even regard green software design as a "threat" that could disrupt their workflow [12]. Our study yields similar findings on energy consumption, but extends our understanding with regard to developer opinions on carbon footprint, current practices regarding both carbon footprint and energy consumption, and opinions on automated improvement tools.

Past research has offered guidelines on how to reduce energy consumption and carbon footprint (e.g., algorithm selection [10], code structure [22], considering server distribution and location [10], or controlling image quality [19]). Such guidelines are highly important, but are not always easy to apply. Nor is it simple to manually improve code after it has been written. Therefore, we are interested in automated carbon footprint reduction techniques.

To date, we are unaware of any automated tools specifically targeting carbon footprint. However, there have been several approaches targeting energy consumption, mostly based on genetic improvement (e.g., [3,6,10,11,20]). Other approaches include specialized compilers [16] and data migration strategies [5]. We hypothesize that GI can also reduce carbon footprint, potentially by extending existing approaches to consider both client and server-side components and additional fitness functions. Other researchers have also recently suggested the use of GI in this area, e.g., to improve Machine Learning frameworks [7,15].

3   Methodology

Our study is guided by the following research questions:

- **RQ1:** What knowledge do developers have about the carbon footprint or energy consumption of software?
- **RQ2:** How do developers assess and control the carbon footprint or energy consumption of their software?

Table 1. Demographic information on interviewees, including location, position, job responsibilities (self-described), and development experience (years).

ID	Country	Position	Responsibility	Exp.
P1	Sweden	Manager	Overlook technical road maps	25
P2	Japan	Developer	Data analysis and development	5
P3	Sweden	Student	Developer testing televisions	4
P4	Sweden	Manager	Technical strategy and development process	20
P5	Japan	Developer	Develops software	5
P6	Japan	Developer	Network operation and maintenance tools	4
P7	Japan	Developer	Service planning and development	7
P8	Japan	Researcher	AI and robotics development	6
P9	Sweden	Student	Machine Learning development	4
P10	Sweden	Developer	C software development	4

- **RQ3:** What requirements and constraints must be satisfied for developers to trust carbon footprint reduction tools?
- **RQ4:** How should a reduction tool fit into the development workflow?
- **RQ5:** How can voluntary adoption of reduction tools be encouraged?

To answer these questions, we conducted semi-structured interviews, then performed thematic analysis following Cruzes and Dyba's guidelines [4], to gain an initial understanding. Then, based on the interview results, we developed a survey to gain additional insights from a broader range of participants.

We do not collect personal information, but rather data on participants' perceptions and practices. All collected information was fully anonymized. Participation in the study was voluntary. Given these considerations, obtaining ethical approval was deemed unnecessary at our institutes.

3.1 Interviews

Population Definition: Our population consists of participants with experience developing software, including professionals and university students studying a related discipline.

Sampling: We interviewed 10 participants. The sampling method was a mix of purposive and convenience sampling. The professionals were gathered from companies in Sweden and Japan using LinkedIn, as well as through personal contacts. After 10 interviews, we had achieved result saturation.

Demographics: Table 1 shows information on participants. To maintain confidentiality, we omit participants' names. These participants come from various roles, with experience ranging from 4–25 years, and experience in a variety of domains (e.g., robotics, machine learning, web applications).

Interview Guide: The interview questions can be found in our replication package [9]. The questions were open-ended, so we could ask follow-up questions if needed, while ensuring we answered the core research questions. The 13 questions were divided into three sections: (1) prior knowledge, (2) experiences and opinions, and (3), requirements for automated carbon footprint reduction tools.

Table 2. Survey respondent demographics.

ID	Country	Position	Software Domain	Experience
I1	China	Developer	Embedded system	1–3 years
I2	Japan	Developer	Sever web service	1–3 years
I3	Denmark	Researcher	Web applications	9 years+
I4	Japan	Developer	Internal tools	4–6 years
I5	Sweden	Developer	Embedded system	7–9 years
I6	Ireland	Researcher	Programming environment	9 years+
I7	Japan	Manager	Web applications	7–9 years
I8	Sweden	Student	Embedded system	4–6 years
I9	UK	Developer	Web applications	<1 year
I10	China	Student	Embedded system	1–3 years
I11	UK	Developer	Web applications	1–3 years
I12	Sweden	Student	Various	1–3 years
I13	USA	Developer	Web applications	<1 year
I14	Sweden	Manager	Analytics	9 years+
I15	Sweden	Developer	Web and desktop applications	7–9 years
I16	Romania	Developer	Web and desktop applications	1–3 years
I17	Sweden	Developer	Data analytics	1–3 years
I18	Sweden	Developer	Various applications	1–3 years
I19	Sweden	Manager	Web applications	9 years+
I20	Sweden	Developer	Data analysis application	4–6 years
I21	Sweden	Developer	Web applications	9 years+
I22	India	Manager	Web applications	9 years+
I23	Ireland	Developer	Windows and Web applications	9 years+
I24	Sweden	Manager	Enterprise software	9 years+
I25	Sweden	Manager	Business intelligence	9 years+
I26	Sweden	Developer	Visual analysis software	9 years+
I27	Sweden	Developer	Visual analysis software	9 years+
I28	Sweden	Developer	On-prem client, cloud service	9 years+
I29	France	Developer	Web applications	4–6 years
I30	Japan	Developer	Mobile mini applications	<1 year
I31	Japan	Developer	Embedded system	1–3 years
I32	Japan	Developer	System software	1–3 years
I33	Japan	Developer	Web applications	<1 year
I34	Japan	Developer	Web applications	1–3 years
I35	Japan	Developer	Cloud web applications	1–3 years
I36	Japan	Developer	Web applications	1–3 years
I37	Japan	Developer	Artificial Intelligence	1–3 years
I38	Japan	Developer	Web applications	1–3 years
I39	Japan	Unemployed	N/A	1–3 years
I40	Sweden	Developer	SAAS	1–3 years

Data Collection: During interviews, we introduced the background and purpose of the research. We then conducted the semi-structured interview. Following completion, we answered their questions and shared information on the project. From November to December 2022, all interviews were conducted online and lasted between 20 and 30 min. Participants were interviewed in English. To analyze the results, we recorded both video and audio. We transcribed our records using a denaturalism approach. Transcriptions were performed using a speech-to-text tool. We referred to the recordings to make clarifications.

Data Analysis: We adopted thematic coding. We familiarized ourselves with the data by reading the transcript repeatedly and identifying relevant segments (codes). These codes were organized and aggregated into themes and sub-themes. After each interview, we modified the codes and themes, and paused for discussion. We stopped when no new codes were found in transcripts. Attention was paid to ensuring that each code was accurate to the original response.

Coding was conducted by the first author. However, the second author independently coded one interview to ensure reliability. As only minor differences were observed, coding of the remaining interviews proceeded.

3.2   Survey

Population and Sampling: Our population and sampling methods are the same as in the interviews. We sent the questionnaire directly to some participants, and also distributed it on LinkedIn, Facebook, Twitter, and Mastadon. Between November–December 2022, 40 respondents completed the survey.

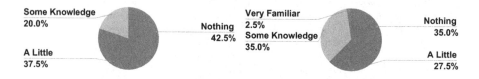

Fig. 1. Knowledge of carbon footprint (left) and energy consumption (right).

Participant Demographics: Table 2 shows demographic information. The participants come from various countries—although most are still from Japan and Sweden—with varied roles, experience levels, and development domains.

Survey Guide: The survey questions are in our replication package [9]. To ensure a high response rate, the survey was designed to be as brief—lasting between 10–15 min. The 26 questions consist of open-ended, multiple choice, ordinal scale, and interval scale questions [17].

Data Collection: The partially-structured questionnaire design method was adopted to ensure participants had freedom to express their opinions. The questionnaire is divided into three parts, mapped to the same topics as the interviews.

Data Analysis: We use descriptive statistics to analyze quantitative data. Qualitative data was incorporated into our previous thematic mapping.

4   Results and Discussion

In this section, we answer the research questions using data from both the interviews and survey.

4.1   Existing Knowledge (RQ1)

As shown in Fig. 1, 80% of survey participants are either unfamiliar with or only have a little knowledge on carbon footprint. Participants had somewhat more knowledge on energy consumption, but 63% still had no or little knowledge. Encouragingly, however, many interviewees had—at least—basic knowledge of factors that impact energy consumption or carbon footprint. For example:

> "That's not something that I think about daily. The only thing I can think about is all the things that we store on service, in the cloud, of course, those computers need electricity. There's been a lot of talk about mining cryptocurrency. It's not a sustainable way of handling money." - **P4**

Another noted how sources of energy affect carbon footprint:

> "[Carbon footprint] depends on where the energy comes from. If the energy is carbon neutral, then the footprint is still small, even if you consume lots of energy ... Most of our customers are not in Sweden, but most of our development is in Sweden. I would say majority of the energy in Sweden is not carbon-based ... water, wind, nuclear, and so on." - **P1**

As shown in Fig. 2, as the experience of developers grows, there is also some increase in their median level of knowledge on both topics. Over time, developers tend to acquire knowledge of specialized topics and be more confident in their knowledge. The median knowledge of carbon footprint remains at a relatively low level—between "little" and "some" knowledge—but does rise. The median level of knowledge on energy consumption rises more noticeably to "some" knowledge.

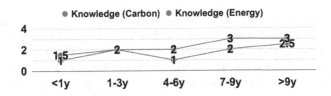

Fig. 2. Median knowledge versus experience (1 = "Nothing", 4 = "Very Familiar").

Fig. 3. Degree of agreement on whether software carbon footprint contributes to climate change (left) and whether software carbon footprint should be considered and controlled (right) (1 = "strongly disagree", 5 = "strongly agree").

Fig. 4. Percentage that believe entity is responsible for controlling footprint.

4.2 Developer Opinions and Practices (RQ2)

Developer Opinions: Figure 3 (left) shows a largely balanced view on whether software carbon footprint contributes to climate change, with a plurality (48%) expressing a neutral view. However, somewhat more participants agree (30%) than disagree (23%). Figure 3 (right) also shows that more participants (40%) agree that carbon footprint should be considered than disagree (18%). Again, however, a plurality are neutral (43%). In both cases, there was no discernible change in opinion as developers gained experience.

Figure 4 shows participants' views on who holds responsibility for considering or controlling energy consumption or carbon footprint. Participants could select more than one option. The majority of respondents felt that both organizations (65%) and regulatory agencies (63%) should bare responsibility. Only 10% believed that no one holds responsibility. Interviewees noted that developers must comply with the company's development rules, business goals, and release criteria. Therefore, they may not have the option of reducing energy consumption.

We suggest that development organizations could take a larger responsibility by raising awareness among their staff, e.g., hosting seminars or training programs that teach sustainable development practices. Companies could also prioritize energy consumption or carbon footprint as part of project goals and impose policies to control their impact on the environment. Regulatory agencies can also formulate stronger policies regarding the IT industry.

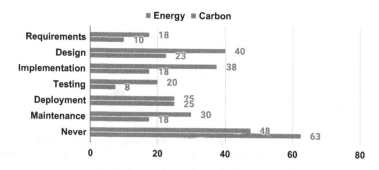

Fig. 5. Percentage that considered energy or carbon footprint at a stage.

Development Stages: Carbon footprint and energy consumption can be considered during multiple development stages. Interviewees considered both during design, testing, and maintenance. During design, developers estimate the number of end users and specify resources (e.g., number and capability of servers):

> "During the design phase, we're going to make some estimations. We're going to decide what technologies are we going to use, how many servers we are going to have, what is the load that we are expecting." - **P2**

Additionally, problematic energy consumption can be observed and mitigated after the system is deployed:

> "... When we actually run something in production and see that ... we are overloading the systems, we need to do something about that." - **P3**

Figure 5 illustrates when survey participants considered energy consumption and carbon footprint. In both cases, the largest percentage of participants— 48% for energy consumption and 63% for carbon footprint—never took action. For energy consumption, the most consideration is given during design (40%) and implementation (38%) phases. During design, decisions are made on the system architecture, which often must incorporate consideration of energy. These decisions are realized during implementation.

Many also considered carbon footprint during design (23%). However, deployment (25%) was the most common phase for carbon footprint. Gaining an accurate estimation of carbon footprint may be difficult before the system is in operation, where usage statistics can be gathered as well as knowledge of where users and data centers are located. Some energy decisions can be made without such information, so energy consumption could be considered early in development to also limit carbon footprint. Once the system is deployed, statistics on carbon footprint can be gathered and changes can be made, if needed.

Automated tools could be deployed at different stages to improve various design and implementation artifacts. The example we proposed—automated source code transformation to reduce carbon footprint from software usage— would be used during the implementation, deployment, or maintenance phases— i.e., any point where source code exists and appropriate measurements can be gathered.

Actions Taken: Most interviewees have not taken concrete actions to address energy or carbon footprint. However, many had reduced resource usage, e.g., by compressing elements or bypassing unnecessary interactions:

> "To make the web pages faster, or save time or resources, we reduced our resources, e.g., we compressed images or music, or [added] some easier way to click to the bottom or go to the next pages." - **P6**

These actions indirectly affect carbon footprint:

> "If I'm a good engineer ... I indirectly reduce cost, indirectly improve code, indirectly reduce carbon footprint." - **P5**

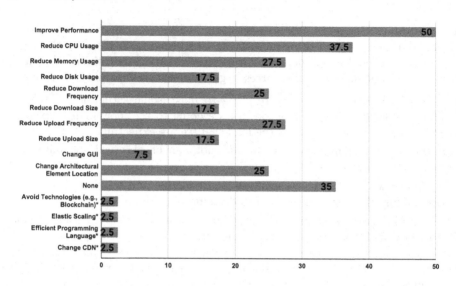

Fig. 6. Percentage of participants that took actions to reduce energy consumption (* indicates a participant-added response).

Figure 6 illustrates the percentage of participants that took certain concrete actions to reduce energy consumption. The most common practice was to improve performance (50%), followed by reducing CPU (38%) and memory consumption (28%) or data upload frequency (28%). Survey participants were also asked what actions they had taken to reduce carbon footprint. They discussed energy and resource consumption, mentioning low-power device states, elastic scaling, memory consumption, and data reuse through instances. Many of these same actions could be invoked by automated tools to improve the software. Performance improvement is already a common target of GI tools [3].

Another participant noted actions developers can take to reduce the footprint of the development process:

> "I have taken steps to reduce energy needed for developing software (by shutting down unused machines and reducing background processes and other things on development machines)." - **I21**

Measurement and Evaluation: While most interviewees have not directly evaluated energy or carbon footprint, several evaluate cost and resource usage:

> "We don't evaluate energy consumption, but we evaluate cost, which is directly related ... [To reduce] cost of service, we design systems ... which are more efficient, consume less cost, and improve user experience." - **P8**

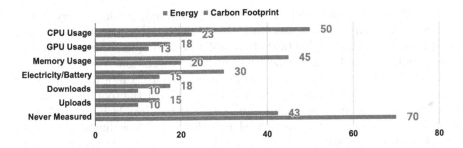

Fig. 7. Percentage that applied a particular measurement.

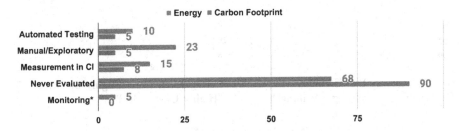

Fig. 8. Percentage that applied a particular evaluation technique.

Figure 7 shows the direct or indirect measures survey participants have used to assess energy or carbon footprint. Many have never measured either (43% for energy, 70% for carbon). Among the respondents who measured either, CPU (50%, 23%) and memory usage (45%, 20%) were the most common methods. These measurements could be used by automated reduction methods to assess potential code transformations.

As shown in Fig. 8, most have also never formally evaluated either (68% for energy, 90% for carbon). For energy consumption, the most common method was manual or exploratory testing (23%), followed by measurement during CI (15%). For carbon footprint, the most common method was during CI (8%). Code transformation could be implemented as part of the CI pipeline, or could be manually invoked as long as executable test cases or other ways of simulating software usage exist.

4.3   Requirements for Automated Tools (RQ3)

During the interviews, all participants expressed a positive attitude toward the idea of an automated carbon footprint reduction tool and regarded the concept as exciting and potentially helpful:

> "We want to reduce the amount of power our software requires. ... it's part of the green message we need to send to the world ... I don't really like bitcoin mining and that kind of thing, so I like what the theory is doing, changing to a much more energy-reduced algorithm for the mining." - **P1**

70% of survey participants were willing or strongly willing to try a tool (Fig. 9(a)), and only 8% were unwilling. However, Fig. 9(b) shows that 35% were either skeptical or highly skeptical of the ability of a tool to successfully reduce carbon footprint, and a further 38% had neutral expectations.

Figure 9(c) indicates that participants may not trust a tool to modify their code, with 50% either unlikely or very unlikely to trust the tool, and a further 28% neutral. Only one respondent indicated that they would be very likely to trust a tool. A participant's experience had little impact on willingness or skepticism. However, participants with <3 years of experience were less likely (median of 2.00) to trust than those with more experience (median 3.00).

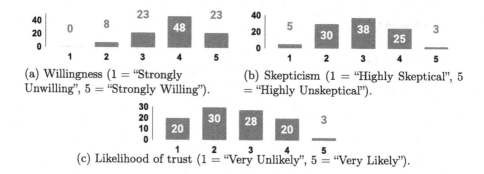

(a) Willingness (1 = "Strongly Unwilling", 5 = "Strongly Willing").

(b) Skepticism (1 = "Highly Skeptical", 5 = "Highly Unskeptical").

(c) Likelihood of trust (1 = "Very Unlikely", 5 = "Very Likely").

Fig. 9. Willingness, skepticism, and likelihood to trust tool results.

Some skepticism seems reasonable. Even if a tool could reduce carbon footprint without supervision, the changes it made could result in incorrect behavior or reduction in other qualities. Care must be taken to prevent such an occurrence.

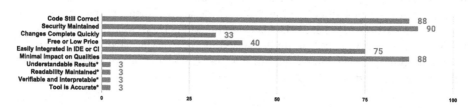

Fig. 10. Percentage of respondents that believe a requirement must be met to trust an automated tool (* indicates a participant-added response).

Interview and survey respondents were asked about the requirements that would have to be met to trust a tool. Among survey participants (Fig. 10), the top requirements are that security is maintained (90%), that the code still operates correctly (88%), and that there is no—or minimal—negative impact on other qualities (88%). Security is one of the most significant qualities of software, with major legal and financial implications. Tools should also not introduce faults, and reducing carbon footprint may not a priority if it comes at the expense of qualities such as performance.

Others asked that the tool be easily integratable into a CI pipeline, be available for free or a low price, and complete changes quickly:

> "If I think I can trust it, it depends on how well it will fit into our development processes and how easy it is to integrate it ... If it's very expensive, then you have to weigh that against how much are we willing to spend on detecting energy consumption." - **P1**

To support integration into CI, the tool should offer an API or CLI, and should be installable through a package manager, (e.g., `pip`).

Further, the tool should produce understandable code and interpretable results—that is, users should understand how and why changes were made. For example, the tool could provide a report with an explanation of code changes and impact on carbon footprint. Such data and rationale can enable verification and trust.

4.4   Use in Development Workflow (RQ4)

Participants were asked about how (and how often) they would apply a tool. Many were interested in integrating this tool into an existing CI pipeline. As shown in Fig. 11, 65% of participants would apply the tool in CI during non-peak times (e.g., overnight) to not interfere with normal development and to increase the likelihood that code is in a working state. The tool could also take more time if results are not needed quickly. 40% would apply the tool as part of CI after a normal commit. 33% of respondents would also apply the tool periodically in CI or before committing code.

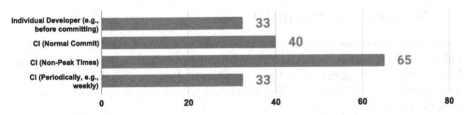

Fig. 11. Percentage of respondents that would use the tool in a particular point in the development workflow.

- Every Commit
- Each Coding Session
- Once Per Day
- Once Per Week
- Once Per Month/Peridically
- Once Per Project
- When Code is Reviewed*
- Depends on Code Size*
- Depends on Tool Requirements*
- After Every Deployment*

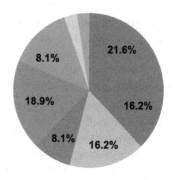

Fig. 12. Frequency that survey participants would apply the tool (* indicates a participant-added response, each 2.5%).

Many indicated (Fig. 12) that they would apply the tool at a relatively high frequency—split between after every commit (22%), after every coding session (16%), or daily (16%). However, a significant portion would instead apply it periodically (19%), possibly to allow code to stabilize before being improved.

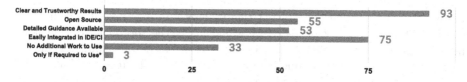

Fig. 13. Percentage of respondents that believe that a factor would encourage voluntary adoption (* indicates a participant-added response)

4.5   Voluntary Adoption (RQ5)

Participants were also asked how to encourage voluntary adoption of tools that reduce software carbon footprint. The views of survey participants are shown in Fig. 13. The most important factor is that the tool shows a track record of clear and trustworthy results (93%). Testimonials from existing users could encourage adoption. One interviewee noted:

> "I will wait until the wider community accepts it. First, I will see if this is doing good. I will try to understand as much as possible what it is doing before I start using this tool." - **P6**

The tool could offer a dashboard or produce a report that visualizes changes to the source code, CPU usage, RAM usage, and carbon footprint so developers can easily understand the changes made.

Easy integration of the tool was essential for 75% of the participants. 33% asked that no additional work be needed to use the tool. An interviewee added:

"I think the main constraint would be that it does not use a lot of resources and ... should not interrupt any development work. It's okay if it takes longer to analyze once the changes are pushed, because it can just run overnight and I don't need to worry about that. But if I use it during development, I would like it to not affect any of my development experience." - **P7**

If the tool is open-source, those who are interested can gain a better understanding of its algorithm and methods. A community could form that expands the tool's capabilities. Additionally, detailed documentation should provide clear and understandable instructions on how to install and use the tool.

5   Threats to Validity

Conclusion Validity: The number of responses may affect conclusion reliability. However, our thematic findings reached saturation. Further interviews or surveys could enrich our findings, but may not produce significant additions.

Construct Validity: The interviews or survey could have missing or confusing questions. There is also a risk that participants may not be familiar with particular terminology. We provided an introduction to reduce this risk. The use of semi-structured interviews allowed us to ask follow-up questions. We also conducted pre-testing of the interview and survey.

External Validity: Generalizability of our findings is influenced by the number and background of participants. Our participants represent many development roles, experience levels, and product domains. Therefore, we believe that our results are relatively applicable to the software development industry. We also contrast results between Sweden and Japan.

Internal Validity: Thematic coding suffers from known bias threats. We mitigated these by performing independent coding and comparing results, finding sufficient agreement. We make our data available, increasing transparency.

6   Conclusions

This study provides a foundation for future research addressing software carbon footprint. We found that many developers lack knowledge. However, some had basic understanding of energy-related factors, and knowledge grows with experience. A plurality were neutral on whether software contributes to climate change and whether carbon footprint should be controlled. However, more agree than disagree with both. The majority feel that both development organizations and regulatory agencies bare responsibility for controlling these factors. Attention should be paid in future work to increasing developer awareness and exploring policy implications of software carbon footprint.

In current practice, energy is considered most often during design and implementation, and is reduced by improving performance or resource consumption. Carbon footprint is considered during deployment and design. Both energy and carbon footprint are most commonly measured through CPU or memory usage.

Energy consumption is often evaluated using manual or exploratory testing, carbon footprint through measurements during Continuous Integration (CI).

The majority are willing to try an automated carbon footprint reduction tool. Developers would apply the tool as part of CI, generally on a regular basis (e.g., daily—possibly at non-peak times). However, many were skeptical of the potential results. To overcome such skepticism, researchers should also explore automated carbon footprint reduction solutions that meet the needs identified by the developers. Such tools must not compromise security, correctness, or other important qualities. They also must integrate into a CI pipeline, be well-documented, be reasonably priced or—preferably—open source, and offer transparent and trustworthy results.

References

1. Andrae, A.S.: New perspectives on internet electricity use in 2030. Eng. Appl. Sci. Lett. **3**(2), 19–31 (2020)
2. Bawdin, T.: Global warming: data centres to consume three times as much energy in next decade, experts warn. Independent **23**, 276 (2016)
3. Bruce, B.R., Petke, J., Harman, M.: Reducing energy consumption using genetic improvement. In: Proceedings of the 2015 Annual Conference on Genetic and Evolutionary Computation, pp. 1327–1334 (2015)
4. Cruzes, D.S., Dyba, T.: Recommended steps for thematic synthesis in software engineering. In: 2011 International Symposium on Empirical Software Engineering and Measurement, pp. 275–284. IEEE (2011)
5. De La Luz, V., Kandemir, M., Kolcu, I.: Automatic data migration for reducing energy consumption in multi-bank memory systems. In: Proceedings 2002 Design Automation Conference (IEEE Cat. No. 02CH37324), pp. 213–218. IEEE (2002)
6. Dorn, J., Lacomis, J., Weimer, W., Forrest, S.: Automatically exploring tradeoffs between software output fidelity and energy costs. IEEE Trans. Software Eng. **45**(3), 219–236 (2017)
7. Georgiou, S., Kechagia, M., Sharma, T., Sarro, F., Zou, Y.: Green AI: do deep learning frameworks have different costs? In: Proceedings of the 44th International Conference on Software Engineering, ICSE 2022, New York, NY, USA, pp. 1082–1094. Association for Computing Machinery (2022)
8. Hao, K.: Training a single AI model can emit as much carbon as five cars in their lifetimes. MIT Technol. Rev. **75**, 103 (2019)
9. Lyu, H., Gay, G., Sakamoto, M.: Replication Data for "Developer Views on Software Carbon Footprint and its Potential for Automated Reduction, February 2023. https://doi.org/10.5281/zenodo.7597662
10. Manotas, I., Pollock, L., Clause, J.: Seeds: a software engineer's energy-optimization decision support framework. In: Proceedings of the 36th International Conference on Software Engineering, pp. 503–514 (2014)
11. Mrazek, V., Vasicek, Z., Sekanina, L.: Evolutionary approximation of software for embedded systems: median function. In: Proceedings of the Companion Publication of the 2015 Annual Conference on Genetic and Evolutionary Computation, pp. 795–801 (2015)

12. Ournani, Z., Rouvoy, R., Rust, P., Penhoat, J.: On reducing the energy consumption of software: from hurdles to requirements. In: Proceedings of the 14th ACM/IEEE International Symposium on Empirical Software Engineering and Measurement (ESEM), pp. 1–12 (2020)
13. Pang, C., Hindle, A., Adams, B., Hassan, A.E.: What do programmers know about software energy consumption? IEEE Softw. **33**(3), 83–89 (2015)
14. Pinto, G., Castor, F., Liu, Y.D.: Mining questions about software energy consumption. In: Proceedings of the 11th Working Conference on Mining Software Repositories, pp. 22–31 (2014)
15. Sarro, F.: Search-based software engineering in the era of modern software systems. In: Proceedings of the 31st IEEE International Requirements Engineering Conference. IEEE (2023)
16. Steinke, S., Wehmeyer, L., Lee, B.-S., Marwedel, P.: Assigning program and data objects to scratchpad for energy reduction. In: Design, Automation and Test in Europe Conference and Exhibition, pp. 409–415. IEEE (2002)
17. Taherdoost, H.: How to design and create an effective survey/questionnaire; a step by step guide. Int. J. Acad. Res. Manage. (IJARM) **5**(4), 37–41 (2016)
18. Taina, J.: How green is your software? In: Tyrväinen, P., Jansen, S., Cusumano, M.A. (eds.) ICSOB 2010. LNBIP, vol. 51, pp. 151–162. Springer, Heidelberg (2010). https://doi.org/10.1007/978-3-642-13633-7_13
19. Thiagarajan, N., Aggarwal, G., Nicoara, A., Boneh, D., Singh, J.P.: Who killed my battery? Analyzing mobile browser energy consumption. In: Proceedings of the 21st International Conference on World Wide Web, pp. 41–50 (2012)
20. White, D.R., Clark, J., Jacob, J., Poulding, S.M.: Searching for resource-efficient programs: low-power pseudorandom number generators. In: Proceedings of the 10th Annual Conference on Genetic and Evolutionary Computation, pp. 1775–1782 (2008)
21. Wiedmann, T., Minx, J.: A definition of 'carbon footprint'. Ecol. Econ. Res. Trends **1**(2008), 1–11 (2008)
22. Zhu, Y., Reddi, V.J.: High-performance and energy-efficient mobile web browsing on big/little systems. In: 2013 IEEE 19th International Symposium on High Performance Computer Architecture (HPCA), pp. 13–24. IEEE (2013)

Search-Based Mock Generation
of External Web Service Interactions

Susruthan Seran[1]([⊠]) [ID], Man Zhang[1] [ID], and Andrea Arcuri[1,2] [ID]

[1] Kristiania University College, Oslo, Norway
{susruthan.seran,man.zhang,andrea.arcuri}@kristiania.no
[2] Oslo Metropolitan University, Oslo, Norway

Abstract. Testing large and complex enterprise software systems can
be a challenging task. This is especially the case when the functionality of the system depends on interactions with other external services
over a network (e.g., external REST APIs). Although several techniques
in the research literature have been shown to be effective at generating test cases in many different software testing contexts, dealing with
external services is still a major research challenge. In industry, a common approach is to *mock* external web services for testing purposes.
However, generating and configuring *mock* web services can be a very
time-consuming task. Furthermore, external services may not be under
the control of the same developers of the tested application.

In this paper, we present a novel search-based approach aimed at *fully
automated* mocking external web services as part of white-box, search-
based fuzzing. We rely on code instrumentation to detect all interactions
with external services, and how their response data is parsed. We then
use such information to enhance a search-based approach for fuzzing.
The tested application is automatically modified (by manipulating DNS
lookups) to rather interact with instances of mock web servers. The
search process not only generates inputs to the tested applications, but
also it automatically setups responses in those mock web server instances,
aiming at maximizing code coverage and fault-finding. An empirical
study on 3 open-source REST APIs from EMB, and one industrial API
from an industry partner, shows the effectiveness of our novel techniques,
i.e., significantly improves code coverage and fault detection.

Keywords: Microservices · Automated Mock Generation ·
Search-Based Test Generation · Search-based Software Engineering

1 Introduction

Enterprise software backends are typically large and complex. Microservice-based
software architecture design helps to tackle the challenges in this domain [20].
In a microservice environment, distributed services are interconnected using
communication protocols like HTTP(S), Remote Procedure Call (RPC), and
Advanced Message Queuing Protocol (AMQP) in a synchronous or asynchronous

© The Author(s), under exclusive license to Springer Nature Switzerland AG 2024
P. Arcaini et al. (Eds.): SSBSE 2023, LNCS 14415, pp. 52–66, 2024.
https://doi.org/10.1007/978-3-031-48796-5_4

manner, to execute a common goal [20]. Likewise, modern web and mobile applications also connect to each other for various reasons, for instance, using services for authentication purposes (e.g., OAuth) or for financial transactions (e.g., Stripe[1] and PayPal[2]). Especially during automated testing, dealing with such external dependencies can be tricky, as what executed in the tested application depends on what returned from those external APIs. Testing for specific error scenarios or specific input data might not be possible in a systematic way if the tester has no control on those external services.

A popular technique in industry to address this limitation is *mocking*. However, for *system-level testing* of web/enterprise applications, instead of using *mock objects*, use of mock external services offers several advantages. For example, the external web service does not even need to be implemented yet, or up and running to execute a test. Furthermore, behavior of the external web service can be extended to test various scenarios (e.g., different returned HTTP status codes). Mocking an external service using a mock HTTP server is a more advanced and possibly less known case. A popular library for the JVM-based applications that can do this is WireMock[3].

In this paper, we provide novel search-based techniques to generate mock web services in a fully automated manner for white-box fuzzing, for the JVM. Using bytecode instrumentation, we can analyze all interactions with external web services during fuzzing, and automatically create mock servers where their responses will be part of the search process. We focus on JavaScript Object Notation (JSON) payloads, where the structure of the responses can be automatically inferred via taint analysis and on how parsing libraries such as Gson and Jackson are used by those tainted values.

Our novel techniques could be adapted and applied to any white-box fuzzer that works on backend web/enterprise applications (or any application that requires communications with external services over a network), for example, RESTful APIs. For the experiments in this paper, we used our open-source fuzzer EVOMASTER [11], as not only it gave the best results among fuzzer comparisons [16,23], but also currently it seems the only fuzzer that supports white-box analyses for this kind of web/enterprise systems [13]. Our extension enables EVOMASTER to generate mock external web service with no need of any manual modification of the System Under Test (SUT). Furthermore, we were able to generate self-contained test suites with integrated mocking capabilities to simulate the same production behavior without relying on any external services up and running.

Our novel developed techniques are evaluated on four RESTful APIs (3 opensource from the EMB corpus [2], and 1 industrial), showing statistically significant improvement in code coverage and fault detection. To enable the replicability of our experiments, our extension to EVOMASTER is open-source.

---

[1] https://stripe.com/.

[2] https://paypal.com/.

[3] https://wiremock.org/.

The novel contributions of this paper are:

- A novel search-based approach in which HTTP mock servers are automatically instantiated when fuzzing web/enterprise applications.
- A novel use of taint-analysis to automatically infer the syntactic structure of the JSON payloads expected to be returned from these external services.
- A novel integration of search-based test generation, in which both inputs to the tested API and outputs from the mocked services are part of a search-based optimization.
- An open-source extension of the existing search-based, white-box fuzzer EVO-MASTER.
- An empirical study on both open-source and industrial APIs, providing empirical evidence that our proposed techniques increase line coverage (e.g., up to 6.9% on average on one of the tested APIs) and find 12 more faults.

2 Related Work

In industry, it is a common practice to use mocking techniques during unit testing to deal with dependencies [21]. The term "mocking" is typically associated in the literature with *unit testing*. For example, instead of passing as input an instance of a class that can make a call to an external service or database, a mock object can be used in which each returned value of its method calls can be configured programmatically directly in the tests (without the need to execute the original code). There are different libraries to help to instantiate and configure *mock objects*. For the JVM, popular libraries are for example Mockito,[4] EasyMock,[5] and JMock,[6] which significantly simplify the writing of mock objects.

Although mocking has several practical benefits [21], it can still require a significant time and effort investment when mocks are created manually, as the returned values of each method call on such mocks needs to be specified.

Besides the case of writing unit tests manually, automated unit test generators can be extended to create mock objects as well for the inputs of the classes under test (CUT). An example is the popular EvoSuite [12], which can generate mock object inputs using Mockito [7]. Similarly, Pex can setup mock objects related to the file system APIs [18].

Interactions with the environment can be mocked away if they are executed on method invocations of input objects (as such input objects can be replaced with configurable mocks in the test cases). However, it cannot be mocked away directly if it is the CUT itself that is doing such interactions with the environment. This is a major issue, especially if the CUT is doing operations on the file system (as random files could be created and deleted during the test generation, which could have disastrous consequences). To overcome such a major issue, tools such as EvoSuite can do bytecode instrumentation on the CUT to replace

---

[4] https://site.mockito.org/.

[5] https://easymock.org/.

[6] https://www.jmock.org/.

different types of environment operations with calls on a virtual file system [5] and a virtual network [6,15]. Still, there are major issues in creating the right data with the right structure (e.g., files and HTTP responses) returned from the calls to the virtual environment [15].

For system testing, in which mock objects cannot be typically used as the SUT is executed through the user interfaces (e.g., a GUI or network calls in the case of web services), there is still the issue of how to deal with network calls to external services during testing. Instead of communicating with the actual external services, the SUT can be modified (e.g., via parameters to change the hostname/IP address of these services) to speak with a different server, on which the tester has full control on how responses are returned. Simulating/mocking entire external web services is different from mocking the network and dependencies through mock objects, although they share the same goal. From the perspective of the SUT, it is not aware of whether it is communicating with a real service or a mocked one, as it will still use the same code to make network calls (e.g., HTTP over TCP) and the same code to read and parse the responses. There are several tools and libraries available in industry which help to setup and run a mocked external web service with less effort, such as Mockoon,[7] Postman,[8] and WireMock.[9] All of them share common functionalities to create configurable mock HTTP(S) web services for testing.

Creating handwritten mock external web services can be tedious and time-consuming. Furthermore, if the third-party interactions are executed using a provided software development kit (SDK), unless the knowledge about the interactions is available or the SDK is reverse-engineered, the process becomes convoluted. A complementary approach is to use *record&replay* where each request and response is captured using a pass-through proxy by the mock server rather than configuring them manually. Later on, the captured information will be used to initiate the mock server. However, the external web service should be owned by the same developers of the SUT to be able to emulate more use cases (especially error scenarios), apart from the common "happy path" scenarios. When the system scales up in size, handwritten mock web services is not a scalable approach. However, record and replay would still be feasible.

The work done in [6,15] is perhaps the closest in the literature to what we present in this paper. However, there are some significant major differences. First, we do not use a limited, artificial virtual network, but rather make actual HTTP calls using external mocked web services (using WireMock). To be able to achieve this automatically, we have to overcome several challenges, especially when dealing with SSL encryption, and when multiple external services use the same TCP port. Furthermore, to enable effective system testing, we need to automatically generate mocked responses with valid syntax (e.g., in JSON representing valid Data Transfer Objects (DTO) for the mocked service), regardless of whether any formal schema is present or not (e.g., the work in [15] requires specifying XSD files manually with the schema of the response messages). Fur-

---

[7] https://mockoon.com/.

[8] https://www.getpostman.com/.

[9] https://wiremock.org/.

thermore, while the work in [15] was evaluated only on an artificial class, we show that our technique can scale on real systems (including an industrial API).

To the best of our knowledge, no technique exists in the scientific literature that can fully automate the process of mock generation for handing external web service dependencies. Moreover, fully automated mock generation of external web services for system level white-box testing is not a topic that has received much attention in the research literature, despite its importance in industry (e.g., considering all the existing popular libraries/tools such as WireMock and Postman).

EVOMASTER is an open-source tool used for fuzzing web services using search-based techniques with white-box and black-box fuzzing [4,11]. EVOMAS-TER provides client-side drivers to enable white-box fuzzing and requires no code modification on the SUT, as instrumentation is done automatically. However, the driver requires writing the necessary steps to cover the three main stages of the API's lifecycle, such as start, reset, and stop. Furthermore, EVOMAS-TER features different search algorithms (e.g., MIO [3] extended with adaptive-hypermutation [22]) and fitness functions (e.g., using advanced testability transformations [9] and heuristics based on the SQL commands executed by the SUT [8]) to generate system level test suites.

3   HTTP Mocking

The objective of our work is to enable automated mocking and configuration of external web services during search-based test generation. We focus on HTTP services that use JSON for the response payloads, as those are the most common types of web services in industry [19]. To achieve this goal, a good deal of research, and technical challenges, need to be addressed, as discussed next in more details.

3.1   Instrumentation

During the search, we need to automatically detect the hostnames/IP addresses and ports of all the external services the SUT communicates with. To achieve this, we applied a form of *testability transformation* [14], relying on the infrastructure of EVOMASTER to apply *method replacements* for common library methods [9] (e.g., the APIs of JDK itself). We extended the white-box instrumentation of EVOMASTER with new replacement methods for APIs related to networking. When classes are loaded into the JVM, method calls towards those APIs are replaced with our methods. Those can track what inputs were used, and then call the original API without altering the semantic of the SUT.

We created method replacements for Java network classes, such as `java.net.InetAddress`, `java.net.Socket`, and `java.net.URL`. This enables us to collect and manipulate various information related to the connection such as hostname, protocol, and port from the different layers of the Open Systems Interconnection (OSI) model.

```
 1 @GetMapping(path = ["/string"])
 2 fun getString() : ResponseEntity<String> {
 3
 4   val url = URL("http://hello.there:8123/api/string")
 5   val connection = url.openConnection()
 6   connection.setRequestProperty("accept", "application/json")
 7   val data = connection.getInputStream()
 8                       .bufferedReader()
 9                       .use(BufferedReader::readText)
10
11   return if (data == "\"HELLO THERE!!!\""){
12         ResponseEntity.ok("YES")
13   } else{
14         ResponseEntity.ok("NOPE")
15   }
16 }
```

Fig. 1. Small example of a REST endpoint written in SpringBoot with Kotlin, making an HTTP call towards an external service using a URL object.

Using the first call made to the external web service, we can capture (and alter) the DNS information about the external web service through the instrumented `java.net.InetAddress`. After the IP address is resolved for the given hostname, when the SUT tries to initiate the `Socket` connection we can capture the port information as well. If the connection is rather created through a `URL` object, such information can be derived directly there.

To make this discussion more clear, let us consider the example in Fig. 1. This is a small artificial example of a REST endpoint written in SpringBoot making an HTTP call towards an external service using a `URL` object. If the request is successful with the response ``HELLO THERE!!!``, the application will respond with an HTTP 200 status code with the string body ``YES``, otherwise with a ``NOPE``.

The `openConnection()` call executed at Line 5 will establish the connection with the remote destination (at the fictional `hello.there:8123`), and it will return a `java.net.URLConnection` to enable to send and receive data to such external endpoint. Our instrumentation will replace the call `url.openConnection()` with our custom `URLClassReplacement.openConnection(url)`. Inside this function, we can get all information about the HTTP connection, and create a new connection where instead of connecting to `hello.there:8123` we connect to an instance of WireMock we control.

Note that this kind of instrumentation is applied to all classes loaded in the JVM, and not just in the business logic of the SUT. For example, if the SUT is using a client library to connect to the external services, this approach will still work. An example in our case study (Sect. 4) is *catwatch*, where it uses the Java library `org.kohsuke:github-api`, which internally connects to `https://api.github.com`.

However, during testing, we want to avoid messing up with the connections with controlled services, such as databases. For this reason, we do not apply any modification when the SUT connects to services running on the hostname `localhost`. This is not a problem when dealing with external services running on internet (e.g., `https://api.github.com`). However, in microservice architectures, the external services are often running on the same host. This is, for example, an issue for the API *cwa-verification* used in our case study (Sect. 4). In this case, the SUT needs to be started with `localhost` replaced with any other hostname, possibly via configuration options. In the case of *cwa-verification*, this was easily achieved by manually overriding the option `--cwa-testresult-server.url`.

3.2   The Mock Server

Once we collect the information on hostnames, protocols, and ports of the external services, we have enough information to initiate mock servers (one per external service).

Writing a mock server that can handle HTTP requests is a major engineering effort. Considering the large amount of work that would be needed to write our own mock server, we rather decided to use an existing mock server library, with a wide use in industry. As the implementation of our techniques is targeting the JVM (e.g., for programs written for example in Java and Kotlin), we needed a mock server capable of running inside the JVM and be programmatically configurable. We chose to use WireMock[10] for this purpose, since it satisfies all our requirements.

WireMock can be configured manually (e.g., by writing all the reposes before staring the server) or programmatically (e.g., during runtime). Apart from that, WireMock supports record and replay as well to configure the mock server. For our purpose, we have used WireMock programmatically. The instrumentation allowed us to reroute the external web service subsequent requests to the respective WireMock server.

Each of the responses can be defined using stubs inside WireMock. A stub can be configured using a static URL path (e.g., `/api/v1/`) or a regular expression-based path (e.g., `/api/v1/.*`). Furthermore, a stub can be extended using various parameters to match a request. The default behavior of WireMock is to throw an exception if a request pattern is not configured. This caused problems during the search. To overcome the difficulties, we set WireMock to return a response with an HTTP 404 for all requests if a stub is not present.

Once initiated, all the requests will be redirected to the respective Wire-Mock server using instrumentation. After a test case is executed, we can query WireMock to retrieve the captured request patterns.

When initiating WireMock servers, we faced difficulties regarding TCP ports. SUT may connect to various external web services using the same TCP port (e.g., HTTP 80 or HTTPS 443). During the search, we have control over the SUT

---

[10] https://wiremock.org/.

through instrumentation. However, it was difficult to maintain the same behavior in the generated test cases (e.g., JUnit files) where no bytecode instrumentation is applied. This means generated test cases should behave the same way without any modification required, like during the search.

Different operating systems (OS) handle TCP ports in different ways, especially regarding available ephemeral TCP ports and the *TCP Time Wait* delays. *TCP Time Wait* defines the amount of time it will take to release a TCP port once it is freed from the previous process. Each of the operating systems has a different default value for *TCP Time Wait*. This is a major issue for empirical research, when running several experiments on the same machine in parallel.

Using different addresses from the loopback subnet range (e.g., *127.0.0.0/8*) is an easy and elegant solution to overcome the challenges we faced with the limitation of available ephemeral TCP ports to initiate WireMock servers. Moreover, it eradicated the dependency on *TCP Time Wait* delays. Furthermore, this allowed us to create and manage mock servers with no code modification required from the SUT. However, some operating systems might handle loopback addresses differently. For example, *macOS* does not allow to access addresses from this range besides *127.0.0.1* by default. So, other addresses from the range should be configured as an alias on the respective network interface (in most cases, it is *lo0*). However, we have not seen this kind of problem when running experiments on *Linux* and *Windows*.

The decision to pick the loopback IP address to host the mock server happens automatically. However, in our tool extension it can be configured using various options. Three different initial local IP address allocation strategies have been developed. This helped to avoid conflicts during running experiments in parallel and to have more control over address allocation (e.g., in the generated test cases). Because of the space limitation, we cannot go into details about explaining each strategy.

Furthermore, in each setting, some of the loopback addresses will be skipped. This includes network addresses *127.0.0.0, 127.0.0.1* and the broadcast address of the range *127.255.255.255*, to avoid unanticipated side effects.

As mentioned earlier, to ensure the same behavior in the generated test cases as the search, we relied on *Java Reflection*, especially needed when hostnames are hard-coded in third-party libraries and cannot be easily modified by the user (e.g., like the case of `https://api.github.com` in *catwatch*). We managed to modify the JVM Domain Name System (DNS) cache through reflection in the generated test cases by using the `dns-cache-manipulator` library from Alibaba. This way, in the generated JUnit tests, we can still remap a hostname such as `api.github.com` to a loopback address where a WireMock instance is running. However, one (arguably minor) limitation here is that we cannot handle in this way the cases in which IP addresses are hard-coded without using any hostname (e.g., using *140.82.121.6* instead of `api.github.com`). But the use of hard-coded IP addresses does not seem a common practice.

3.3 Requests and Responses

As previously mentioned, the instantiated WireMocks will run with a default response HTTP 404 for all the request patterns. However, mocking the external web services with different correct responses is necessary to achieve better code coverage. Recall the example in Fig. 1, where the result of an if statement depends on whether the external service returns the string ''HELLO THERE!!!''. To reach this point of execution, the mock server should give the response as expected. It would be extremely unlikely to get the right needed data at random. Performance improvement of the search requires better heuristics in a case like this.

Besides body payloads, there could be a possibility for SUT to check for other HTTP response parameters as well (e.g., HTTP status code and headers). To maximize code coverage in the SUT (and so indirectly increase the chances of detecting faults), there is the need to have various HTTP responses in each stage of the search to cover all these possible cases.

To address these issues, we have extended the fuzzer engine of EVOMASTER to create mock responses. Besides evolving the parameters and payloads of the REST API calls towards the SUT, now our EVOMASTER extension can also evolve the data in the mock responses.

Internally, each REST API call "action" in a test will have associated actions related to setup these mock. Once a test is executed, and its fitness evaluation is computed, through the instrumentation we gather information about the interactions the SUT had with the external services from the respective WireMock servers. In the subsequent steps of the search, when the test is selected again for mutation, these newly created actions will be mutated, and the respective WireMock server will have a new response for the request pattern besides the default HTTP 404. Initially, the genotype of these WireMock setup actions will contain mutable genes to handle the returned HTTP status code and an optional body payload (for example, treated as random strings). Throughout the search, actions will enhance the respective WireMock responses by mutating those genes, and then collecting their impact on the fitness function.

It is possible to easily randomize some parameters in a typical HTTP response while searching, such as HTTP status code (e.g., typically range is from 100 to 599). But, creating correct values in parameters like headers and response bodies is not a straightforward task. With no information available at the beginning of the search, it is necessary to find a way to gather this information to create a response schema. For example, when the SUT expects a specific JSON schema as a response, sending a random string as body payload will lead to throwing an exception in the data parsing library of the SUT.

In case the schema is available in a commonly used format such as OpenAPI/Swagger, it is possible to infer it from that. However, it is not always possible. An alternative, more general solution is to use instrumentation to analyze how such body payloads are parsed by the SUT.

The JSON is a common choice as data transfer format for the interactions between web services [19]. Use of Data Transfer Objects (DTO) is a known practice in most of the statically typed programming languages to represent the schema in code. When a JSON payload is received from an HTTP request, a library can be used to parse such text data into a DTO object. By instrumenting the relevant libraries, at runtime during the test evaluation we can analyze these DTOs to infer the structure of the schema of these JSON messages.

On the JVM, the most popular libraries for JSON parsing are *Gson* and *Jackson* [17]. For these two libraries, we provide method replacements for their main entry points related to parsing DTOs, for example `<T> T fromJson(String json, Class<T> classOfT)`. In these method replacements, we can see how any JSON string data is parsed to DTOs (analyzing as well all the different Java annotations in these libraries used to customize the parsing, for example `@Ignored` and `@JsonProperty`). This information can then be fed back to the search engine: instead of evolving random strings, EvoMaster can then evolve JSON objects matching those DTO structures.

There is one further challenge that needs to be addressed here: how to trace a specific JSON text input to the source it comes from. It can come from an external web service we are mocking, but that could use different DTOs for each of its different endpoints. Or, it could come from a database, or as input to the SUT, and have nothing to do with any of our WireMock instances. The solution here is to use *taint analysis*. In particular, we extend the current input tracking system in EvoMaster [9]. Each time a string input is used as body payload in the mocked responses, it will not be a random string, but rather a specific tainted value matching the regex _EM_\d+_XYZ_, e.g., _EM_0_XYZ_. In each of our method replacements (e.g., for `fromJson`) we check if the input string does match that regular expression. If so, we can check the genotype of the executed test case to see where that value is coming from. The gene representing that value is then modified in the next mutation operation to rather represent a JSON object valid for that DTO.

During the search, modifications/mutations to an evolving test case might lead the SUT to connect to new web services, or not connect anymore to any (e.g., if a mutation leads the test case to fail input validation, and then the SUT directly returns a 400 status code without executing any business logic). If no matching request exists to the existing actions after a fitness evaluation, it will be disabled. The rest will be marked as active for further use. If an action representing a call to the SUT is deleted, then all the WireMock stubs associated with it are deleted as well.

4   Empirical Study

To evaluate the effectiveness of our novel techniques presented in this paper, we carried out an empirical study to answer the following research question:

What is the impact on code coverage and fault-finding of our novel search-based approach for external service mocking?

Table 1. Descriptive statistics of case studies. Note that, for each case study, #Endpoints represents several endpoints, #Classess represents numerous classes and #File LOCs represents numerous lines of code (LOC).

SUT	#Endpoints	#Classes	#File LOCs
catwatch	23	106	9636
cwa-verification	5	47	3955
genome-nexus	23	832	64339
ind1	54	115	7112
Total	105	1100	85042

4.1   Experiment Setup

To evaluate our approach, we conducted our empirical study with three case studies from EMB [2] and one industrial case study (i.e., *ind1*). EMB is an open-source corpus composed of open-source web/enterprise APIs for scientific research [2].

To assess the effectiveness of our mock generation, we selected from EMB all the REST APIs which require to communicate with external web services for their business logic (i.e., *catwatch*, *cwa-verification*, and *genome-nexus*). Descriptive statistics of the selected case studies are reported in Table 1. In total, 105 endpoints and $85k$ lines of codes were employed in these experiments. Note that these statistics only concern code for implementing the business logic in these APIs. The code related to third-part libraries (which can be millions of lines [2]) is not counted here.

catwatch is a web application which allows fetching GitHub statistics for GitHub accounts, processes, and saves the data in a database and provides them via a RESTful API. The application heavily relies on GitHub APIs to perform its core functions.

cwa-verification is a component of the official Corona-Warn-App for Germany. This case study is a part of a microservice-based architecture which contains various other services, including mobile and web apps. The tested backend server relies on other services in the microservice architecture to complete its tasks.

genome-nexus is an interpretation tool which aggregates information from various other online services about genetic variants in cancer.

ind1 is a component in an e-commerce system. It deals with authentication using an external Auth0 server, and it processes monetary transactions using Stripe[11].

To assess our novel approach, we integrated it into our open-source, white-box fuzzer EvoMaster. Then we conducted experiments to compare the baseline and our novel proposed approach, i.e., *Base* refers to EvoMaster with its

---

[11] https://stripe.com/.

default configuration, and *WM* refers to our approach which enables our handling of mock generation with EvoMASTER. Considering the randomness nature of search algorithms, we repeated each setting 30 times using the same termination criterion (i.e., 1 h), by following common guidelines for assessing randomized techniques in software engineering research [1].

Interactions with real external services are often non-deterministic, as the external services might not be accessible and change their behavior at any time. For instance, with a preliminary study, we found that *catwatch* communicates with Github API, but there exists a rate limiter (a typical method to prevent DoS attacks) to control the access to this API[12] based on IP address, e.g., up to 60 requests per hour for unauthenticated requests. Considering the network setup of our university, we may share the same IP address with all our colleagues and students (e.g., when behind a NAT router). Then, such rate limit configuration will strongly affect results on this study, e.g., depending on the time of the day in which the experiments are running, in some experiments we might be able to fetch data from GitHub, but not in others. As this can lead to completely unreliable results when comparing techniques, we decided to run all the experiments with internet disabled. This also provides a way to evaluate our techniques in the cases in which the external services are not implemented yet (e.g., at the beginning of a new project) or are temporarily down.

With two settings (i.e., Base and WM) on four case studies using 1 h as search budget, 30 repetitions of the experiments took 240 h (10 days), i.e., $2 \times 4 \times 30 \times 1$. All experiments were run on the same machine, i.e., HP Z6 G4 Workstation with Intel(R) Xeon(R) Gold 6240R CPU @2.40 GHz 2.39 GHz, 192 GB RAM, and 64-bit Windows 10 OS.

4.2 Experiment Results

To answer our research question, we report line coverage and number of detected faults on average (i.e., **mean**) with 30 repetitions achieved by Base and WM, as shown in Table 2. We employed a Mann-Whitney U test (i.e., *p*-value) and Vargha-Delaney effect size (i.e., $\hat{A}_{12}$) to perform comparison analyses between Base and WM in terms of line coverage and fault detection. With Mann-Whitney U test, if *p*-value is less than the standard significance level (i.e., 0.05), it indicates that the two compared groups (i.e., Base and WM) have statistically significant differences. Otherwise, there is no enough evidence to support the claim the difference is significant. Comparing WM with Base, the Vargha-Delaney effect size (i.e., $\hat{A}_{12}$) measures how likely WM can perform better than Base. $\hat{A}_{12} = 0.5$ represents no effect. If $\hat{A}_{12}$ surpasses 0.5, it indicates that WM has more chances to achieve better results than Base.

Based on the analysis results reported in Table 2, compared to Base, we found that WM achieved consistent improvements on both metrics, i.e., line coverage and detected faults. The results show that, for all the four selected APIs,

---

[12] https://docs.github.com/en/rest/overview/resources-in-the-rest-api?
apiVersion=2022-11-28.

Table 2. Results of line coverage and detected faults achieved by Base and WM. We also report pair comparison results between Base and WM using Vargha-Delaney effect size (i.e., $\hat{A}_{12}$) and Mann-Whitney U test (i.e., p-value at significant level 0.05).

SUT	Line Coverage %				Detected Faults %			
	Base	WM	$\hat{A}_{12}$	p-value	Base	WM	$\hat{A}_{12}$	p-value
catwatch	46.4	53.3	**0.99**	<0.001	41.5	45.4	**0.82**	<0.001
cwa-verification	57.4	59.9	**0.95**	<0.001	12.3	13.8	**0.87**	<0.001
genome-nexus	27.9	30.3	**1.00**	<0.001	21.2	22.0	**0.71**	<0.001
ind1	14.2	15.1	**0.70**	0.002	59.7	65.1	**0.97**	<0.001
Average	36.5	39.7	0.91		33.7	36.6	0.84	

our approach (i.e., WM) significantly outperformed Base with low p-values and high $\hat{A}_{12}$. Such results demonstrate effectiveness of our approach with white-box heuristic and taint analysis to guide mock object generation.

For *genome-nexus*, we found that most of the interactions from the SUT with external services is to fetch data, then save the data into a database (i.e., MongoDB). In this case, it is not necessary to extract the data when fetching them, and such data extraction can be performed when saving data into the database. Code snippet of an interaction and data extraction in *genome-nexus* is shown as below (complete code can be found in `BaseCachedExternalResourceFetcher.java`[13]).

```
1  rawValue = this.fetcher.fetchRawValue(this.buildRequestBody(
     subSet));
2  ...
3  rawValue = this.normalizeResponse(rawValue);
4  ...
5  List<T> fetched = this.transformer.transform(rawValue, this.
     type);
6
```

Based on the code, line 1 does fetch to get raw data. By checking the implementation of `fetchRawValue` (e.g., `BaseExternalResourceFetcher.java`[13]), a general type (such as `BasicDBList`[14]) is provided. With such type info, we can only know it is a list. The actual data extraction based on the raw value is performed later in Line 5 before saving it into database. Our current handling does not support such response schema extraction yet. It can be considered as a future work.

Unfortunately, for reasons of space, we cannot discuss in more details the results obtained on the other APIs.

---

[13] https://github.com/EMResearch/EMB.

[14] https://mongodb.github.io/mongo-java-driver/3.4/javadoc/com/mongodb/BasicDBList.html.

> *RQ: Our approach with white-box heuristics and taint analysis demonstrates its effectiveness to guide mock object generation, increasing code coverage and fault detection. Such improvements for a search-based fuzzer (i.e., EvoMASTER) are statistically significant on all the four selected APIs.*

5 Conclusion

In this paper, we have provided a novel search-based approach to enhance white-box fuzzing with automated mocking of external web services. Our techniques have been implemented as an extension of the fuzzer EvoMASTER [11], using WireMock for the mocked external services. Experiments on 3 open-source and 1 industrial APIs show the effectiveness of our novel techniques, both in terms of code coverage and fault detection.

To the best of our knowledge, this is the first work in the literature that provides a working solution for this important problem. Therefore, there are several avenues for further enhancements of our techniques in future work. An example is how to effectively deal with APIs that have a 2-phase parsing of JSON payloads (like in the case of *genome-nexus* in our case study).

Our tool extension of EvoMASTER is released as open-source, with a replication package for this study currently available on GitHub[15].

Acknowledgment. This work is funded by the European Research Council (ERC) under the European Union's Horizon 2020 research and innovation programme (EAST project, grant agreement No. 864972).

References

1. Arcuri, A., Briand, L.: A Hitchhiker's Guide to Statistical Tests for Assessing Randomized Algorithms in Software Engineering **24**(3), 219–250 (2014)
2. Arcuri, A., Zhang, M., Golmohammadi, A., Belhadi, A., Galeotti, J.P., Marculescu, B., Susruthan, S.: Emb: A curated corpus of web/enterprise applications and library support for software testing research. IEEE (2023)
3. Arcuri, A.: Test suite generation with the Many Independent Objective (MIO) algorithm. Inf. Softw. Technol. **104**, 195–206 (2018)
4. Arcuri, A.: Automated black-and white-box testing of restful apis with evomaster. IEEE Softw. **38**(3), 72–78 (2020)
5. Arcuri, A., Fraser, G., Galeotti, J.P.: Automated unit test generation for classes with environment dependencies. In: Proceedings of the 29th ACM/IEEE international conference on Automated software engineering. pp. 79–90 (2014)
6. Arcuri, A., Fraser, G., Galeotti, J.P.: Generating tcp/udp network data for automated unit test generation. In: Proceedings of the 2015 10th Joint Meeting on Foundations of Software Engineering. pp. 155–165 (2015)
7. Arcuri, A., Fraser, G., Just, R.: Private api access and functional mocking in automated unit test generation. In: 2017 IEEE international conference on software testing, verification and validation (ICST). pp. 126–137. IEEE (2017)

---

[15] https://github.com/researcher-for/es-mocking.

8. Arcuri, A., Galeotti, J.P.: Handling sql databases in automated system test generation **29**(4), 1–31 (2020)
9. Arcuri, A., Galeotti, J.P.: Enhancing Search-based Testing with Testability Transformations for Existing APIs. ACM Transactions on Software Engineering and Methodology (TOSEM) **31**(1), 1–34 (2021)
10. Arcuri, A., Galeotti, J.P.: Enhancing search-based testing with testability transformations for existing apis. ACM Transactions on Software Engineering and Methodology (TOSEM) **31**(1), 1–34 (2021)
11. Arcuri, A., Galeotti, J.P., Marculescu, B., Zhang, M.: Evomaster: A search-based system test generation tool. Journal of Open Source Software **6**(57), 2153 (2021)
12. Fraser, G., Arcuri, A.: Evosuite: automatic test suite generation for object-oriented software. In: Proceedings of the 19th ACM SIGSOFT symposium and the 13th European conference on Foundations of software engineering. pp. 416–419 (2011)
13. Golmohammadi, A., Zhang, M., Arcuri, A.: Testing restful apis: A survey (2023)
14. Harman, M., Hu, L., Hierons, R., Wegener, J., Sthamer, H., Baresel, A., Roper, M.: Testability transformation. IEEE Trans. Software Eng. **30**(1), 3–16 (2004)
15. Havrikov, N., Gambi, A., Zeller, A., Arcuri, A., Galeotti, J.P.: Generating unit tests with structured system interactions. In: 2017 IEEE/ACM 12th International Workshop on Automation of Software Testing (AST). pp. 30–33. IEEE (2017)
16. Kim, M., Xin, Q., Sinha, S., Orso, A.: Automated test generation for rest apis: No time to rest yet. In: Proceedings of the 31st ACM SIGSOFT International Symposium on Software Testing and Analysis. p. 289–301. ISSTA 2022, Association for Computing Machinery, New York, NY, USA (2022). https://doi.org/10.1145/3533767.3534401 , https://doi.org/10.1145/3533767.3534401
17. Maeda, K.: Performance evaluation of object serialization libraries in xml, json and binary formats. In: 2012 Second International Conference on Digital Information and Communication Technology and it's Applications (DICTAP). pp. 177–182. IEEE (2012)
18. Marri, M.R., Xie, T., Tillmann, N., De Halleux, J., Schulte, W.: An empirical study of testing file-system-dependent software with mock objects. In: Automation of Software Test, 2009. AST'09. ICSE Workshop on. pp. 149–153 (2009)
19. Neumann, A., Laranjeiro, N., Bernardino, J.: An analysis of public rest web service apis. IEEE Transactions on Services Computing (2018)
20. Newman, S.: Building microservices. " O'Reilly Media, Inc." (2021)
21. Spadini, D., Aniche, M., Bruntink, M., Bacchelli, A.: To mock or not to mock? an empirical study on mocking practices. In: 2017 IEEE/ACM 14th International Conference on Mining Software Repositories (MSR). pp. 402–412. IEEE (2017)
22. Zhang, M., Arcuri, A.: Adaptive hypermutation for search-based system test generation: A study on rest apis with evomaster. ACM Transactions on Software Engineering and Methodology (TOSEM) **31**(1) (2021)
23. Zhang, M., Arcuri, A.: Open problems in fuzzing restful apis: A comparison of tools (may 2023). https://doi.org/10.1145/3597205 ,https://doi.org/10.1145/3597205, just Accepted

Exploring Genetic Improvement
of the Carbon Footprint of Web Pages

Haozhou Lyu[1], Gregory Gay[1(✉)] (iD), and Maiko Sakamoto[2]

[1] Chalmers and University of Gothenburg, Gothenburg, Sweden
haozhou@student.chalmers.se, greg@greggay.com
[2] University of Tokyo, Tokyo, Japan
m-sakamoto@k.u-tokyo.ac.jp

Abstract. In this study, we explore automated reduction of the carbon footprint of web pages through genetic improvement, a process that produces alternative versions of a program by applying program transformations intended to optimize qualities of interest. We introduce a prototype tool that imposes transformations to HTML, CSS, and JavaScript code, as well as image resources, that minimize the quantity of data transferred and memory usage while also minimizing impact to the user experience (measured through loading time and number of changes imposed).

In an evaluation, our tool outperforms two baselines—the original page and randomized changes—in the average case on all projects for data transfer quantity, and 80% of projects for memory usage and load time, often with large effect size. Our results illustrate the applicability of genetic improvement to reduce the carbon footprint of web components, and offer lessons that can benefit the design of future tools.

Keywords: Carbon Footprint · Energy Consumption · Web Development · Genetic Improvement · Genetic Programming

1 Introduction

Climate change, caused by increasing concentrations of greenhouse gases in the atmosphere, is expected to have profound long-term consequences to the human health, safety, and quality of life. The carbon dioxide emitted through development and use of software is a major contributor to climate change [2].

In this study, we focus on the carbon footprint of web pages. Web pages are some of the most commonly used programs in the world—presently, there are estimated to be approximately two billion websites, with 400 million actively maintained, and almost four billion internet users around the world [10]. Therefore, reductions in the carbon footprint of web pages could contribute significantly to reducing the overall carbon footprint of the software industry.

Reducing software carbon footprint is not a straight-forward task. Researchers have begun to make recommendations (e.g., [14,22,24]). Such guidelines are highly important, but can be difficult to apply—especially after the code has been written. Therefore, we are interested in exploring *automated* reduction

P. Arcaini et al. (Eds.): SSBSE 2023, LNCS 14415, pp. 67–83, 2024.
https://doi.org/10.1007/978-3-031-48796-5_5

of carbon footprint through transformation of existing source code—e.g., reducing energy consumption while maintaining the semantics of the original code.

A promising technique to impose such changes is *genetic improvement* [3], where alternative versions of a program are scored according to qualities of interest—called fitness functions—then evolved over many generations to optimize these scores. Genetic improvement has been applied to energy consumption (e.g., [3,9,14,15,23]), but not to carbon footprint or web pages.

In this study, we have explored the use of genetic improvement to automatically reduce the carbon footprint of web pages through the development of an extendable tool. This tool imposes transformations to HTML, CSS, and JavaScript code, as well as image resources, to identify web page modifications that minimize fitness functions that correlate with carbon footprint—the quantity of data transferred and memory usage—and functions intended to preserve the user experience—the page load time and number of changes imposed.

In an experimental evaluation on 10 open-source projects of varying complexity, we compare our tool to two baselines—the original, unmodified page and randomized changes. In the average case, our tool was able to reduce the quantity of data transferred for all projects, and the memory consumption and loading time for eight of the projects. Our tool outperformed the random baseline with large effect size in 92.50% of comparisons. Compressing and converting images and removing unused CSS were the most common actions performed by the tool, with major effects on solution fitness.

Our results illustrate the applicability of genetic improvement to reduce the carbon footprint of web components, and offer lessons that can benefit the design of future tools for this purpose. We make our tool[1], comparison baselines[2], and experiment data[3] available to researchers and practitioners to use or extend.

2   Background and Related Work

Carbon Footprint and Energy Consumption of Software: The carbon footprint of a software product is the quantity of carbon dioxide emissions associated with its development. There are sources of emission at multiple points, including implementation, testing, delivery, usage, and maintenance [21]. In this research, our scope is restricted to emissions associated with energy consumption during *usage*—i.e., when interactions take place with the software.

Carbon footprint is affected by the *quantity* of energy consumed and *where and how* that energy is produced or consumed, as some energy sources have a greater carbon footprint than others. Software carbon footprint is potentially affected by energy usage on both the client-side (i.e., consumer devices) and server-side (i.e., data centers in disparate geographic areas), as well as by network transmissions between the two [1]. In this study, we focus on energy usage.

---

[1] https://github.com/haozhoulyu416/ARCFW-Tool.
[2] https://github.com/haozhoulyu416/ARCFW-Random-Solution-Generation.
[3] https://doi.org/10.5281/zenodo.8347915.

Genetic Improvement: Genetic improvement is the automated improvement of non-functional qualities (e.g., performance) of software through transformations to the source code [3]. Transformations are imposed using genetic programming [3], a process where population of patches are produced, their quality is measured according to one or more "fitness functions" related to the qualities of interest, and then patches are evolved over a series of generations. The patches that yield the best scores in each generation form a new population through mutation—where stochastic changes are introduced—or crossover—where aspects of "parent" patches combine to form new "children". Carbon footprint can be considered a quality. Thus, genetic programming could be used to automate its reduction through appropriate transformation actions and fitness functions.

Related Work: Past research has offered guidelines on how to reduce energy consumption and carbon footprint (e.g., algorithm selection [14], code structure [24], considering server distribution and location [14], or controlling image quality [22]). Such guidelines are highly important, but are not always easy to apply. Nor is it simple to manually improve code after it has been written. Therefore, we are interested in automated carbon footprint reduction techniques.

We are unaware of automated tools targeting carbon footprint. However, there have been several approaches targeting energy consumption. Much of this research utilizes genetic improvement—for example, Bruce et al. targeted C implementations of MiniSAT [3], Dorn et al. explore trade-offs between energy consumption and output fidelity [9], Manotas et al. optimize applications that use Java collections [14], Mrazek et al. targeted microcontrollers [15], and White et al. targeted pseudorandom number generators [23]. Other approaches include, e.g., specialized compilers [20] and data migration strategies [6]. None of these approaches target web pages, despite their prevalence, and their approaches are not applicable to this domain. Our approach is the first to target web page carbon footprint using genetic improvement.

3 Methodology

Our study is guided by the following research questions:

- **RQ1:** What factors of web page design suggest code transformations or fitness functions for genetic improvement of carbon footprint?
- **RQ2:** What impact does our prototype genetic improvement tool have on the carbon footprint of web pages?
- **RQ3:** Which program modifications are used most often by the tool?

To answer these questions, we applied the Design Science methodology to develop a prototype automated carbon footprint reduction tool for web pages. Design science is a systematic, cyclic methodology for the creation and evaluation of artifacts. This prototype tool was designed over three iterations. In Iteration I

(Sect. 3.1), we identified factors of web page design that have a potential impact on carbon footprint. These factors form the basis of fitness functions and transformation actions in our tool. In Iteration II (Sect. 3.2), genetic programming—based on the NSGA-II algorithm—was utilized to develop the automated carbon footprint reduction tool. In Iteration III (Sect. 3.3), we conducted parameter tuning experiments, then we conducted final experiments comparing the tool against two baselines—the original web page and random solution generation.

3.1 Iteration I (Scoping, Fitness Functions, and Transformations)

The purposes of this iteration were to identify the scope of the genetic improvement tool, then—based on that scoping—identify web page design factors that have a potential relationship with the carbon footprint of a web page and develop fitness functions and code transformations based on those factors. The identification of fitness functions and actions was conducted by, first, performing a literature review of past work in this area. We then implemented actions and fitness functions and performed exploratory experiments to identify those that could be performed and measured reliably.

Scoping: A web page can consist of both *front-end* and *back-end* components, implementing user interfaces and underlying functionality, respectively. Front-end and back-end components can be built using many different programming or markup languages, and often make use of additional resources such as images, videos, or audio. Web page components can also be *localized* to a single computing unit or *geographically distributed*.

Our aspiration was to develop a tool that could be expanded over time to additional web page components, web programming languages, fitness functions, and code transformation actions. However, for the initial prototype, it was important to establish a clear scope that could be later enlarged.

In this study, we focus on **front-end, localized** web page components. Specifically, we modify **HTML, CSS, and JavaScript** components related to the user-facing interface of a web page. We also include **images** in this scope. In the current prototype, we focus on **the quantity of energy consumed**, and not the sources of energy (e.g., some geographic areas may use more renewable sources of energy than others).

Fitness Functions: To identify factors affecting a web page's carbon footprint, it is necessary to identify factors affecting its energy consumption. After examining past literature and exploring the feasibility of implementing measurement in a manner that (a) could be performed reliably[4], and (b) could be performed without specialized equipment[5], we implemented the following fitness functions:

---

[4] That yield relatively deterministic readings and are not heavily affected by the specific hardware and software configuration where the prototype tool is executed.

[5] Our desire was to develop a framework that could be used on any computer, without the need for dedicated equipment that measures energy consumption.

- **Memory Usage:** Philippot et al. [17] identified a high correlation between memory and energy consumption for web pages. There is a correlation between the number of requests, the page size, and the consumed memory on the client. `Selenium`, a suite of tools for automating web browsers, is used to simulate the user environment of the web page to gather memory usage[6].
- **Quantity of Transferred Data:** Wholegrain Digital have developed a "Website Carbon Calculator" [5]. Their calculation is based on the quantity of data transferred to the end user, the energy intensity of the data, and the carbon intensity of the energy consumed. The latter two factors take into account the locations where energy is consumed. As these are not considered in the current prototype, we focus solely on the quantity of data transferred. To measure this factor, we utilize the `PageSpeed Insights` API[7].

We also implemented, **but ultimately abandoned**, the following:

- **CPU Usage:** Many researchers use CPU usage to measure energy consumption, e.g., [4, 24]. However, after several experiments, we found that it was difficult to measure and isolate the CPU usage of the web page accurately. As a result, we decided to abandon this factor.

Reduction of carbon footprint must not negatively affect the user experience of the web page. Therefore, we also balance carbon footprint reduction against the following fitness functions, representing the user experience:

- **Page Load Time:** Load time is an important aspect of web page performance, as slow load times lead to many users leaving the page [19]. Load time and energy consumption are not strongly correlated [4]. Thus, we ensure performance is not negatively impacted while reducing the carbon footprint. We apply `Selenium` and `PageSpeed Insights` to capture load time.
- **Number of Changes:** The automated carbon footprint reduction tool should not overtly change the original code, as this may negatively affect the user experience, e.g., reducing usability or readability.

The prototype tool attempts to *minimize* the selected subset of fitness functions. This set of functions can be expended in future work as well. To address RQ1:

RQ1 (Factors): The carbon footprint of a web page is affected by the quantity and location of energy consumed. We focused on quantity, and identified *memory usage* and *quantity of transferred data* as approximations that could be measured reliably and without specialized equipment.

Web Page Modifications: Through modification of code and resource elements, carbon footprint can potentially be reduced. These actions are intended

---

[6] https://www.selenium.dev/.
[7] https://pagespeed.web.dev/.

to be applied to one compatible element at a time, e.g., a single image, HTML tag, or file. That way, the minimal set of actions that most strongly affect the carbon footprint can be identified. We have identified the following actions through analysis of literature and exploratory experimentation:

- **Change Image Format:** Energy consumption of image formats varies [22]. The WebP format has been found to yield smaller images than JPEG and PNG formats, leading to smaller data transmission quantity and improved page performance. Therefore, we convert images to WebP.
- **Compress Images:** Compressing images can reduce energy consumption [16]. Over-compressing images can reduce usability, but high image quality is not often required and users may not notice a difference after compression.
- **Swap HTML Tags:** `<strong¿` elements use less energy and load faster than unstyled `<span>` tags [18]—the former requires 14% less loading time and energy, and `<span>` tags are particularly inefficient in mobile device browsers. Thus, we change the `<span>` tag to `<strong>` automatically.
- **Remove Unused CSS:** When a page is loaded, an HTML file is fetched and converted into a DOM object model. Afterwards, CSS stylesheets are fetched by the browser and converted to the CSSOM model [13]. A render tree is constructed by combining the DOM and CSSOM. The first content is produced by a browser only after this render tree has been constructed. Because of this, CSS files heavily affect the rendering time and quantity of data transferred [8]. When a CSS file contains unused CSS, it takes longer to build under the render tree. Thus, we remove unused CSS rules.
- **Remove CSS Opacity:** Translucent elements are rendered more slowly than opaque elements [18]. Consequently, removing opacity could potentially reduce energy consumption.
- **Move JavaScript Invocation:** Moving the JavaScript `<script>` to the end of the body can improve performance because the script invocation blocks parallel downloads, e.g., of image files [12].

We also implemented the following actions, but decided to discontinue their use following experimentation:

- **Remove HTML or CSS Whitespace:** Removing whitespace in the HTML or CSS source code can reduce the file size. This operation could be conducted before deploying the website to the server to avoid negatively impacting the readability of the code. However, due to this potential for reducing readability, we did not utilize this action in our initial prototype tool.
- **Use of async and defer:** The `async` attribute, used when invoking a JavaScript file in HTML, enables scripts to be loaded asynchronously. If a script uses this attribute, it will load independently and will not impede loading of other elements. Loading several scripts asynchronously can increase page loading speed and reduce total resource consumption. Similarly, when using the `defer` attribute, the browser will load the script after loading the page. This can also situationally improve resource consumption. However, we determined through initial experimentation that these changes could affect the behaviour of a web page in inadvertent ways.

Like with fitness functions, additional actions can be added in future work.

RQ1 (Factors): The initial prototype attempts to reduce the carbon footprint by changing image formats, compressing images, swapping energy-consuming HTML tags for alternatives, removing unused CSS, removing opacity from elements, and moving JavaScript invocations.

3.2   Iteration II (Design of the Prototype Tool)

In the second iteration, we developed our prototype genetic improvement tool—making use of the fitness functions and actions developed in Iteration I. This tool performs multi-objective genetic improvement based on the NSGA-II algorithm (Non-Dominated Sorting Genetic Algorithm-II) [7]. The process followed by this tool is, as follows:

- An initial population of N solutions—alterations of the original web page—is generated by making random changes.
- This population is evolved over a series of generations. In each generation:
  - The best solutions in the population are identified (selection).
  - These solutions ("parents") are used to create a new "child" population, using the mutation and crossover operations.
  - The best N solutions from the parent and child populations form the population considered in the next generation, preventing the best solutions from being lost.
- After the final generation, the best solutions—those that cannot be dominated by any other solutions—are returned.

Parameters: The following parameters are user-adjustable:
- **Population Size:** The number of individuals in the population.
- **Search Budget:** The number of generations of evolution.
- **Fitness Functions:** The fitness functions to optimize. NSGA-II is generally considered efficient with up to three objectives [11]. Thus, we allow the selection of one to three fitness functions.

Solution Representation: Each individual represents an altered version of a web page. Solutions are represented using an array, where each item represents an action that can be applied to an element (e.g., compressing a particular image). The length of the array is fixed to the number of actions that could be applied to the particular page being optimized. A value of 0 means the original version of the element is kept, while a value of 1 means the element should be modified using the appropriate action.

Selection: NSGA-II uses the selection operator to select the most qualified candidates from the population as the basis for a new population. Each individual is evaluated according to how many of the others in the population dominate it and how many it dominates, measured using the set of fitness function. If no individual dominates another individual, that individual is considered to be in the first non-domination level, or Pareto frontier. To create the next population, individuals with higher non-domination ranks are selected, and if two individuals have the same non-domination rank, the selection operator favors the one with a greater crowding distance to preserve diversity. The crowding distance estimates the density of candidate solutions surrounding a particular individual in a Pareto frontier, with individuals from a less-dense region of the frontier preferred.

Tournament selection is used to select the parent population for creating the new child population. In a K-way tournament selection, K individuals are selected at random and compared from the previous population. The best two candidates are identified from this subset of the population.

Mutation and Crossover: At a certain probability, the mutation and crossover operations are applied to transform the "parent" solutions identified by the tournament selection into new, potentially improved, "child" solutions.

Mutation selects one action from a solution randomly and swaps the value in the array, i.e., replaces 0 with 1 or 1 with 0. Crossover creates two child solutions by blending elements from the parent solutions. A simple form of crossover is utilized where two indexes are chosen at random, and the items at those indexes are swapped between the two parents. In the current prototype, the mutation probability is 0.4 and the crossover probability is 0.7. These values were identified through exploratory experimentation.

Table 1. Project name and GitHub link for the final experimental subjects.

Project Name	Project Link
Poke-Dex	https://github.com/AM1CODES/Poke-Dex
Ecommerce-Website-main	https://github.com/MOUSTAFAAMIN25/Ecommerce-Website-main
htmlBurger-website	https://github.com/Marius-MPA/htmlBurger-website
complex-storm-html	https://github.com/kasumaputu06/complex-storm-html
module1-capstone-project	https://github.com/MahdiAghaali/module1-capstone-project
awesome-portfolio-websites	https://github.com/smaranjitghose/awesome-portfolio-websites
OpenWISP-Website	https://github.com/openwisp/OpenWISP-Website
project-website-template	https://github.com/yenchiah/project-website-template
ProjectSakura	https://github.com/ProjectSakura/ProjectSakura.github.io
Books-bootstrap-website	https://github.com/akashyap2013/Books-bootstrap-website

Table 2. Metadata on the web pages used for the final experiment.

Project Name	Num. Images	CSS Lines	HTML Lines	JS Lines
Poke-Dex	41	324	6713	111
Ecommerce-Website-main	33	275	415	319
htmlBurger-website	26	750	730	91
complex-storm-html	53	125	519	318
module1-capstone-project	10	206	192	83
awesome-portfolio-websites	2	1696	217	20
OpenWISP-Website	3	396	243	402
project-website-template	64	1841	1086	7
ProjectSakura	19	706	473	36
Books-bootstrap-website	6	422	355	51

3.3 Iteration III (Refinement and Final Evaluation)

In the final iteration, we performed parameter tuning experiments for the tool, then used the identified parameter settings in a final evaluation. There are two main aims for conducting the evaluation. The first is to see if the prototype tool is able to reduce the carbon footprint of web pages. To this end, we compare to the *baseline of the initial fitness values for each web page with no changes made*. The second aim is to see if the prototype tool is more effective than picking transformation actions at random. The corresponding *baseline is imposing changes with a random generation tool*. That is, we generate a random solution and compare to the final solution produced by our tool.

Experiment Subjects: We evaluate our tool and the baselines using ten web page projects, selected from GitHub to represent varying degrees of complexity. Table 1 shows the project names and GitHub links, Table 2 presents metadata on each subject, and Table 3 shows the fitness values for the unmodified pages.

Experiment Configurations: We execute two configurations of our tool, each targeting three fitness functions: (1) *(Data Transferred Quantity) + (Number of Changes) + (Page Load Time)* (**Configuration DNT**), and (2), *(Data Transferred Quantity) + (Number of Changes) + (Memory Usage)* (**DNR**).

Table 3. Baseline fitness values of the web pages used for the final experiment.

Project Name	Data Transferred (KB)	Load Time (ms)	Memory Usage (KB)
Poke-Dex	5158908	3372	275528
Ecommerce-Website-main	3021120	1870	189700
htmlBurger-website	1907546	1937	163008
complex-storm-html	645713	2476	406188
module1-capstone-project	947203	1540	228976
awesome-portfolio-websites	843424	5802	238592
OpenWISP-Website	1238487	6077	172708
project-website-template	5141268	1743	273548
ProjectSakura	1422532	7052	223280
Books-bootstrap-website	1734210	2119	173412

The number of generation of evolution and population size found optimal by the parameter tuning were employed—a population of 20 solutions and a 20-generation search budget.

We perform 20 trials for each subject for each fitness function configuration. For every trial of our tool, we also perform one trial where the random baseline is executed. We refer to random trials paired with DNT-trials as "Random-DNT" and random trials paired with DNR-trials as "Random-DNR".

Data Collection and Analysis: We record the final value for each selected fitness function. Based on the collected data, we compared the performance of multi-objective optimization to the two baselines defined above first using the median fitness values for each fitness function and each experimental subject.

In addition, we compared the performance of the tool and the random baseline using statistical analysis for each fitness function. Data collected for each subject are drawn from an unknown distribution, and normality cannot be assumed. The Mann-Whitney Wilcoxon rank-sum test is used, with $\alpha = 0.05$, to determine whether the multi-objective tool and the random baseline yield fitness values drawn from different distributions. The following null hypothesis and alternative hypothesis are proposed for the analysis of the data collected:

– H0: Observations of results from the prototype tool are drawn from the same distribution as the random generation tool.
– H: Observations of results from the prototype tool are drawn from a different distribution than the random generation tool.

If the distributions are different, the Vargha-Delaney effect size test is used to measure the magnitude. We interpret effect sizes > 0.5 as the first technique performing better than the second. We follow the general interpretation, where an effect size of $0.56 \leq A < 0.64$ is classified as small, while $0.64 \leq A < 0.71$ is considered medium, and $A \geq 0.71$ is deemed large.

4   Results and Discussion

Median Fitness Values: Table 4 shows the median data transfer quantity for each baseline and the two configurations of the tool.

> **Performance (RQ2):** In the median case, our tool reduces the quantity of data transferred by the original web page by 39.14% (DNT) and 40.68% (DNR) and by randomized changes by 25.42% (DNT) and 15.60% (DNR).

Table 4. Median quantity of data transferred (KB) for the original page, randomized baseline, and our tool. Lower values are better, and the lowest is bolded.

Project Name	Original	Random-DNT	Random-DNR	DNT	DNR
Poke-Dex	5158908	4942889	5069008	**4088047**	4181722
Ecommerce-Website-main	3021120	2136636	2167752	1477222	**1403839**
htmlBurger-website	1907546	1848460	1076644	928236	**881270**
complex-storm-html	645713	519497	444831	415664	**383898**
module1-capstone-project	947203	824963	824964	**803259**	818164
awesome-portfolio-websites	843424	767178	767155	**524879**	563573
OpenWISP-Website	1238487	766532	721795	736714	**716632**
project-website-template	5141268	4574004	4179609	4126205	**4110037**
ProjectSakura	1422532	1218049	1083724	**762353**	841990
Books-bootstrap-website	1734210	1090758	1026710	**651616**	1014127

Table 5. Median values for load time and memory usage for the original page, randomized baseline, and our tool. Lower values are better, the lowest is bolded.

Project Name	Load Time (ms)			Memory Usage (KB)		
	Original	Random-DNT	DNT	Original	Random-DNR	DNR
Poke-Dex	**3372**	3637	3526	275528	273394	**263079**
Ecommerce-Website-main	**1870**	1999	1883	189700	170972	**169447**
htmlBurger-website	1937	1870	**1836**	163008	165868	165013
complex-storm-html	2476	2474	**1873**	406188	444831	**402963**
module1-capstone-project	1540	1409	**1396**	228976	148444	**139848**
awesome-portfolio-websites	5802	6306	**5132**	238592	195604	**182057**
OpenWISP-Website	6077	985	**937**	172708	160578	**142629**
project-website-template	1743	1409	**1403**	273548	232752	**206689**
ProjectSakura	7052	6826	**6366**	223280	180134	**107218**
Books-bootstrap-website	2119	1859	**1855**	**173412**	182876	176933

Our tool's performance—generally for both fitness function configurations—is better than both baselines for all experiment subjects. The random baseline only attains comparable results for OpenWISP-Website. As discussed in Sect. 3.1, the quantity of transferred data is highly correlated with the carbon footprint of a web page [5]. Therefore, this is an indication that our tool can reduce a web page's carbon footprint significantly.

Table 5 shows the median memory usage for each baseline and the DNR configuration of the tool.

> **Performance (RQ2):** In the median case, our tool reduces memory consumption of the page by 10.64% and of randomized changes by 3.96%.

Our tool yields lower memory consumption than both baselines for the majority of the subject projects, with the exception of the original versions of `htmlBurger-website` and `Books-bootstrap-website`. As memory usage is highly correlated with energy consumption [17], these results offers further evidence that our tool can reduce the carbon footprint of a web page.

The page load time was considered not because of a relationship with carbon footprint—past research found that it was not always correlated [4]—but because long load times can create a negative user experience [19]. We, therefore, minimize page load time to balance carbon footprint reductions with potentially negative changes to user experience. Table 5 also shows the median page load time for each baseline and the DNT configurations of the tool.

> **Performance (RQ2):** In the median case, our tool reduces the load time of the original page by 14.05% and of randomized changes by 6.36%.

We can see that our tool also yields lower load times for the majority of the experiment subjects, with the exception of `Poke-Dex` and `Ecommerce-Website-main`. In other words, in many cases, reductions in data transfer quantity can also yield an improved user experience through faster loading times.

However, we can also see from the deviating cases that improvements to these fitness functions do not always correlate. Changes intended to reduce the data transferred can reduce memory consumption and load time as well, but they can also have a slight negative impact in some cases.

Table 6. Median number of changes made by randomized baseline and our tool.

Project Name	Random-DNT	Random-DNR	DNT	DNR
Poke-Dex	18.00	15.00	18.50	17.50
Ecommerce-Website-main	19.50	17.00	22.00	20.00
htmlBurger-website	13.50	12.50	16.50	16.00
complex-storm-html	9.50	9.50	12.50	13.00
module1-capstone-project	6.00	5.00	9.00	9.00
awesome-portfolio-websites	2.00	3.00	4.00	4.00
OpenWISP-Website	4.00	3.00	5.00	5.00
project-website-template	19.00	30.50	32.50	33.00
ProjectSakura	11.00	11.00	13.00	13.00
Books-bootstrap-website	4.00	8.50	12.00	13.00

Table 6 shows the median number of changes made by the randomized baseline and our tool. Our tool tries to balance improvements in other fitness functions against the number of changes made to preserve the usability of the page. More changes are made by our tool than by random generation in the average case. However, for many pages, the set of changes is still relatively small.

Statistical Analysis: Table 7 shows that there is a statistical difference in the data transfer quantity between our tool and random solution generation for almost all subjects, with the exception of `OpenWISP-Website` under the DNT configuration. In all cases where such a difference exists, the DNT configuration outperforms that random baseline with a large effect size. In all ten subjects, the DNR configuration outperforms the random generation with a large effect size with regard to quantity of data transferred.

Table 7. Effect sizes for data transfer quantity, load time, and memory usage in cases where a statistically significant difference exists between our tool and the random baseline. Large effect sizes are in bold.

Project Name	Transfer (DNT)	Transfer (DNR)	Load Time	Memory Usage
Poke-Dex	0.99	0.88	0.96	0.76
Ecommerce-Website-main	0.93	0.88	0.80	0.76
htmlBurger-website	0.82	0.84	0.77	-
complex-storm-html	0.88	0.84	0.81	0.75
module1-capstone-project	0.96	0.93	0.91	0.87
awesome-portfolio-websites	0.89	0.94	0.80	0.87
OpenWISP-Website	-	0.78	0.70	0.88
project-website-template	0.93	0.99	0.75	0.85
ProjectSakura	0.91	0.82	0.83	0.77
Books-bootstrap-website	0.95	1.00	0.77	0.91

With regard to load time and memory usage, Table 7 shows that statistical differences exist for almost all subject projects, with the exception of the memory usage of `htmlBurger-Website`. Our tool outperforms the random baseline in each case where a statistical difference was observed. In terms of page load time, the tool outperforms the random baseline with a large effect size for nine projects and one with a medium effect size. In terms of memory usage, the tool outperforms the random baseline with a large effect size for nine projects.

> **Performance (RQ2):** Our tool outperforms the random baseline in 95.00% of comparisons with statistical significance—with a large effect size in 92.50% of comparisons.

We can also compare the two configurations of our tool in terms of the quantity of data transferred—a fitness function shared in both configurations. Table 8

Table 8. Effect size results for data transfer quantity when comparing the two fitness function configurations. Large effect sizes are in bold.

Project Name	Effect Size
Poke-Dex	**0.07**
Ecommerce-Website-main	–
htmlBurger-website	**0.89**
complex-storm-html	**0.92**
module1-capstone-project	**0.03**
awesome-portfolio-websites	**0.00**
OpenWISP-Website	**1.00**
project-website-template	**0.73**
ProjectSakura	**0.27**
Books-bootstrap-website	**0.00**

shows that there are statistically significant differences in the results in nine of the ten projects. However, there is not a clear pattern in *which* configuration is better. In four of ten projects, the DNR fitness function combination outperforms the DNT fitness function combination with a large effect size. However, in the other five projects where a distribution difference was detected, the DNT fitness function combination outperforms the DNR configuration.

It is not clear exactly why one configuration outperforms another in these cases with regard to the quantity of data transferred. It may be that pursuit of one of the other fitness functions—memory usage or load time—may offer feedback on how to further reduce the quantity of transferred data. Future research should explore both additional fitness functions as well as different combinations of fitness functions to identify the tool configurations most widely effective.

Table 9. The percentage of final solutions that apply an action of a particular type to at least one compatible element for the **DNT** configuration.

Project Name	Move Script (%)	Remove Opacity (%)	ChangeHTML (%)	Remove Unused CSS (%)	Compress Image (%)	Convert Image (%)
Poke-Dex	25.00	75.00	65.00	80.00	100.00	100.00
Ecommerce-Website-main	30.00	55.00	55.00	60.00	100.00	100.00
htmlBurger-website	35.00	35.00	55.00	65.00	95.00	100.00
complex-storm-html	45.00	40.00	50.00	50.00	100.00	100.00
module1-capstone-project	35.00	50.00	75.00	80.00	100.00	100.00
awesome-portfolio-websites	25.00	25.00	40.00	90.00	100.00	100.00
OpenWISP-Website	45.00	25.00	65.00	50.00	100.00	100.00
project-website-template	15.00	15.00	60.00	75.00	100.00	100.00
ProjectSakura	10.00	40.00	70.00	70.00	100.00	100.00
Books-bootstrap-website	25.00	55.00	55.00	90.00	100.00	100.00
Overall	28.50	52.00	59.00	71.50	99.50	100.00

Modifications Used: We also examine which modifications are applied most often. Table 9 shows the percentage of final solutions where a particular type of action has been taken for at least one compatible element when targeting the DNT configuration. Table 10 shows the same for the DNR configuration.

Table 10. The percentage of final solutions that apply an action of a particular type to at least one compatible element for the **DNR** configuration.

Project Name	Move Script (%)	Remove Opacity (%)	ChangeHTML (%)	Remove Unused CSS (%)	Compress Image (%)	Convert Image (%)
Poke-Dex	15.00	40.00	45.00	80.00	100.00	100.00
Ecommerce-Website-main	35.00	50.00	50.00	55.00	100.00	100.00
htmlBurger-website	30.00	50.00	65.00	55.00	100.00	100.00
complex-storm-html	15.00	60.00	65.00	70.00	100.00	100.00
module1-capstone-project	55.00	40.00	50.00	50.00	95.00	100.00
awesome-portfolio-websites	40.00	30.00	40.00	65.00	100.00	100.00
OpenWISP-Website	30.00	15.00	70.00	65.00	100.00	100.00
project-website-template	25.00	30.00	50.00	80.00	100.00	100.00
ProjectSakura	15.00	15.00	55.00	65.00	100.00	100.00
Books-bootstrap-website	10.00	50.00	65.00	80.00	100.00	100.00
Overall	26.50	43.00	57.00	62.50	99.50	100.00

As might be anticipated, changes to the images—both compression and format changes—are applied particularly often and clearly have an impact on the quantity of transferred data, memory usage, and page loading time. However, the other actions are applied as well. In particular, unused CSS is frequently removed, perhaps because many websites make use of existing templates and their creators do not optimize the templates. Addressing RQ3:

> **Modifications (RQ3):** Compressing, converting images and removing unused CSS are the most common modifications applied by our tool.

5   Threats to Validity

Conclusion Validity: When using statistical analyses, we have attempted to ensure the base assumptions behind these analyses are met. We have favored non-parametric methods, as distribution characteristics are not generally known a priori, and normality cannot be assumed.

To control experiment cost, we have only performs twenty trials for each tool configuration and case example. It is possible that larger sample sizes may yield different results. However, given the consistency of our experiment results, we believe that this is a sufficient number of repetitions to draw stable conclusions.

External Validity: Our results are specific to HTML and CSS, and our techniques and findings cannot be expected to map to additional languages or file formats. Our study has also focused on ten subject web pages—a relatively small sample. Nevertheless, we attempted to identify open-source web pages representing a range of sizes and use cases. We believe that our subjects are generally representative of small-to-medium-sized web pages.

6   Conclusions

We have explored the use of genetic improvement to automatically reduce the carbon footprint of web pages. In the average case, our tool was able to reduce the quantity of data transferred for all projects, and the memory consumption and loading time for eight of the projects. Our tool outperformed the random baseline with large effect size in 92.50% of comparisons. Compressing and converting images and removing unused CSS were the most common actions performed by the tool, with major effects on solution fitness.

In future research, we will expand the range of actions and fitness functions, as well as the scope of experiment subjects considered. We will also perform a user study to qualitatively assess the acceptability of the applied transformations. We are also particularly interested in examining the impact of the location where components are hosted on the carbon footprint of web applications. We will also explore ways to encourage users to regularly use and trust such tools as part of their workflow.

References

1. Andrae, A.S.: New perspectives on internet electricity use in 2030. Eng. Appl. Sci. Lett. **3**(2), 19–31 (2020)
2. Bawden, T.: Global warming: data centres to consume three times as much energy in next decade experts warn (2016). https://www.independent.co.uk/ climate-change/news/global-warming-data-centres-to-consume-three-times-as-much-energy-in-next-decade-experts-warn-a6830086.html. Accessed 12 Nov 2022
3. Bruce, B.R., Petke, J., Harman, M.: Reducing energy consumption using genetic improvement. In: Proceedings of the 2015 Annual Conference on Genetic and Evolutionary Computation, pp. 1327–1334 (2015)
4. Cao, Y., Nejati, J., Maguluri, P., Balasubramanian, A., Gandhi, A.: Analyzing the power consumption of the mobile page load. In: Proceedings of the 2016 ACM SIG-METRICS International Conference on Measurement and Modeling of Computer Science, pp. 369–370 (2016)
5. Adams, T.F.C., Baouendi, R.: Website carbon calculator (2022)
6. De La Luz, V., Kandemir, M., Kolcu, I.: Automatic data migration for reducing energy consumption in multi-bank memory systems. In: Proceedings 2002 Design Automation Conference (IEEE Cat. No. 02CH37324), pp. 213–218. IEEE (2002)
7. Deb, K., Pratap, A., Agarwal, S., Meyarivan, T.: A fast and elitist multiobjective genetic algorithm: NSGA-II. IEEE Trans. Evol. Comput. **6**(2), 182–197 (2002)
8. Developers, C.: Remove unused css (2020). https://developer.chrome.com/docs/ lighthouse/performance/unused-css-rules/. Accessed 09 Nov 2022
9. Dorn, J., Lacomis, J., Weimer, W., Forrest, S.: Automatically exploring tradeoffs between software output fidelity and energy costs. IEEE Trans. Softw. Eng. **45**(3), 219–236 (2017)
10. Haan, K.: How many websites are there? (2023). https://www.forbes.com/advisor/ business/software/website-statistics/. Accessed 04 Oct 2022
11. Khare, V., Yao, X., Deb, K.: Performance scaling of multi-objective evolutionary algorithms. In: Fonseca, C.M., Fleming, P.J., Zitzler, E., Thiele, L., Deb, K. (eds.) EMO 2003. LNCS, vol. 2632, pp. 376–390. Springer, Heidelberg (2003). https:// doi.org/10.1007/3-540-36970-8_27
12. Kirupa. Running your code at the right time (2020). https://www.kirupa.com/ html5/running_your_code_at_the_right_time.html. Accessed 01 Dec 2022

13. Lazaris, L.: An introduction and guide to the css object model (cssom) (2018). https://css-tricks.com/an-introduction-and-guide-to-the-css-object-model-cssom/. Accessed 08 Nov 2022
14. Manotas, I., Pollock, L., Clause, J.: Seeds: a software engineer's energy-optimization decision support framework. In: Proceedings of the 36th International Conference on Software Engineering, pp, 503–514 (2014)
15. Mrazek, V., Vasicek, Z., Sekanina, L.: Evolutionary approximation of software for embedded systems: median function. In: Proceedings of the Companion Publication of the 2015 Annual Conference on Genetic and Evolutionary Computation, pp. 795–801 (2015)
16. Philippot, O.: Which image format choose to reduce energy consumption and environmental impact? (2022). https://greenspector.com/en/which-image-format-to-choose-to-reduce-its-energy-consumption-and-its-environmental-impact/. Accessed 15 Jan 2023
17. Philippot, O., Anglade, A., Leboucq, T.: Characterization of the energy consumption of websites: impact of website implementation on resource consumption. In: ICT for Sustainability 2014 (ICT4S-2014), pp. 171–178. Atlantis Press (2014)
18. Sampson, A., Caşcaval, C., Ceze, L., Montesinos, P., Gracia, D.S.: Automatic discovery of performance and energy pitfalls in html and css. In: IEEE International Symposium on Workload Characterization (IISWC), pp. 82–83. IEEE (2012)
19. Stadnik, W., Nowak, Z.: The impact of web pages' load time on the conversion rate of an e-commerce platform. In: Borzemski, L., Swiatek, J., Wilimowska, Z. (eds.) ISAT 2017. AISC, vol. 655, pp. 336–345. Springer, Cham (2018). https://doi.org/10.1007/978-3-319-67220-5_31
20. Steinke, S., Wehmeyer, L., Lee, B.-S., Marwedel, P.: Assigning program and data objects to scratchpad for energy reduction. In: Proceedings Design, Automation and Test in Europe Conference and Exhibition, pp. 409–415. IEEE (2002)
21. Taina, J.: How green is your software? In: Tyrväinen, P., Jansen, S., Cusumano, M.A. (eds.) ICSOB 2010. LNBIP, vol. 51, pp. 151–162. Springer, Heidelberg (2010). https://doi.org/10.1007/978-3-642-13633-7_13
22. Thiagarajan, N., Aggarwal, G., Nicoara, A., Boneh, D., Singh, J.P.: Who killed my battery? analyzing mobile browser energy consumption. In: Proceedings of the 21st International Conference on World Wide Web, pp. 41–50 (2012)
23. White, D.R., Clark, J., Jacob, J., Poulding, S.M.: Searching for resource-efficient programs: Low-power pseudorandom number generators. In: Proceedings of the 10th Annual Conference on Genetic and Evolutionary Computation, pp. 1775–1782 (2008)
24. Zhu, Y., Reddi, V.J.: High-performance and energy-efficient mobile web browsing on big/little systems. In: 2013 IEEE 19th International Symposium on High Performance Computer Architecture (HPCA), pp. 13–24. IEEE (2013)

A Novel Mutation Operator
for Search-Based Test Case Selection

Aitor Arrieta$^{(\boxtimes)}$ and Miren Illarramendi

Mondragon University, Mondragon, Spain
{aarrieta,millarramendi}@mondragon.edu

Abstract. Test case selection has been a widely investigated technique
to increase the cost-effectiveness of software testing. Because the search
space in this problem is huge, search-based approaches have been found
effective, where an optimization algorithm (e.g., a genetic algorithm)
applies mutation and crossover operators guided by corresponding objective functions with the goal of reducing the test execution cost while
maintaining the overall test quality. The de-facto mutation operator is
the bit-flip mutation, where a test case is mutated with a probability of
$1/N$, N being the total number of test cases in the original test suite.
This has a core disadvantage: an effective test case and an ineffective one
have the same probability of being selected or removed. In this paper,
we advocate for a novel mutation operator that promotes selecting effective test cases while removing the ineffective ones. To this end, instead of
applying a probability of $1/N$ to every single test case in the original test
suite, we calculate new selection and removal probabilities. This is carried
out based on the adequacy criterion of each test case, determined before
executing the algorithm (e.g., based on historical data). We integrate
our approach in the domain of Cyber-Physical Systems (CPSs) within a
widely applied dataset. Our results suggests that the proposed mutation
operator can increase the effectiveness of search-based test case selection
methods, especially when the time budget for executing test cases is low.

Keywords: Search-based test case selection · Regression test
optimization

1 Introduction

Search algorithms have been found to be effective in solving multiple software
engineering tasks, including test case generation [1,15–17,26], fault localization [23], and regression test optimization [8,10,12,14,19,29,31,32,35]. Because
of the time it requires for test cases to execute, in the last few years, significant effort has been devoted to the field of test case selection [6,8,28,29,31,35].
Test case selection aims at reducing the number of test cases to execute, while
maintaining as high as possible the overall test quality. As the search space of
the test case selection problem is huge (i.e., 2^N, N being the total number of
test cases), search algorithms have been found appropriate in multiple domains,
including, software product lines [33], cyber-physical systems [21] and deep neural networks [4].

P. Arcaini et al. (Eds.): SSBSE 2023, LNCS 14415, pp. 84–98, 2024.
https://doi.org/10.1007/978-3-031-48796-5_6

The test case selection problem has been investigated from different perspectives. On the one hand, a large corpus of studies investigate the effect of different fitness functions (and their combination) in the cost-effectiveness of the selected test cases [7,8]. On the other hand, other studies investigate how different search algorithms perform when selecting test cases [33]. A third group of studies focus on giving algorithmic solutions adapted to the context of test case selection. For instance, Panichella et al. [29] propose the inclusion of diversity in multi-objective genetic algorithms. This was carried out by using orthogonal design and orthogonal evolution mechanisms during the search process [29]. Arrieta et al. [5,6] propose a set of seeding strategies adapted to the test case selection problem. Specifically, instead of generating the initial population pure randomly, they propose different strategies, e.g., generating solutions in the population with a different amount of test cases selected or injecting diversity in the initial population [5,6]. Olsthoorn and Panichella [27] proposed a linkage learning approach to optimize test case selection by using unsupervised learning techniques at the crossover level to yield new individuals by inferring structures. Despite all the work in the field of search-based test case selection, to the best of our knowledge, there is no study that has investigated how to enhance the test case selection problem from the mutation operator perspective. Indeed, most of the studies employ the default value of bit-flip mutation with a probability of $1/N$, N being the number of test cases in the initial test suite [5–7,27,29,31,33].

In this paper we propose a novel mutation operator specifically designed for targeting the test case selection problem. Instead of giving the same probability for being selected or removed from the initial test suite to all test cases, we advocate for giving different probabilities for each test case based on their effectiveness. This way, the mutation operator has higher probabilities of selecting effective test cases and higher probabilities of removing ineffective ones.

Our evaluation was conducted by using a well-known test case selection dataset for Cyber-Physical Systems (CPSs), using four different case study systems and a total of 15 instances (i.e., four different instances for each case study system, except for one of them, where we used three different instances). Our approach showed superiority in 8 out of 15 instances with statistical significance. Conversely, in 5 out of 15 instances, the performance was worse than the traditionally employed mutation operator. Overall, we can summarize the key contributions of this paper as follows:

- Technique: We propose a novel mutation operator that fosters selection of effective test cases and reduction of weak test cases.
- Evaluation: We evaluate the approach in four CPS case study systems of a well-known test case selection dataset.
- Replication package: We provide a replication package with the code, experiments, results and analysis: https://dx.doi.org/10.6084/m9.figshare.23998029

The rest of the paper is structured as follows. Section 2 proposes the mutation operator. Section 3 explains the conducted evaluation to assess the approach. Section 4 positions our work with the current state-of-the-art. Lastly, we conclude and discuss future research avenues in Sect. 5.

2 The Mutation Operator

2.1 Formalization

Let $TS = \{tc_1, tc_2, ..., tc_N\}$ be a test suite composed of N test cases (tc). Because executing all test cases in TS is often not practical, the test case selection problem aims at selecting a subset of test cases from TS, such that $TS' = \{tc_{x1}, tc_{x2}, ..., tc_xM\}$ is a subset of TS (i.e., $TS' \subseteq TS$) and $M \leq N$. To guide the search algorithm, the test quality and cost of TS' needs to be measured. In the context of multi-objective test case selection, this is carried out by a set of p objective functions, i.e., $OF = \{of_1, of_2, ..., of_p\}$. Usually, the objective functions cover at least one quality objective function (e.g., code coverage [35], failure detection rate [31]) and one cost function (e.g., test execution time [35]).

The most typical way for representing a solution in multi-objective test case selection is through binary coding representation [5–7,27,29,31,33], where the i-th digit of the binary string represents whether a test case has been selected (when the digit is 1) or not selected (when the digit is 0). For instance, given a test suite of $N = 6$ test cases, an individual k can be represented as $s_k = (1, 0, 0, 1, 1, 0)$. For the individual s_k, test cases tc_1, tc_4 and tc_5 are selected whereas test cases tc_2, tc_3 and tc_6 are not.

2.2 Approach

When selecting a set of test cases from TS, it is necessary to measure the cost and overall effectiveness of the subset of selected test cases. To this end, each test case encompasses certain degree of adequacy, which can be measured based on different criteria. For instance, one typical criterion is *test coverage*, where, if tc_1 is able to exercise a larger portion of code than tc_2, it is said that tc_1 is more adequate than tc_2. Another typical criterion is the *fault detection capability* of test cases, which can be measured based on the number of failures the test cases have triggered during their historical executions.

In this paper we advocate for promoting the selection of adequate test cases and deselection of non-adequate test cases. To this end, we propose to consider the adequacy of a test case during the mutation process of the search-based test case selection algorithm. Our technique is simple, yet effective. For each test case, instead of having a mutation probability of $1/N$, we obtain two probabilities based on a predefined adequacy criterion: the selection probability (p_{sel_i}) and the removal probability (p_{rem_i}). The former provides the probability for the i-th test case for being selected when this is not selected in s_k. The latter provides the probability for the i-th test case for being removed when it is selected in s_k. An effective test case, (i.e., that with a high adequacy score) should have a higher p_{sel_i} and a lower p_{rem_i} than $1/N$. Conversely, a non-effective test case should have a lower p_{sel_i} and a higher p_{rem_i} than $1/N$.

Let as_{tc_i} be the normalized adequacy score of test case i, where the higher the value, the higher its adequacy. Given a test suite of N test cases, we obtain the selection probability for tc_i as follows:

$$p_{sel_i} = \frac{as_{tc_i}}{\sum_{i=1}^{N} as_{tc_i}} \tag{1}$$

On the other hand, the removal probability for tc_i can be obtained as follows:

$$p_{rem_i} = \frac{1 - as_{tc_i}}{\sum_{i=1}^{N}(1 - as_{tc_i})} \tag{2}$$

It is important to recall that p_{sel_i} is only applied when the tc_i is not selected in the individual (i.e., it has a 0 in the binary string representation of the solution). Conversely, p_{rem_i} is only applied when the tc_i is selected in the individual (i.e., it has a 1 in the binary string representation of the solution). That is, our mutation operator iterates the status of each test case in each solution provided by the search algorithm and applies the corresponding probability depending on the test case selection status (i.e., selected or not selected).

2.3   Applicability and Limitations

Our approach requires to retrieve the predefined probabilities for being selected/removed from the initial test suite during the mutation process. To address this, the adequacy of a test case needs to be obtained. As a result, our approach is applicable for regression testing contexts, where data from previous executions exists.

Conversely, our approach is not applicable for cases in which the similarity of test cases is the only metric to assess the adequacy of a test case. A potential way could be to extract the adequacy of each test case by measuring the distance to the closest test case. However, this would require to compute distance metrics of each test case every time a new test case is selected or removed during the mutation process as well as every time the mutation operator is invoked. Consequently, this approach would not scale in terms of computational cost, especially in those cases with large test suites.

3   Evaluation

3.1   Research Questions

In our evaluation, we aimed at answering the following two research questions (RQs):

- **RQ1 – Overall cost-effectiveness:** How does the proposed mutation operator perform when compared to the traditionally employed bit-flip mutation operator in terms of overall cost-effectiveness?
- **RQ2 – Fault detection capabilities:** Is the proposed mutation operator capable of detecting more faults than the traditional bit-flip mutation operator given a test execution time budget? When is it beneficial to use the proposed mutation operator?

With the first RQ, we aimed at assessing the overall cost-effectiveness of the new mutation operator compared to the traditional mutation operator. With the second RQ, we aimed at assessing the effectiveness of the new mutation operator in terms of fault detection when a decision maker selects one solution of the Pareto-frontier given a time-budget [3]; this may provide us some insights about when the proposed approach is beneficial.

3.2   Experimental Design

Dataset and Case Study Systems: We employed the dataset and case study systems provided by Arrieta et al., [8] for test case selection. This dataset has been widely used by different researchers for test case selection studies [3,5,6,20, 21]. Moreover, a recent study [3] confirmed with this dataset that the revisited hypervolume metric (i.e., one of the metrics used to in our evaluation setup) is an appropriate metric to assess multi-objective test case selection approaches. The dataset involves a total of 6 Simulink models (encompassing each a different CPS case study) of different characteristics and complexities (i.e., in terms of size, number of inputs and outputs). Similar to other studies [3,20,21], we did not use two of the Simulink models due to their simplicity. Table 1 summarizes the main characteristics of the selected Simulink models. Each Simulink model encompassed between 120 to 150 test cases. Moreover, the dataset employs a set of mutants, appropriately filtered out in order to remove duplicate and trivial mutants [8].

Table 1. Key characteristics of the selected Simulink models in the first application context

Simulink models	# of Blocks	# of Inputs	# of Outputs	# of Test Cases	Initial set of mutants	Final set of mutants
CW	235	15	4	133	250	98
EMB	315	1	1	150	40	10
AC Engine	257	4	1	120	20	12
Two Tanks	498	11	7	150	34	6

Fitness Functions and Adequacy Scores: Similar to recent test case selection studies using the dataset used in this paper, we derived a total of four different fitness function combinations. Each of the combinations encompassed one effectiveness metric and the test execution time (TET) as the cost metric. Related to the effectiveness metrics, we employed four black-box metrics defined by Arrieta et al. [8], which are commonly employed by other researchers too [20,21]. Similar to recent studies, we discarded similarity metrics because (1) their performance was low [8] and (2) distance-based metrics cannot be applied with our mutation operator as an adequacy criterion (see Sect. 2.3 for details).

For the adequacy criterion in the mutation operator, for each of the combinations used, we employed the same as the one used in the effectiveness fitness function. Although our approach permits the use of an adequacy criterion different to the one used to compute the fitness, we opted to use the same as this would be a natural choice by a developer (i.e., the fitness function employed in the algorithm should be the most adequate one). This would also permit to have a "synchronization" between the mutation operator and the effectiveness fitness function (Table 2).

Table 2. Selected fitness function combinations based on the metrics proposed by Arrieta et al., [8]

	Effectiveness metric	Cost metric
c2	Growth to infinity	Test Execution Time
c2	Growth to infinity	Test Execution Time
c3	Instability	Test Execution Time
c4	MinMax	Test Execution Time

Evaluation Metrics: To answer the first RQ, we employed the revisited Hypervolume (rHV). Proposed first by Panichella et al. [29], this metric determines the overall cost-effectiveness of the algorithm by deriving a second Pareto-frontier from the original Pareto-frontier returned by the multi-objective test case selection algorithm. This second Pareto-frontier is derived by considering the actual fault detection capability (e.g., obtained through mutation testing) and the cost. In a recent empirical study [3] (using the dataset from this paper), it was demonstrated that this metric is appropriate for multi-objective test case selection.

As for the second RQ, since the goal was to measure to which extent the proposed mutation operator showed benefits when detecting faults, we employed the mutation score. Multi-objective search algorithms return a set of solutions, i.e., the Pareto-frontier. Therefore, to obtain the mutation score, a decision maker (DM) needs to select one solution among all. To this end, we implemented a DM proposed in our previous study [3], which takes as input (1) a set of non-dominated solutions returned by the search algorithm and (2) a given time-budget provided by the user. Since in our experiments we only considered two fitness functions (i.e., test execution time and an effectiveness function), the DM returns the solution which is closer to the time-budget without exceeding it. If such solution does not exist, it returns a null (i.e., it is not possible to execute a test suite given that time budget). It is noteworthy that the DM does not have prior information of the detected faults. Specifically, we configured the DM to select solutions incorporating a test suite that does not exceed the 1%, 5%, 10%, 15%, 20%, 30%, 40% and 50% of the original test suite's test execution time, i.e., the same as Arrieta [3].

Algorithms Setups: We used the NSGA-II algorithm as it is the most widely used algorithm for test case selection [5–7,27,29,31,33]. We use the parameters used in prior studies [5–7,31,35]. The population size was set to 100, the crossover probability was 0.8 and we used the binary tournament selection operator. Regarding the baseline mutation operator, we employed the bit-flip mutation operator with probability $1/N$, N being the number of test cases in the test suite.

Runs and Statistical Tests: As the employed Pareto-based search algorithm (i.e., NSGA-II) is stochastic, based on recommendations by Arcuri and Briand [2], we repeated its execution 50 times. In addition, we analyzed the results through statistical tests. We first measured the normality distribution of the obtained results through the Shapiro-Wilk test. As most of the data was not normally distributed (i.e., p-value in Shapiro-Wilk test < 0.05) we used the Mann-Whitney U-test to assess the significance of the results produced by the different algorithms. Moreover, the Vargha and Delaney $\hat{A}_{12}$ value was employed to assess the difference between the different algorithms.

3.3 Analysis of the Results

RQ1 – Overall Cost-Effectiveness. Table 3 provides the $\hat{A}_{12}$ and p-values when comparing the proposed mutation operator with the traditional one for the rHV metric. On the one hand, the $\hat{A}_{12}$ value provides the probability of a technique being better than the other one. The higher the $\hat{A}_{12}$, the higher probability that the traditional mutation operator (i.e., 1/N) was better than the proposed one in this study. On the other hand, the p-value indicates whether there was statistical significance. We consider so if the p-value was below 0.05.

Table 3. RQ1 – Summary of the statistical test results rHV metric for the different case study systems and different cost-effectiveness metrics

	c1		c2		c3		c4	
	$\hat{A}_{12}$	p-val	$\hat{A}_{12}$	p-val	$\hat{A}_{12}$	p-val	$\hat{A}_{12}$	p-val
ACEngine	0.71	<0.001	0.68	0.002	0.53	0.6466	0.61	0.048
CW	0.06	<0.001	–	–	0.15	<0.001	0.99	<0.001
EMB	0.29	<0.001	0.98	<0.001	0.25	<0.001	0.50	0.967
TwoTanks	0.33	0.003	0.36	0.017	0.16	<0.001	0.30	<0.001

The results indicate that in 8 out of 15 of the analyzed fitness function combinations, there was statistical significance in favor of our mutation operator. Specifically, in three out of four case study systems (i.e., CW, EMB and TwoTanks), there was at least two fitness function combinations for which our mutation operator outperformed with statistical significance the commonly used mutation operator. Conversely, for 5 out of 15 of the studied scenarios, the proposed operator was not favorable. In fact, for the ACEngine case study system, our approach seemed to rather reduce the overall cost-effectiveness. A potential explanation for this could be that the test execution time of each test case also has an important impact in this specific case study, which was not considered in the mutation operator.

It is noteworthy that the results seemed more beneficial when employing the c1 and c3 fitness function combinations, which relate to the combinations that employ the discontinuity and instability anti-patterns to measure the effectiveness fitness function. Based on prior results employing these case study systems [6,8], these two fitness functions were found to be the most effective ones. We recall that to obtain the selection and removal probabilities of each test case, we employed the same as those used for the fitness function calculations. Therefore, if those attributes are not appropriate, it is expectable that the mutation operator does not favor the multi-objective search algorithm towards obtaining better results. Therefore, RQ1 can be answered as follows:

RQ1: In more than half of the studied cases, the proposed mutation operator showed positive results with statistical significance for the rHV metric. However, in some of the cases, the mutation operator showed a negative impact, which may be attributed to (1) ineffective adequacy criterion used to compute the probability array and (2) need for considering the test execution time too in the mutation operator.

RQ2 – Fault Detection Capability. The graphs from Fig. 1 show the average mutation scores obtained for the different configurations in which our novel mutation operator showed a positive influence according to the results from RQ1. Specifically, it can be appreciated that when employing our technique, the mutation scores were higher when the time budgets were low. Some eye-catching results in which the benefit of our proposed mutation operator were high involve (1) CW case study system for the c1 and c3 configurations; (2) EMB case study system for c1 and c3 configurations; and (3) TwoTanks case study system for c3 and c4 configurations. For instance, in the CW case study system, when the time budget for executing the test suite should not exceed a 5% of the original test suite's test execution time, the mutation score increased over 3-fold and 2-fold for c1 and c3, respectively.

Conversely, the graphs in Fig. 2 show those cases in which our mutation operator had a negative effect according to the previous RQ. This is also confirmed when plotting the mutation scores based on the decision provided by the DMs. Specifically, the results for CW-c4 and EMB-c2 were significantly worse than those used by the traditional mutation operator. The core reason is that those fitness function configurations involved the anti-patterns related to the growth to infinity (GTI) and the difference between minimum and maximum values. When looking more into the detail of these results, we found that the test cases that had high MinMax and GTI values also involved long test cases in terms of execution time. As a result, in both cases, there were no solutions in the Pareto-frontier that involved test suites with test cases that encompassed lower time

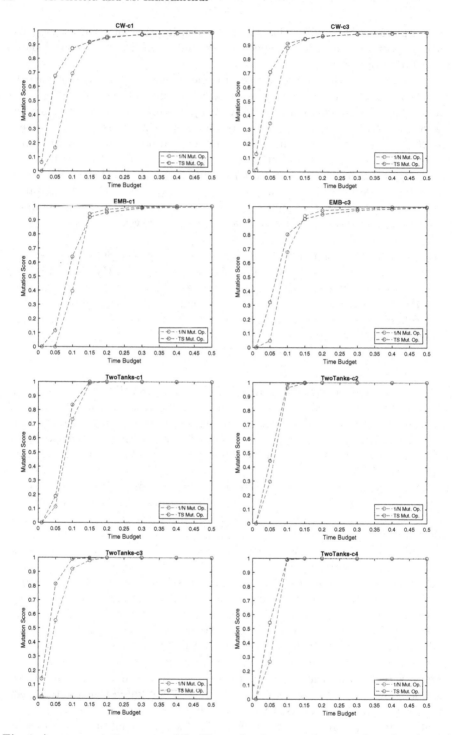

Fig. 1. Average mutation scores of the 50 runs for the cases where our algorithm showed a positive effect in the mutation score

budgets than the 15% it took to execute the original test suite. Consequently, the mutation score values for three of the configurations for these cases were 0, as no test case could be executed. We conjecture that a potential way of solving this issue could be to include information of the test execution time when obtaining the selection and removal probabilities. This could be carried out, for instance, by employing a weighted approach.

Lastly, the graphs in Fig. 3 show the mutation score values for those cases in which, for RQ1, there was no statistical significance. We show that the average value for the 50 runs was mostly the same in all cases. This could be attributed to the low effectiveness of the fitness functions used in those specific combinations.

Based on the obtained results, the second RQ can be answered as follows:

> **RQ2:** The proposed mutation operator helped increase the mutation score in 8 out of the 15 studied cases. The approach shows benefits when the time budget to execute test cases is low, showing significant increase in the fault detection capabilities in those cases.

3.4   Threats to Validity

Internal Validity: An internal validity threat of our study relates to the mutants. Specifically, the number of mutants was not large, but it is comparable to similar studies in which CPS models are employed [9,11,22–25]. This is mainly because such kind of systems take a long time to execute and therefore, it is not practical to use a large amount of mutants. However, to reduce this threat, we employed the same mutants as previous studies [6–8,21]. Moreover, such studies already removed duplicated and trivial mutants as suggested by Papadakis et al. [30]. Another internal validity threat refers to the employed algorithm, which was the NSGA-II. Further validation of our approach is required to see how the proposed mutation operator performs with other algorithms. Note, however, that the NSGA-II is the most widely used multi-objective algorithm in test case selection studies [7,8,34,35]. Lastly, the parameters of the algorithms might have an influence in the obtained results. We used the same parameters as previous studies [5–8,35] to mitigate this internal validity threat.

External Validity: The main external validity threat of our evaluation relates to the generalizability of the results. We only employed four different case study systems and more case studies are required to further validate the approach, which we foresee to target it in the close future. However, the selected case study systems were diverse in terms of complexity and characteristics and have been widely used for multi-objective test case selection research.

Conclusion Validity: A conclusion validity threat of our evaluation relates to the non-determinism of the search algorithms. This was mitigated by running each algorithm instance 50 times and using statistical tests to analyze the results, as recommended by related guidelines [2].

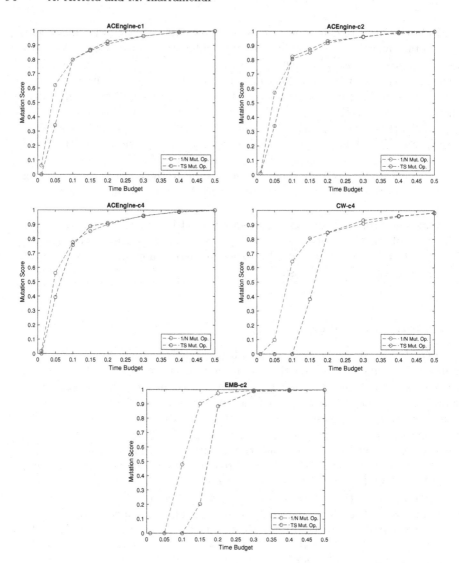

Fig. 2. Average mutation scores of the 50 runs for the cases where our mutation score showed a negative effect in the mutation score

Construct Validity: To mitigate construct validity threats of our study, we employed the same setup for all algorithms in terms of population size and number of generation. This way, the NSGA-II configured to use our mutation operator or the commonly used one (i.e., probability of 1/N) employ the same number of fitness function computations.

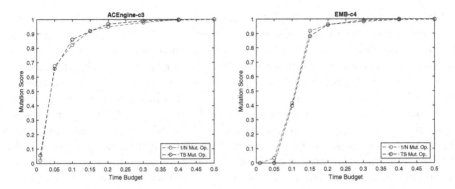

Fig. 3. Average mutation scores of the 50 runs for which the proposed mutation score did not have any effect

4   Related Work

As previously explained, search-based test case selection studies can be divided in three main groups: (1) studies that investigate which search algorithms perform best when selecting test cases (in specific domains); (2) studies that investigate which are the fitness functions that yield best cost-effectiveness; and (3) studies that propose algorithmic enhancement focused on test case selection. This paper focuses on this last group. Within this last group, different perspectives have been proposed, such as, seeding the initial population [5,6], injecting diversity during the search process [29] and proposing novel crossover operators [27]. Unlike all these studies, our algorithm investigates enhancements in the mutation operator. To the best of our knowledge, this is the first paper that investigates enhancing search-based test case selection from the mutation operator perspective.

Besides test selection, other studies have studied different mutation operators with different goals, such as, enhancing differential evolution [13]. As for software engineering tasks, to the best of our knowledge, the only work focusing on the mutation operator relates to Guizzo et al., [18] who focus on pattern-based mutation operators to optimize product line architectures, i.e., a different goal as our's.

5   Conclusion and Future Work

Search-based test case selection requires different genetic operators. This paper lies in the context of the mutation operator, for which, up to now, to the best of our knowledge, has not been investigated for the context of test case selection. Specifically, instead of all test cases having the same probability for being selected or removed from the original test suite, we advocate for having different probabilities based on their adequacy score. This fosters the removal of weak test cases and the selection of the strong ones. We evaluate this novel approach for selecting test cases in a dataset involving 4 case study systems related to

CPSs and 4 different fitness function combinations for each (except for the CW, for which one of them did not have sense to be applied). The mutation operator showed higher cost-effectiveness in 8 of the 15 studied scenarios. Specifically, our findings suggest that our approach is beneficial when the time budget to execute test cases is low. However, in 5 of the 15 studied cases, the cost-effectiveness of the approach was reduced when compared to the traditional mutation operator.

Future research avenues include approaches to gain confidence in our technique so as to be appropriate in all situations. To this end, we aim at investigating two core aspects. Firstly, we want to investigate strategies to include the test execution time in the mutation operator, as we found that many most "adequate" test cases took longer execution time. Secondly, we want to investigate the combination of metrics between fitness function and the adequacy criterion used for extracting the probability metrics. Besides these aspects, we would like to further validate the performance of our approach in other contexts and domains, such as those related to continuous integration (CI).

Replication Package: The full replication package can be found here: https://dx.doi.org/10.6084/m9.figshare.23998029

Acknowledgments. This work was partially founded by the Basque Government through their Elkartek program (EGIA project, ref. KK-2022/00119). The authors are part of the Software and Systems Engineering research group of Mondragon Unibertsitatea (IT1519-22), supported by the Department of Education, Universities and Research of the Basque Country.

References

1. Almulla, H., Gay, G.: Learning how to search: generating effective test cases through adaptive fitness function selection. Empir. Softw. Eng. **27**(2), 1–62 (2022)
2. Arcuri, A., Briand, L.: A practical guide for using statistical tests to assess randomized algorithms in software engineering. In: 2011 33rd International Conference on Software Engineering (ICSE), pp. 1–10. IEEE (2011)
3. Arrieta, A.: Is the revisited hypervolume an appropriate quality indicator to evaluate multi-objective test case selection algorithms? In: Proceedings of the Genetic and Evolutionary Computation Conference, pp. 1317–1326 (2022)
4. Arrieta, A.: Multi-objective metamorphic follow-up test case selection for deep learning systems. In: Proceedings of the Genetic and Evolutionary Computation Conference, pp. 1327–1335 (2022)
5. Arrieta, A., Agirre, J.A., Sagardui, G.: Seeding strategies for multi-objective test case selection: an application on simulation-based testing. In: Proceedings of the 2020 Genetic and Evolutionary Computation Conference, pp. 1222–1231 (2020)
6. Arrieta, A., Valle, P., Agirre, J.A., Sagardui, G.: Some seeds are strong: seeding strategies for search-based test case selection. ACM Trans. Softw. Eng. Methodol. **32**(1), 1–47 (2023)
7. Arrieta, A., Wang, S., Arruabarrena, A., Markiegi, U., Sagardui, G., Etxeberria, L.: Multi-objective black-box test case selection for cost-effectively testing simulation models. In: Proceedings of the Genetic and Evolutionary Computation Conference, pp. 1411–1418 (2018)

8. Arrieta, A., Wang, S., Markiegi, U., Arruabarrena, A., Etxeberria, L., Sagardui, G.: Pareto efficient multi-objective black-box test case selection for simulation-based testing. Inf. Softw. Technol. **114**, 137–154 (2019)
9. Arrieta, A., Wang, S., Sagardui, G., Etxeberria, L.: Search-based test case prioritization for simulation-based testing of cyber-physical system product lines. J. Syst. Softw. **149**, 1–34 (2019)
10. Assunção, W.K.G., Colanzi, T.E., Vergilio, S.R., Pozo, A.: A multi-objective optimization approach for the integration and test order problem. Inf. Sci. **267**, 119–139 (2014)
11. Binh, N.T., Tung, K.T., et al.: A novel fitness function of metaheuristic algorithms for test data generation for simulink models based on mutation analysis. J. Syst. Softw. **120**, 17–30 (2016)
12. Birchler, C., Khatiri, S., Derakhshanfar, P., Panichella, S., Panichella, A.: Single and multi-objective test cases prioritization for self-driving cars in virtual environments. ACM Trans. Softw. Eng. Methodol. **32**(2), 1–30 (2023)
13. Das, S., Abraham, A., Chakraborty, U.K., Konar, A.: Differential evolution using a neighborhood-based mutation operator. IEEE Trans. Evol. Comput. **13**(3), 526–553 (2009)
14. De Lucia, A., Di Penta, M., Oliveto, R., Panichella, A.: On the role of diversity measures for multi-objective test case selection. In: 2012 7th International Workshop on Automation of Software Test (AST), pp. 145–151. IEEE (2012)
15. Fraser, G., Arcuri, A.: Whole test suite generation. IEEE Trans. Software Eng. **39**(2), 276–291 (2012)
16. Fraser, G., Arcuri, A., McMinn, P.: A memetic algorithm for whole test suite generation. J. Syst. Softw. **103**, 311–327 (2015)
17. Gay, G.: Generating effective test suites by combining coverage criteria. In: Menzies, T., Petke, J. (eds.) SSBSE 2017. LNCS, vol. 10452, pp. 65–82. Springer, Cham (2017). https://doi.org/10.1007/978-3-319-66299-2_5
18. Guizzo, G., Colanzi, T.E., Vergilio, S.R.: A pattern-driven mutation operator for search-based product line architecture design. In: Le Goues, C., Yoo, S. (eds.) SSBSE 2014. LNCS, vol. 8636, pp. 77–91. Springer, Cham (2014). https://doi.org/10.1007/978-3-319-09940-8_6
19. Lachmann, R., Felderer, M., Nieke, M., Schulze, S., Seidl, C., Schaefer, I.: Multi-objective black-box test case selection for system testing. In: Proceedings of the Genetic and Evolutionary Computation Conference, pp. 1311–1318 (2017)
20. Ling, X., Menzies, T.: Faster multi-goal simulation-based testing using doless (domination with least square approximation). arXiv preprint arXiv:2112.01598 (2021)
21. Ling, X., Menzies, T.: What not to test (for cyber-physical systems). IEEE Trans. Softw. Eng. **49**, 3811–3826 (2023)
22. Liu, B., Lucia, Nejati, S., Briand, L.C., Bruckmann, T.: Simulink fault localization: an iterative statistical debugging approach. Softw. Test. Verif. Reliabi. **26**(6), 431–459 (2016)
23. Liu, B., Nejati, S., Briand, L.C., et al.: Effective fault localization of automotive simulink models: achieving the trade-off between test oracle effort and fault localization accuracy. Empir. Softw. Eng. **24**(1), 444–490 (2019)
24. Matinnejad, R., Nejati, S., Briand, L.C., Bruckmann, T.: Automated test suite generation for time-continuous simulink models. In: proceedings of the 38th International Conference on Software Engineering, pp. 595–606 (2016)
25. Matinnejad, R., Nejati, S., Briand, L.C., Bruckmann, T.: Test generation and test prioritization for simulink models with dynamic behavior. IEEE Trans. Software Eng. **45**(9), 919–944 (2018)

26. McMinn, P.: Search-based software test data generation: a survey. Softw. Test. Verif. Reliab. **14**(2), 105–156 (2004)
27. Olsthoorn, M., Panichella, A.: Multi-objective test case selection through linkage learning-based crossover. In: O'Reilly, U.-M., Devroey, X. (eds.) SSBSE 2021. LNCS, vol. 12914, pp. 87–102. Springer, Cham (2021). https://doi.org/10.1007/978-3-030-88106-1_7
28. Pan, R., Ghaleb, T.A., Briand, L.: ATM: black-box test case minimization based on test code similarity and evolutionary search. In: 2023 IEEE/ACM 45th International Conference on Software Engineering (ICSE), pp. 1700–1711. IEEE (2023)
29. Panichella, A., Oliveto, R., Di Penta, M., De Lucia, A.: Improving multi-objective test case selection by injecting diversity in genetic algorithms. IEEE Trans. Software Eng. **41**(4), 358–383 (2014)
30. Papadakis, M., Jia, Y., Harman, M., Le Traon, Y.: Trivial compiler equivalence: a large scale empirical study of a simple, fast and effective equivalent mutant detection technique. In: 2015 IEEE/ACM 37th IEEE International Conference on Software Engineering, vol. 1, pp. 936–946. IEEE (2015)
31. Pradhan, D., Wang, S., Ali, S., Yue, T., Liaaen, M.: CBGA-ES: a cluster-based genetic algorithm with elitist selection for supporting multi-objective test optimization. In: 2017 IEEE International Conference on Software Testing, Verification and Validation (ICST), pp. 367–378. IEEE (2017)
32. Saber, T., Delavernhe, F., Papadakis, M., O'Neill, M., Ventresque, A.: A hybrid algorithm for multi-objective test case selection. In: 2018 IEEE Congress on Evolutionary Computation (CEC), pp. 1–8. IEEE (2018)
33. Wang, S., Ali, S., Gotlieb, A.: Cost-effective test suite minimization in product lines using search techniques. J. Syst. Softw. **103**, 370–391 (2015)
34. Wang, S., Ali, S., Yue, T., Li, Y., Liaaen, M.: A practical guide to select quality indicators for assessing pareto-based search algorithms in search-based software engineering. In: Proceedings of the 38th International Conference on Software Engineering, pp. 631–642 (2016)
35. Yoo, S., Harman, M.: Pareto efficient multi-objective test case selection. In: Proceedings of the 2007 International Symposium on Software Testing and Analysis, pp. 140–150 (2007)

RENE/NIER Track

Multi-objective Black-Box Test Case Prioritization Based on Wordnet Distances

Imara van Dinten[(✉)] [iD], Andy Zaidman [iD], and Annibale Panichella[(✉)] [iD]

Delft University of Technology, Delft, The Netherlands
{I.vanDinten,A.E.Zaidman,A.Panichella}@tudelft.nl

Abstract. Test case prioritization techniques have emerged as effective strategies to optimize this process and mitigate the regression testing costs. Commonly, black-box heuristics guide optimal test ordering, leveraging information retrieval (e.g., cosine distance) to measure the test case distance and sort them accordingly. However, a challenge arises when dealing with tests of varying granularity levels, as they may employ distinct vocabularies (e.g., name identifiers). In this paper, we propose to measure the distance between test cases based on the shortest path between their identifiers within the WordNet lexical database. This additional heuristic is combined with the traditional cosine distance to prioritize test cases in a multi-objective fashion. Our preliminary study conducted with two different Java projects shows that test cases prioritized with WordNet achieve larger fault detection capability ($APFD_C$) compared to the traditional cosine distance used in the literature.

Keywords: Empirical software engineering · Search-based software testing · Test case prioritization · Wordnet · Natural language processing

1 Introduction

Regression testing is the process of retesting a software project to evaluate whether changes in the production code have any unintended effects on the unchanged portions [12]. The simplistic approach to regression testing involves executing the entire test suite within a CI/CD pipeline. However, this strategy may not be feasible for systems that require extensive resources or have large test suites. Therefore, researchers have proposed different techniques to reduce the cost of regression testing [12], including removing redundant tests, selecting a subset of tests for execution, and sorting the test cases to detect regression faults earlier through test case prioritization (TCP).

Black-box TCP techniques have emerged as effective strategies to optimize this process and mitigate the regression testing costs [8]. The main advantage of black-box heuristics is that they do not require access to the source code and, thus, can be applied to any software project. Black-box heuristics commonly guide optimal test ordering by leveraging diversity/distance metrics. The idea is

P. Arcaini et al. (Eds.): SSBSE 2023, LNCS 14415, pp. 101–107, 2024.
https://doi.org/10.1007/978-3-031-48796-5_7

that diverse test cases cover different parts/behaviors of the system under test and, thus, would be more effective in detecting faults [12].

To this aim, researchers have reduced the TCP problem into a traditional information retrieval (IR) task [8,10], where test cases are treated as textual *queries* and used to retrieve the more diverse (less related) test cases in the test suite. However, these methods statically inspect test case keywords and compare them using well-known similarity functions, such as cosine similarity, hamming distance, etc. Static keyword comparison might only partially capture the semantic distance between test cases if they employ different vocabularies. While unit-level tests that target the same classes may share common identifiers or keywords, system-level tests invoke components and call specific APIs.

To address these limitations, we proposed to leverage WordNet [7], a large lexical database of English words interlinked with each other through semantic and lexical relations. While two words can have different meanings, they may share a common ancestor in the WordNet hierarchy. For example, the words "chapter" and "paragraph" are not identical, but they are semantically related as they are both part of a "document". Our intuition is that WordNet can provide additional information about how two test cases can be related to one another.

Our paper introduces `TestScheduler`, a novel black-box TCP method that combines the traditional cosine distance with the WordNet distances. Our approach relies on multi-objective evolutionary algorithms (and NSGA-II [5] in particular) to prioritize the test cases based on (1) their cosine distance, (2) their WordNet distance, and (3) past test execution cost.

We evaluated `TestScheduler` on two open-source Java projects, namely `Javaparser` and `Apache Commons Lang`. The former is a parser for Java source code, while the latter is part of the Defects4J dataset [6]. We analyze the fault detection capability produced by `TestScheduler`. And compare its performance against a baseline that relies on the traditional IR distance and past execution cost. Our results indicate that TCP by `TestScheduler` can detect more faults than the baseline while incurring a lower execution cost. This confirms our conjecture that WordNet can complement the traditional IR-based methods.

2   Test Case Prioritization Based on WordNet

WordNet [7] is a well-established lexical database of English words grouped in sets of synonyms, called *synsets*. Synsets are connected via synonym relationships, i.e., distinct synsets that share the same meaning. In addition to synonyms, WordNet also includes additional relationships between synsets, such as hypernyms (superordinate terms), hyponyms (subordinate terms), meronyms (part-whole relationships), and holonyms (whole-part relationships). We proposed a novel approach, called `TestScheduler`, that prioritizes test cases based on their semantic distance in WordNet. We elaborate on its main steps below.

Pre-processing. Before using WordNet, the test cases undergo a pre-/processing phase aiming to extract words to query on WordNet and exclude programming language-specific keywords that do not contribute to the test semantics. TestScheduler pre-processes the tests by applying various IR steps: (i) *tokenization, removing stop words*, and (ii) *stemming*. First, *tokenization* extracts words in the tests and removes non-relevant characters. After which, the compound names are split into tokens [1]. Further, it applies the *stop-word list* function to remove words that do not contribute to the semantic content of the tests [1]. Our stop-list includes the standard list for the English language (e.g., prepositions and articles) [1], plus a list of words that are specific to the programming languages (i.e., keywords like class in Java). The stop-word function also removes words that contain less than three characters [4]. Finally, *stemming* algorithms reduce the words to their root form using the Porter stemming algorithm [1].

WordNet Distance. Given two test cases t_i and t_j, we measure their semantic distance as the average pairwise distance between their composing words/synsets (after pre-processing) in the WordNet taxonomy/database:

$$\text{WD}(t_a, t_b) = \frac{1}{m \times n} \sum_{i=1}^{m} \sum_{j=1}^{n} d(w_i, w_j) \tag{1}$$

where w_i is the i-th word in t_a; w_j is the j-th word in t_b; m and n are the number of words in t_a and t_b, respectively; $d(w_i, w_j)$ denotes the distance between the words/synsets w_i and w_j in the WordNet taxonomy/graph.

Multiple distances have been defined for the WordNet database, such as the simple *path distance*, the *Leacock Chodorow* similarity, *Resnik*, and the *Wu & Palmer* similarity. In this preliminary study, we focus on the *Wu & Palmer* (WUP) similarity [11] while we aim to experiment with other metrics in the future. The WUP similarity between two synsets/words is defined as: $d(w_1, w_2) = 2 \times [depth(lcs(w_1, w_2))] / [depth(w_1) + depth(w_2)]$, where $lcs(.)$ is the *Least Common Subsumer* (LCS), also called the most specific ancestor node, and $depth(.)$ is the depth of a given node in the WordNet graph.

Multi-objective Optimization. Our approach uses the WordNet distance as an additional heuristic/objective to guide the search for optimal test case ordering rather than as an alternative to existing black-box heuristics. Given a test suite $T = \{t_1, \ldots, t_n\}$, we consider the following three objectives to optimize:

$$min \left[f_1(T) = \sum_{i=1}^{n} \frac{cost(t_i)}{i}, \ f_2(T) = -\sum_{i=2}^{n} \frac{\text{WD}(t_i, t_{i-1})}{i}, \ f_3(T) = -\sum_{i=2}^{n} \frac{cosine(t_i, t_{i-1})}{i} \right] \tag{2}$$

f_1 measures the contribution of each test case t_i ($cost(t_i)$) to the cumulative execution cost divided by its position i in the test case ordering. It corresponds to the traditional cost-based objective used in the literature [2] for test case prioritization. f_2 measures the contribution of each test case t_i to the cumulative diversity divided by its position i in the test case ordering. $WD(t_i, t_{i-1})$ denotes the WordNet distance between a test t_i and its predecessor t_{i-1} in the order. Finally, f_3 considers the traditional cosine distance between two consecutive test cases. These three objectives promote solutions where the least expensive or the more diverse test cases are prioritized first (i.e., executed earlier).

Finding optimal solutions for problems with multiple criteria requires trade-off analysis. Given the conflicting nature of our two objectives[1], it is not possible to obtain one single solution optimal for all objectives. Hence, we are interested in finding the set of solutions that are optimal trade-offs between the three objectives. To this aim, we use NSGA-II [5] as it provides well-distributed Pareto fronts and performs best when dealing with two or three search objectives [5].

3   Preliminary Study

The goal of our preliminary study is to answer the following research question:

RQ1: *To what extent does the use of WordNet improve the effectiveness of diversity-based test case prioritization?*

We compare `TestScheduler` against a baseline that prioritizes the test cases without using WordNet data. The baseline is set up as follows: it uses NSGA-II [2,12] and prioritizes the test cases based on (1) past execution cost and (2) cosine distance between the test cases. We assess the *effectiveness* of the prioritized tests in terms of fault detection capability, *i.e.*, detecting faults earlier when executing the test suite with a given test order.

Benchmark. For our preliminary study, we consider two open-source projects: `Javaparser` and `Apache commons lang`. The former is a Java library for parsing, analyzing, and manipulating Java code and it is publicly available on `GitHub`[2] (containing 2,864 test cases). For test execution cost (f_1 in Eq. 2), we collected the execution times available in the past build logs on the `GitHub` repository of the project. For the fault detection capability, we analyzed the *git* history and identified failing builds due to test failures and later fixed by developers via source code changes (patches). We consider only faults (7 in total) for which the developers provided a patch, and their commits do not include unrelated changes (e.g., documentation and refactoring).

The second project, *i.e.*, `Apache commons lang`, is a library with a set of utility functions for the Java programming language (e.g., numerical function and string manipulation). We have selected this project since it is part of the Defects4J dataset [6]. The project has 2,223 test cases written in *JUnit* and has 65 isolated faults. The dataset also provides, for each isolated bug, the list of failing (fault-revealing) test cases. As for the execution cost, we run the test suites in a dedicated `Docker` container set up with the correct JVM version and

---

[1] Diverse tests are not necessarily the least expensive to run.

[2] https://github.com/javaparser/javaparser.

Table 1. Median APFD$_c$ values (with IQR) achieved with the WordNet Similarity vs. the traditional cosine distance. Best performance is highlighted in grey color.

Project Name	Baseline	TestScheduler	p-value	$\hat{A}_{12}$
Javaparser	0.8834 (0.0415)	0.9139 (0.0390)	0.004	0.7600 (large)
Apache commons lang	0.5230 (0.0335)	0.5778 (0.0455)	<0.001	0.8575 (large)

the required dependencies. We run each test case 10 times, and consider the median execution time as the (past) execution cost.

Experimental Setup. We run the `TestScheduler` (with WordNet) and the baseline (without WordNet) 20 times (each) to address their randomized nature. Both approaches rely on NSGA-II and are configured with the same default parameter values: (1) population size of 200 randomly sampled permutations; (2) 400 generations; (3) *partially-mapped crossover* (PMX) [2] with the probability μ_p=0.; (4) hybrid mutation operator [2] that combines three different mutation operators, namely *swap*, *insert*, and *invert*; (5) mutation probability of μ_c0.1/| T | with T being the test suite to prioritize; (6) *tournament selection* with tournament size $k = 2$. Since the two approaches differ in the number of objectives they optimize for, we could not compare them based on traditional metrics, e.g., HV and IGD. Among the non-dominated solutions generated at the end of each search run, we selected the extreme (corner) points that achieved the lowest past execution cost. We have tried other solutions from the generated fronts (e.g., the knee or elbow solutions [2]), but they did not lead to consistent results. Therefore, we compared the two approaches based on the *cost-cognizant* variant of the *average percentage of faults detected* (APFD$_c$) [2,12] for the corner points described above. APFD$_c$ is a well-established metric in TCP, and it reflects practitioners' needs, interested in maximizing the number of detected regression faults at the same level of test execution cost. To assess the significance of the differences between `TestScheduler` and the baseline, we use the Wilcoxon rank-sum test with the α=0.05. We further complement the test for significance with the Vargha-Delaney statistic ($\hat{A}_{12}$).

Preliminary Results. Table 1 reports the median and the interquartile range (IQR) of the APFD$_c$ values achieved by `TestScheduler` and the baseline over 20 independent runs. We observe that `TestScheduler` achieves a larger (better) APFD$_c$ value than the baseline for both projects. For `javaparser`, `TestScheduler` leads to a median increase in the APFD$_c$ value of 3.05%; for `Apache commons lang`, the use of Wordnet leads to a median increase in APFD$_c$ of 5.48%. It is also worth noticing that simply relying on the cosine distance (the baselines) leads to APFD$_c$ values slightly above (very close) to what a random prioritization would do (i.e., APFD$_c$=0.5). From a statistical standpoint, the differences are all statistically significant according to the Wilcoxon rank-sum test (all p-values<0.01) and with a *large* effect size according to the Vargha-Delaney statistic ($\hat{A}_{12}$=0.76 and $\hat{A}_{12}$=0.86 for `javaparser` and `Apache commons lang`, respectively). These preliminary results confirm our intuition/hypothesis that the use of WordNet can improve the fault detection capability.

Threats to Validity. The main threats to external validity regard the generalizability of our results. In this preliminary study, we have considered only two open-source projects. However, `javaparser` and `Apache common langs` are well-known and widely used projects in the software engineering community. The latter project is also part of the Defects4J dataset, which is a well-known benchmark for software testing research. Replicating our results with more projects and different application domains is part of our future plan.

4   Conclusion and Future Work

Diversity-based heuristics are widely used in TCP. In this paper, we propose to use WordNet to complement existing diversity metrics based on IR. We implemented a proof-concept in `TestScheduler`, and demonstrated the feasibility and usefulness of WordNet in a preliminary study. In the future, we plan to extend our study to more projects and different application domains. We also plan to investigate multiple distances for the WordNet taxonomy, such as the Leacock-Chodorow distance, and the Lin distance. Finally, we have considered only NSGA-II as the multi-objective algorithm. We plan to investigate other algorithms, such as AGE-MOEA [9] and NSGA-III.

Acknowledgements. This work has been partially supported by the European Union's Horizon 2020 Research and Innovation Programme under grant agreement No. 957254, project COSMOS [3].

References

1. Baeza-Yates, R., Ribeiro-Neto, B., et al.: Modern information retrieval, vol. 463. ACM press New York (1999)
2. Birchler, C., Khatiri, S., Derakhshanfar, P., Panichella, S., Panichella, A.: Single and multi-objective test cases prioritization for self-driving cars in virtual environments. ACM Trans. Softw. Eng. Methodol. (TOSEM) (2022)
3. COSMOS: Devops for complex cyber-physical systems. https://www.cosmos-devops.org (2021)
4. De Lucia, A., Di Penta, M., Oliveto, R., Panichella, A., Panichella, S.: Applying a smoothing filter to improve IR-based traceability recovery processes: an empirical investigation. Inform. Softw. Technol. (IST) **55**(4), 741–754 (2013)
5. Deb, K., Pratap, A., Agarwal, S., Meyarivan, T.: A fast and elitist multiobjective genetic algorithm: NSGA-II. IEEE Trans. on evol. Comput. **6**(2), 182–197 (2002)
6. Just, R., Jalali, D., Ernst, M.D.: Defects4J: a database of existing faults to enable controlled testing studies for Java programs. In: International Symposium on Software Testing and Analysis, pp. 437–440. ISSTA, ACM (2014)

7. Miller, G.A.: Wordnet: a lexical database for English. Commun. ACM **38**(11), 39–41 (1995)
8. Nguyen, C.D., Marchetto, A., Tonella, P.: Test case prioritization for audit testing of evolving web services using information retrieval techniques. In: International Conference on Web Services, pp. 636–643. IEEE (2011)
9. Panichella, A.: An adaptive evolutionary algorithm based on non-euclidean geometry for many-objective optimization. In: Proceedings of the Genetic and Evolutionary Computation Conference, pp. 595–603 (2019)
10. Peng, Q., Shi, A., Zhang, L.: Empirically revisiting and enhancing IR-based test-case prioritization. In: Proceedings of the 29th ACM SIGSOFT International Symposium on Software Testing and Analysis, pp. 324–336 (2020)
11. Wu, Z., Palmer, M.: Verb semantics and lexical selection. arXiv preprint cmp-lg/9406033 (1994)
12. Yoo, S., Harman, M.: Regression testing minimization, selection and prioritization: a survey. Softw. Testing, Verification Reliab. **22**(2), 67–120 (2012)

On the Impact of Tool Evolution and Case Study Size on SBSE Experiments: A Replicated Study with EvoMaster

Amid Golmohammadi[1]([✉])[iD], Man Zhang[1][iD], and Andrea Arcuri[1,2][iD]

[1] Kristiania University College, Oslo, Norway
{amid.golmohammadi,man.zhang,andrea.arcuri}@kristiania.no
[2] Oslo Metropolitan University, Oslo, Norway

Abstract. In the dynamic landscape of Search-Based Software Engineering (SBSE), tools and algorithms are continually improved, possibly making past experimental insights outdated. This could happen if a newly designed technique has side-effects compared to techniques and parameters settings studied in previous work. Re-tuning all possible parameters in a SBSE tool at each new scientific study would not be viable, as too expensive and too time consuming, considering there could be hundreds of them. In this paper, we carried out a series of experiments to study the impact that such re-tuning could have. For such a study, we chose the SBSE tool EvoMaster. It is an open-source tool for automated test generation for REST APIs. It has been actively developed for over six years, since November 2016, making it an appropriate choice for this kind of studies. In these experiments, we replicated four previous studies of EvoMaster with 15 REST APIs as case studies, using its latest version. Our findings reveal that updated parameter settings can offer improved performance, underscoring the possible benefits of re-tuning already existing parameters. Additionally, the inclusion of a broader range of case studies provides support for the replicated study's outcomes compared to the original studies, enhancing their external validity.

Keywords: White-Box Test Generation · SBST · RESTful APIs · Parameter Tuning · Replicating Studies

1 Introduction

In this paper, we examine the effects of tool evolution and case study size on Search-Based Software Engineering (SBSE) experiments.

The first objective of this study is to focus on the ongoing evolution of SBSE tools. We are interested in how a tool's maturity over an extended period of time might necessitate a re-examination of earlier experiments. As tools grow and integrate new techniques, there is a possibility that past studies, including how parameters were tuned, might no longer offer accurate insights. For example, if in a scientific study a new technique X is found to have best setting x', would a new study in which Y is introduced with best value y' still imply that x' is still best for X? Or maybe x'' would be a better choice when $Y = y'$? In essence, we aim to find out if the integration of new techniques into the tool, typically operated with default parameter values based on existing scientific studies, would necessitate any changes that would require re-adjusting those default settings.

The second objective aims to reduce the limitations imposed by the small size of case studies in the original, existing research work. In simpler terms, we want to test whether the conclusions of the original studies are still true when applied to a more extensive and diverse set of case studies. Threats to external validity are common to most empirical studies. In our work, we want to evaluate how serious such threats could be when replicating existing studies, but by using a larger body of artifacts for the experiments.

For the empirical experiments in this study, we use EvoMaster [9] as our subject tool. EvoMaster is a tool designed for automatically generating system-level test cases for RESTful APIs. It utilizes search-based software engineering techniques (e.g., Many Independent Objective (MIO) algorithm [5]) to optimize the generated test cases, aiming to maximize code coverage and number of found faults.

There could be many parameters and studies that could be replicated. To be able to run all the needed experiments within a viable amount of time, we selected four parameters to re-tune. The choice of these four parameters of the search algorithm was based on a review of three foundational studies on EvoMaster, spanning from 2018 to 2021 [6,18,19].

To enable such a comprehensive evaluation, we employed the latest version of EvoMaster, which was 1.6.2-SNAPSHOT at the time of conducting the experiments. In relation to the case studies used for this research, we opted for a comprehensive approach by selecting 14 different open-source REST APIs from the EMB repository [2]. This includes the case studies that were part of the original studies we replicate. Additionally, to augment the robustness of our study and make it more relevant to real-world applications, we also incorporated one industrial REST API into our set of case studies. This diverse selection aims to provide a well-rounded view of how the tool performs across a range of scenarios, thereby enhancing the external validity of our findings.

For the current study, every parameter, which is based on an earlier article, was assigned distinct values. This approach aimed to capture any emerging patterns or unique outcomes associated with the parameter variations.

The results of the varied configurations were gauged against three fundamental metrics: line coverage, which measures the extent of the codebase executed; branch coverage, measuring the percentage of decision points, such as if and else statements, that have been executed; and fault detection, indicating the capability to identify potential issues.

After the experimental phase, a comprehensive analysis ensued. This sought to identify the standout parameter configuration for each of the 15 REST APIs, assessing line and branch coverage, as well as fault detection. The findings enable us to see if previous results could be confirmed or invalidated. This could have an impact on how new experiments should be evaluated and analyzed, especially compared to all previous experiments on all the other configurations/parameters previously introduced. This type of research work deepens the knowledge on search-based software testing, possible pointing out some existing shortcomings when dealing with advanced, complex tools with many parameter settings.

2 Related Work

Parameter tuning has a critical role in the design and performance of Evolutionary Algorithms (EAs). The choice of parameter values can substantially influence the EA's performance, to the extent that an EA with well-chosen parameters can outperform one with poorly chosen parameters [11].

The study by Freisleben and Hartfelder [13] presents a method for finding the best Genetic Algorithm (GA) for a problem by treating it as an optimization problem and using another GA to solve it. It proposes a two-level optimization approach for finding the best Genetic Algorithm (GA) for a given problem. The bottom level consists of a secondary GA operating on gene strings that represent potential solutions. The top level involves a primary GA working on a population of secondary GAs represented as separate gene strings. Each secondary GA runs independently to produce a solution, and its fitness influences the primary GA's operation. The generations on the two levels are independent, and the primary GA aims to find the highest fitness string as the best GA for the original problem.

There have been multiple studies conducted to investigate the impact of parameter tuning on the performance of search-based test generation. Arcuri and Fraser [7] conducted over one million experiments in test data generation for object-oriented software using the EvoSuite tool. The results indicate that parameter tuning has an impact on search algorithm performance, but it is difficult to find settings that significantly outperform default values. This finding suggests that using default values is a reasonable choice for researchers and practitioners, as parameter tuning is a costly process with uncertain benefits.

Zamani and Hemmati [17] introduced a novel metric called *Tuning Gain* to determine the efficiency of tuning a specific class. The authors suggest predicting the Tuning Gain by analyzing the static characteristics of source code classes. Subsequently, they prioritize classes for tuning based on the estimated Tuning Gains and allocate the tuning budget specifically to the classes with higher rankings. For low-tuning budgets, it only distributes the tuning budget to a subset of classes with the greatest anticipated Tuning Gain, which increased the overall tuning outcomes by ten times.

Beyond the area of tuning, the importance of replication in search-based software engineering has also been examined. Tawosi *et al.* [16] focused on replicating and extending an existing study on CoGEE, a state-of-the-art tool for multi-objective software effort estimation. By using an independent implementation and a robust baseline, LP4EE, they enhanced the study's internal and external validity. CoGEE is also tested with four additional evolutionary algorithms and a Java framework, JMetal, to further validate its effectiveness. The results not only confirmed CoGEE's superior performance and accuracy, but also showed that its effectiveness is not dependent on a specific algorithm.

There is another study [10] which addressed the challenges of replicating and comparing computational experiments in the field of applied evolutionary computing. It highlighted the frequent lack of adequate documentation in existing studies, which made replication difficult. The paper also discussed the importance of adhering to scientific standards of experimentation and statistical precision, given the random nature of evolutionary algorithms. The primary goal was to provide guidelines to avoid common pitfalls and thereby improve the quality and reproducibility of future research in this domain.

3   Considered Parameters

Parameters in search algorithms are pivotal for optimizing performance and efficiency, affecting everything from the search space and convergence rate to runtime. Poorly chosen or untuned parameters can lead to inefficiencies, while well-selected ones can significantly improve the quality of results, making parameter tuning essential for effective algorithmic performance.

The *Many Independent Objective (MIO)* [5,6] is an evolutionary algorithm tailored based on the specific properties of test suite generation. The MIO algorithm has been employed not only by EVOMASTER for test generation but also by other tools such as *EvoSuite* [12] and *Pynguin* [15]. The effectiveness and efficiency of test case generation with the MIO algorithm is controlled by particular parameters. When carefully adjusted, these variables could have a major impact on the results, ensuring a balance between the exploration and exploitation of the search landscape.

In this section, we discuss the four parameters used in EVOMASTER that we chose for this study, namely: feedbackDirectedSampling, probOfApply-SQLActionToCreateResources, probOfRandomSampling and focusedSearch-ActivationTime. We could have examined more than 100 different parameters in EVOMASTER, but we decided to focus on just four important ones. We picked these four because they were studied in three major research articles [6,18,19] in which EVOMASTER has been extended with new techniques. This leaded us to consider these settings as they are potentially quite important for how the tool works.

Feedback-Directed Sampling (FDS) in the MIO algorithm is a technique that guides the generation of test inputs based on feedback from previous tests. Instead of randomly exploring the input space, it prioritizes areas more likely to produce valuable test cases quicker, making test generation possibly more efficient, especially when the search budget is limited. This feedback mechanism can help guide the evolution process, ensuring that the population of test cases evolves in a direction that is more likely to achieve the desired objectives, like finding faults or maximizing coverage. In a *many objective* problem (i.e., when there are several objectives to optimize for, and that are not necessarily conflicting, like in a multi-objective problem), it can make sense to first focus on the objectives that show a gradient in the fitness function. This approach also helps avoid spending excessive time on infeasible targets (as there would be no gradient there). In EvoMaster, this is controlled by the parameter feedbackDirectedSampling. In the original study in [6], three different values were studied: NONE, LAST and FOCUSED. The value LAST was selected as new default for EvoMaster. According to the Git history of the repository of EvoMaster, such default value has not been changed since 2017.

REST API testing is challenging, especially when creating system-level tests due to the potential complexity of their relationships with SQL databases. Endpoints are typically created in REST architectures around resources and the operations that can be performed on them. In order to improve code coverage, especially in white-box testing scenarios, it is beneficial to interact with these resources in all of their different states via the HTTP endpoints [21,22]. Moreover, resource manipulation is improved through the direct use of SQL commands such as INSERT [19], to create new data directly into the database. The parameter probOfApplySQLActionToCreateResources specifies the probability of applying such resource manipulation through the execution of SQL commands. The default value 0.5 currently in EvoMaster is based on the study in [19], which has not been changed since 2021.

The probability of applying random sampling is one of the most crucial parameters in the MIO algorithm [5]. It serves as one of the key parameters for managing the trade-off between *exploration*, which seeks out new, untested solutions, and *exploitation*, which fine-tunes known good solutions. Finding the right balance is key to the algorithm's effectiveness. Focusing too much on one can neglect the other, either missing new opportunities or failing to optimize what is already known. An excessive emphasis on randomness could make the search less effective, while a low value could restrict the exploration and put the algorithm at risk of getting stuck in local optima.

Within EvoMaster, the probOfRandomSampling parameter plays a pivotal role. The likelihood that EvoMaster will create a test case entirely from scratch as opposed to using pre-existing test cases or other search-based techniques is determined by this parameter. A probOfRandomSampling value of 0.2, for example, indicates a 20% likelihood that a new test case will be generated randomly, without relying on the knowledge gathered from previous test cases (i.e., no population in the MIO algorithm is used for mutation).

The parameter probOfRandomSampling was not studied on any concrete API in the articles introducing MIO [5,6]. However, due to its potential major impact on the search, it was studied in a followup work where MIO was extended with adaptive hyper-mutation [18]. Still, its default value 0.5 (which was confirmed still best in [18]) has not been changed since 2016.

The parameter focusedSearchActivationTime in EvoMaster denotes the percentage of the total search duration after which the tool switches from an exploratory approach to a targeted, focused search. For instance, a setting of 20% means that after completing 20% of the total search time in an exploratory manner, EvoMaster will transition to a more focused search for the remaining 80%.

It is worth noting that quite a few parameters, such as `probOfRandomSampling`, decrease linearly over time until this focus search phase begins. For example, `probOfRandomSampling` goes to 0 when the focused search starts [5]. Proper tuning of this parameter is essential to ensure a balance between broad exploration and efficient, targeted searching.

Like in the case of `probOfRandomSampling`, the parameter `focusedSearch-ActivationTime` was not studied on any concrete API in the articles introducing MIO [5,6]. It was studied in the work that extended MIO with adaptive hypermutation [18]. Still, its default value `0.5` (which was confirmed still best in [18]) has not been changed since 2017.

4   Empirical Study

4.1   Research Questions

In this study, we aim at answering the following two research questions:

RQ1: How do the results of the replicated study compare to the original findings for each parameter in terms of line coverage, branch coverage, and found faults?

RQ2: What is the impact of increasing the number of case studies on the generalizability and reliability of the original study's findings?

4.2   Experiment Setup

We conducted our experiments using an existing corpus of Web/Enterprise Applications for REST API testing, namely EMB [2,4], which has been used in various recent studies (e.g., [8,14,20]). Note that all of the selected studies that we replicate [6,18,19] also employed the EMB corpus. However, over the years, the corpus has been extended with new Web APIs, i.e., from the five REST APIs[1] in the first release in 2017, to the 14 REST APIs[2] in the latest release 1.6.1 in 2023.

In our replicated study, we involved all of the 14 open-source REST APIs from EMB plus one industrial REST API. This enables a broader range of SUTs compared to the original studies we replicate [6,18,19]. To distinguish these new APIs from the ones used in the original studies, we reported our results in terms of **Original SUTs** and **Other SUTs**. Descriptive statistics of all case studies (i.e., the number of source files #SourceFiles, the line of code #LOCs, and the number of endpoints #Endpoints of each REST API) are shown in Table 1.

In the context of search-based algorithms, the term *time budget* represents a user-defined limitation on the duration for which the search process will be left running. EVOMASTER utilizes evolutionary algorithms (e.g., the default is MIO [5]) to generate test cases, and these algorithms function by continuously

---

[1] https://github.com/EMResearch/EMB/tree/v0.1.1.

[2] https://github.com/EMResearch/EMB/tree/v1.6.1.

Table 1. Descriptive statistics of 15 REST APIs in our replicated study

SUT	#SourceFiles	#LOCs	#Endpoints
catwatch	106	9,636	14
cwa-verification	47	3,955	5
features-service	39	2,275	18
genome-nexus	405	30,004	23
gestaohospital	33	3,506	20
ind0	103	17,039	20
languagetool	1,385	174,781	2
market	124	9,861	13
ocvn	526	45,521	258
proxyprint	73	8,338	74
rest-ncs	9	605	6
rest-news	11	857	7
rest-scs	13	862	11
restcountries	24	1,977	22
scout-api	93	9,736	49
Total 15	2,991	318,953	542

refining and improving a set of solutions over numerous iterations. By setting a time budget, users provide a boundary to ensure that EVOMASTER delivers results within the desired amount of time. However, there is a balancing act involved: if a user allocates a very short time budget, the tool may not have ample opportunity to explore diverse test cases, potentially resulting in tests that are not as comprehensive or effective. On the other hand, granting a longer time budget allows the evolutionary algorithm more iterations to evolve the test cases, leading to potentially higher-quality results. Still, this comes at the cost of waiting longer for the process to complete. This flexibility allows users to tailor the tool's operation based on their specific needs and constraints. For conducting this replication study, we allocated a one-hour time budget, as it is the stopping criterion used in the most recent study of EVOMASTER [20].

In addition, search-based algorithms incorporate some level of randomness in their nature. Therefore, we followed the guidelines in [3] for conducting SBSE experiments, and repeated each setting of experiments 10 times. Multiple runs help to reduce the impact of randomness on the experimental results. To properly draw conclusions based on these results, we applied statistical analysis using the *Vargha-Delaney* effect size ($\hat{A}_{12}$) and the *Mann-Whitney-Wilcoxon U-test* (*p-value*) [3] for comparing the results yielded by each parameter setting.

All settings of re-tuning the four different parameters have three configurations for each parameter (recall Sect. 3), which resulted in $1 + (4 \times 2) = 9$ distinct configurations, i.e., the base settings plus 2 variants for each of the 4 parameters.

Considering 15 REST APIs with one-hour time budget and 10 repetitions, all these experiments took over 50 d of computation time, i.e., $9 \times 15 \times 10 \times 1h$. The experiments were executed on a machine with the following specifications: Processor Intel(R) Xeon(R) Gold 6240R CPU @2.40 GHz, 2394 Mhz, 24 Core(s), 48 Logical Processor(s); RAM 192 GB; Operating System Windows 10 Pro for Workstations.

Table 2. Pair comparison of Line Coverage, Branch Coverage, and Faults achieved by different settings of Feedback-Directed Sampling (FDS). For instance, comparing x with y, $\hat{A}_{xy}$, values in **bold** mean x is statistically significant better than y, whereas values in *italic* mean y is statistically significant better than x.

feedbackDirectedSampling A=LAST, B=FOCUSED, C=NONE									
SUT	Line Coverage			Branch Coverage			Faults		
	$\hat{A}_{AB}$	$\hat{A}_{AC}$	$\hat{A}_{BC}$	$\hat{A}_{AB}$	$\hat{A}_{AC}$	$\hat{A}_{BC}$	$\hat{A}_{AB}$	$\hat{A}_{AC}$	$\hat{A}_{BC}$
Original SUTs									
catwatch	0.49	0.58	0.59	0.51	0.62	0.60	0.55	0.56	0.51
features-service	0.48	0.48	0.49	0.56	0.53	0.47	**0.71**	**0.65**	0.48
proxyprint	0.48	0.56	0.58	0.56	0.57	0.53	0.56	0.58	0.54
rest-ncs	*0.23*	*0.23*	0.50	*0.25*	*0.28*	0.56	0.50	0.50	0.50
rest-news	0.40	0.40	0.49	0.45	0.45	0.49	0.56	0.54	0.48
rest-scs	*0.23*	*0.16*	*0.34*	*0.30*	*0.23*	0.38	*0.23*	*0.23*	0.50
scout-api	0.44	0.43	0.46	0.46	0.59	**0.68**	0.46	*0.33*	0.40
Average (original)	0.39	0.40	0.49	0.44	0.47	0.53	0.51	0.48	0.49
Median (original)	0.44	0.43	0.49	0.46	0.53	0.53	0.55	0.54	0.50
Other SUTs									
cwa-verification	0.45	0.45	0.50	0.41	0.44	0.53	0.43	0.44	0.52
genome-nexus	0.63	0.65	0.54	0.57	**0.68**	0.60	**0.94**	**0.93**	0.46
gestaohospital-rest	0.61	0.63	0.53	0.54	0.50	0.46	0.50	0.50	0.50
ind0	*0.26*	*0.32*	0.53	*0.27*	*0.33*	0.53	*0.26*	*0.25*	0.46
languagetool	0.46	0.36	*0.32*	0.45	*0.34*	*0.35*	0.49	0.37	0.37
market	0.48	0.59	0.60	0.47	0.60	0.61	0.52	0.46	0.44
ocvn-rest	0.57	0.51	0.44	0.60	0.54	0.44	*0.19*	0.40	**0.71**
restcountries	0.43	0.44	0.53	0.44	0.48	0.55	0.50	0.50	0.50
Average (other)	0.49	0.49	0.50	0.47	0.49	0.51	0.48	0.48	0.49
Median (other)	0.47	0.48	0.53	0.46	0.49	0.53	0.50	0.45	0.48
Average (all)	0.44	0.45	0.50	0.46	0.48	0.52	0.49	0.48	0.49
Median (all)	0.46	0.45	0.50	0.46	0.50	0.53	0.50	0.50	0.50

4.3 Experiment Results

Results of Re-Tuning the Strategy of Enabling Feedback-Directed Sampling. The original study [6] was published in 2018, and studied the performance of three configurations of FDS, i.e., FDS $\in$ {NONE, FOCUSED, LAST}. The original study showed that, in two cases (*proxyprint* and *rest-news*), FOCUSED provided statistically superior outcomes. Yet, in two different situations (*rest-scs* and *scout-api*), FDS yielded statistically lower coverage (i.e., NONE was better). The study was inconclusive regarding which value was the best, with LAST chosen as default based on the experiments on synthetic, artificial examples.

Table 2 represents results in our replicated study. Based on *Average* and *Median* results (see *Average (original)* and *Median (original)*) of the original case studies, NONE (i.e., not applying FDS) performed slightly better in terms of line coverage, FOCUSED had a slight advantage for branch coverage, and LAST showed a slight advantage in fault detection. A comparison of the results from the eight additional case studies (see *Average (other)* and *Median (other)*) revealed that, while there is no significant difference between the three configurations, FOCUSED had a slight overall advantage. It yielded slightly better branch coverage and almost the same line coverage and found faults compared to LAST and NONE. In total of 15 REST APIs, there is no clear winner among the three settings in terms of all of the three metrics, confirming the same conclusions as in the original study.

Results of Re-Tuning the Probability of Applying SQL Handling to Prepare Resources. In the original study [19], the highest setting of 0.5 for probOfApplySQLActionToCreateResources yielded the best results for three projects: *rest-news*, *proxyprint*, and *scout-api*. This suggested that using just HTTP methods, like POST or PUT, to add new resources could be tricky in these cases. So, a higher chance of using SQL commands directly seemed to perform better. On the other hand, in projects like *features-service* and *catwatch*, a lower setting was better (i.e., 0.1 and 0.3 respectively). Based on these results, the authors of EVOMASTER chose 0.5 as the default setting for this parameter.

In the current study, we carried out a replication of the original study to compare results and draw more robust conclusions. As it is shown in Table 3, in terms of achieving the highest code coverage, the findings are mixed. While a setting of 0.5 delivered the best coverage for *rest-news*, it was not the optimal choice for *proxy-print* and *scout-api*. These two SUTs performed best with settings of 0.3 and 0.1, respectively. Interestingly, this diverges from the results of the original study where 0.5 was optimal across the board. For *feature-service* and *catwatch*, the setting of 0.5, which was not the best choice in the original study, actually produced the highest code coverage in our replicated study. On average, when we looked at the five SUTs featured in the original study, a setting of 0.5 proved to deliver the best code coverage. Another intriguing observation was related to the detection of faults. A setting of 0.1 surprisingly led to the identification of the highest number of faults, which merits further investigation.

Furthermore, when we expanded our scope to include an additional 10 SUTs, we found 0.5 yielded slightly better line and branch coverage. Nonetheless, the count of detected faults remained unchanged.

Regarding results of all of the 15 REST APIs, the setting of 0.5 achieved the overall best performance, that is consistent with the original study.

Results of Re-Tuning the Probability of Applying Random Sampling. In the original study [18], two distinct parameters were examined: probOfRandomSampli-ng and focusedSearchActivationTime. We aimed to

Table 3. Pair comparison of Line Coverage, Branch Coverage, and Faults achieved by different configurations of probability of applying SQL handling to prepare resources. For instance, comparing x with y, $\hat{A}_{xy}$, values in **bold** mean x is statistically significant better than y, whereas values in *italic* mean y is statistically significant better than x

SUT	Line Coverage			Branch Coverage			Faults		
probOfApplySQLActionToCreateResources A=0.5, B=0.1, C=0.3									
	$\hat{A}_{AB}$	$\hat{A}_{AC}$	$\hat{A}_{BC}$	$\hat{A}_{AB}$	$\hat{A}_{AC}$	$\hat{A}_{BC}$	$\hat{A}_{AB}$	$\hat{A}_{AC}$	$\hat{A}_{BC}$
Original SUTs									
catwatch	0.53	0.65	0.60	0.53	**0.69**	0.64	0.40	0.64	**0.73**
features-service	0.54	0.53	0.47	0.54	0.59	0.54	0.39	0.52	0.63
proxyprint	0.46	0.38	0.45	0.47	0.45	0.49	0.47	0.44	0.46
rest-news	**0.70**	0.60	0.39	**0.77**	0.63	0.35	0.62	0.44	*0.33*
scout-api	0.48	0.54	0.54	0.43	0.48	0.54	0.43	0.49	0.57
Average (original)	0.54	0.54	0.49	0.55	0.57	0.51	0.46	0.50	0.54
Median (original)	0.53	0.54	0.47	0.53	0.59	0.54	0.43	0.49	0.57
Other SUTs									
cwa-verification	0.47	0.47	0.50	0.45	0.51	0.56	0.47	0.41	0.44
genome-nexus	0.51	0.54	0.54	0.46	0.50	0.57	0.53	0.50	0.48
gestaohospital-rest	0.62	0.62	0.51	0.51	0.50	0.50	0.50	0.50	0.50
ind0	0.45	0.40	0.42	0.50	0.43	0.42	0.55	0.53	0.48
languagetool	0.38	0.46	0.59	0.36	0.44	0.58	0.44	0.40	0.46
market	0.56	0.59	0.51	0.56	0.59	0.51	0.54	0.44	0.41
ocvn-rest	0.42	0.53	0.61	0.46	0.56	0.58	0.48	0.54	0.55
rest-ncs	0.45	0.43	0.46	0.46	0.46	0.48	0.50	0.50	0.50
rest-scs	0.57	0.57	0.50	0.58	0.57	0.51	0.58	0.58	0.51
restcountries	0.53	0.60	0.55	0.53	0.59	0.55	0.50	0.50	0.50
Average (other)	0.50	0.52	0.52	0.49	0.51	0.53	0.51	0.49	0.48
Median (other)	0.49	0.54	0.51	0.48	0.51	0.53	0.50	0.50	0.49
Average (all)	0.51	0.53	0.51	0.51	0.53	0.52	0.49	0.49	0.50
Median (all)	0.51	0.54	0.51	0.50	0.51	0.54	0.50	0.50	0.50

extend and replicate this study by incorporating eight additional case studies and adjusting these two parameters. For our research, we approached these parameters as independent entities and assessed each in isolation. The primary research indicated that a value of 0.5 was optimal for both parameters. However, our expanded investigation revealed divergent findings.

Regarding the `probOfRandomSampling` parameter, a glance at the original SUTs displayed in Table 4 shows that a value of 0.8 yielded the most favorable results (see *Average (original)* and *Median (original)*). Based on the results obtained by the additional eight SUTs, all of the three settings achieved similar results in terms of line coverage and branch coverage. Regarding fault detection, we observed one significant outperformance achieved by the setting of 0.8 on *ocvn-rest*, while the difference is not significant on the other seven case studies. However, based on results of all case studies in terms of all three metrics, the advantage of 0.8 over 0.5 is modest.

Results of Re-Tuning the Time of Activating Focused Search. As we assess the `focusedSearchActivationTime` parameter from Table 5, we note that

Table 4. Pair comparison of Line Coverage, Branch Coverage, and Faults achieved by different settings of probability of applying random sampling. For instance, comparing x with y, $\hat{A}_{xy}$, values in **bold** mean x is statistically significant better than y, whereas values in *italic* mean y is statistically significant better than x.

probOfRandomSampling A=0.5, B=0.2, C=0.8									
SUT	Line Coverage			Branch Coverage			Faults		
	$\hat{A}_{AB}$	$\hat{A}_{AC}$	$\hat{A}_{BC}$	$\hat{A}_{AB}$	$\hat{A}_{AC}$	$\hat{A}_{BC}$	$\hat{A}_{AB}$	$\hat{A}_{AC}$	$\hat{A}_{BC}$
Original SUTs									
rest-ncs	0.52	0.48	0.48	0.52	0.51	0.50	0.50	0.55	0.55
rest-scs	0.60	0.50	0.43	0.63	0.47	0.37	0.60	0.47	0.38
rest-news	0.56	0.52	0.43	**0.71**	*0.33*	*0.17*	0.58	0.45	*0.38*
catwatch	**0.75**	0.40	*0.16*	**0.80**	0.41	*0.11*	**0.67**	0.44	*0.27*
features-service	**0.68**	0.57	*0.35*	0.57	0.64	0.58	0.51	0.45	0.45
proxyprint	0.64	0.38	*0.23*	0.60	0.45	0.36	0.49	0.37	0.35
scout-api	0.56	0.56	0.50	0.51	0.56	0.55	0.57	0.49	0.38
Average (original)	0.62	0.49	0.37	0.62	0.48	0.38	0.56	0.46	0.39
Median (original)	0.60	0.50	0.43	0.60	0.47	0.37	0.57	0.45	0.38
Other SUTs									
cwa-verification	0.43	0.44	0.52	0.47	0.45	0.50	0.47	0.46	0.49
genome-nexus	0.52	0.48	0.44	0.55	0.44	0.40	0.49	0.49	0.51
gestaohospital-rest	0.62	**0.66**	0.54	0.52	0.52	0.50	0.52	0.50	0.48
ind0	*0.31*	0.50	**0.70**	*0.35*	0.59	**0.72**	0.49	0.57	0.55
languagetool	0.47	0.41	0.45	0.44	0.41	0.47	0.52	0.50	0.48
market	0.46	0.52	0.56	0.47	0.52	0.56	0.49	0.48	0.49
ocvn-rest	0.54	0.47	0.45	0.53	0.50	0.48	**0.98**	*0.00*	*0.00*
restcountries	0.57	0.55	0.48	0.56	0.55	0.49	0.50	0.50	0.50
Average (other)	0.49	0.51	0.52	0.49	0.50	0.51	0.56	0.44	0.44
Median (other)	0.50	0.49	0.50	0.50	0.51	0.49	0.50	0.50	0.49
Average (all)	0.55	0.50	0.45	0.55	0.49	0.45	0.56	0.45	0.42
Median (all)	0.56	0.50	0.45	0.53	0.50	0.49	0.51	0.48	0.48

while a value of 0.5 seemed significantly more effective for certain SUTs, such as *catwatch* and *feature-service*, a broader perspective considering other SUTs and the number of detected faults suggests a different story. Contrary to the findings of the original study [18], a value of 0.5 did not outperform others. Specifically, it resulted in lower code coverage and found fewer faults compared to 0.8. This observation was consistent across the additional case studies.

4.4   Findings Summary

Results for RQ1. In the case of our first replicated study, focusing on the FDS parameter, the outcomes revealed a slight advantage of FOCUSED had a minor advantage in branch coverage but no configuration was a clear winner in all metrics, reaffirming the conclusions of the original study.

Our second replicated study looked into the probOfApplySQLActionToCreateResources parameter. Here, we found a consistent pattern with the original study: a setting of 0.5 did lead to better line and branch coverage. The number of detected faults were consistent with the original study, reaffirming its initial findings.

Table 5. Pair comparison of Line Coverage, Branch Coverage, and Faults achieved by different settings of time of activating focused search For instance, comparing x with y, $\hat{A}_{xy}$, values in **bold** mean x is statistically significant better than y, whereas values in *italic* mean y is statistically significant better than x.

SUT	Line Coverage			Branch Coverage			Faults		
	$\hat{A}_{AB}$	$\hat{A}_{AC}$	$\hat{A}_{BC}$	$\hat{A}_{AB}$	$\hat{A}_{AC}$	$\hat{A}_{BC}$	$\hat{A}_{AB}$	$\hat{A}_{AC}$	$\hat{A}_{BC}$
Original SUTs									
rest-ncs	0.49	0.48	0.50	0.51	0.47	0.47	0.52	0.50	0.48
rest-scs	0.54	0.60	0.56	0.57	0.59	0.53	0.53	0.55	0.52
rest-news	0.62	0.55	0.42	0.52	0.49	0.47	**0.67**	0.48	*0.32*
catwatch	**0.67**	0.42	*0.29*	**0.74**	0.45	*0.20*	**0.73**	0.38	*0.16*
features-service	0.60	0.47	*0.35*	0.57	0.44	0.36	**0.70**	0.49	*0.30*
proxyprint	**0.66**	*0.29*	*0.17*	**0.67**	0.35	*0.20*	0.44	0.40	0.44
scout-api	0.57	*0.34*	*0.25*	0.50	*0.29*	*0.26*	**0.65**	0.36	*0.17*
Average (original)	0.59	0.45	0.36	0.58	0.44	0.36	0.61	0.45	0.34
Median (original)	0.60	0.47	0.35	0.57	0.45	0.36	0.65	0.48	0.32
Other SUTs									
cwa-verification	0.48	0.41	0.43	0.49	0.43	0.45	0.55	0.44	0.39
genome-nexus	**0.71**	0.51	*0.27*	**0.67**	0.50	*0.28*	0.58	0.53	0.44
gestaohospital-rest	**0.72**	0.59	0.37	0.52	0.52	0.50	0.50	0.50	0.50
ind0	0.57	0.38	*0.32*	0.64	0.43	*0.30*	**0.65**	0.52	0.37
languagetool	0.51	0.47	0.44	0.48	0.46	0.48	0.49	0.39	0.40
market	0.55	0.55	0.51	0.54	0.55	0.51	**0.65**	0.39	*0.26*
ocvn-rest	0.60	0.45	0.36	0.60	0.56	0.46	**0.99**	*0.03*	*0.00*
restcountries	0.62	0.61	0.47	0.60	0.58	0.48	0.50	0.50	0.50
Average (other)	0.59	0.50	0.40	0.57	0.50	0.43	0.61	0.41	0.36
Median (other)	0.58	0.49	0.40	0.57	0.51	0.47	0.56	0.47	0.40
Average (all)	0.59	0.48	0.38	0.57	0.47	0.40	0.61	0.43	0.35
Median (all)	0.60	0.47	0.37	0.57	0.47	0.46	0.58	0.48	0.39

focusedSearchActivationTime A=0.5, B=0.2, C=0.8

For the third and fourth replicated studies, which investigated the `probOf Ran-domSampling` and `focusedSearchActivationTime` parameters respectively, our results took a different turn. Unlike the original studies that found `0.5` as the optimal setting, our study showed that a `0.8` setting yielded better results across various APIs.

> *RQ1: While certain initial parameter suggestions remain valid, especially in the second study, other results indicate the necessity to reassess them as the* EVOMASTER *tool continues to be developed and evolved.*

Results for RQ2. By examining the results across the four replicated studies, there was a consistent pattern observed. The results derived from the original case studies were generally affirmed by the newly added case studies introduced in our research. For instance, while there was an anomaly in the second replicated study where the parameter setting of `0.1` detected slightly more faults for the original case studies, this distinction was neutralized when taking into account the results from the expanded set of SUTs.

> *RQ2: The inclusion of additional case studies in our replicated research generally confirmed the findings from the original studies' SUTs, enhancing the external validity of the results.*

5   Threats to Validity

Conclusion Validity. To take into account the randomness of SBST techniques, our experiments were repeated 10 times. In order to draw reliable conclusions, we used statistical analysis techniques, including Mann-Whitney-Wilcoxon U-tests (p-value) and Vargha-Delaney effect sizes ($\hat{A}_{12}$), following common guidelines in software engineering research [3].

Internal Validity. The implementation of EVOMASTER and the case studies in EMB, except one industrial API, are open-source and available online. As the authors of EVOMASTER, we provide as well all the scripts used to setup experiments in most of our previous work. To reduce threats of running EVOMASTER differently, we re-used those scripts as starting point to setup our experiments. We have published those modified scripts online on EvoMaster's GitHub repository [1]. This allows anyone to review and replicate this study.

External Validity. It is important to acknowledge that our study is specifically tailored to evolutionary algorithms in the domain of search-based software testing. Moreover, our case studies exclusively involved REST APIs and the tool EVOMASTER. Our findings in this study may not be directly generalizable to other types of software, tools, algorithms, or problem domains. However, we incorporated all the JVM (i.e., Java/Kotlin) REST APIs in the EMB corpus for Web/Enterprise API testing research and an industrial REST API to ensure having a broad range of case studies (i.e., 15 REST APIs, 318k LOC and 542 endpoints). Furthermore, different results might have been reached if a selection of different parameters was done. Due to the high cost of running experiments on system test generation (50 d in our case, if experiments are run in sequence), our research concentrated on a restricted set of parameters, leaving potential for other parameter effects to be investigated in future research. Also, we only considered one value for the search budget, i.e., 1 h. Different search budgets would have different impacts on tuning. For example, a "short" search budget might reward settings that put more emphasis on the "exploitation" of the search landscape, in contrast to a wider "exploration" of the search landscape which would require more time.

6   Conclusion

Our study had two primary goals: first, to re-evaluate the effectiveness and parameter tuning of EVOMASTER with respect to its ongoing development; and second to determine whether the findings of the original studies still apply when a larger set of SUTs are used for the experiments.

Our results show that some of the original parameter suggestions still hold true, but other choices might need to be re-evaluated. This could also underline the importance of periodic retuning for SBSE tools such as EVOMASTER. The inclusion of additional case studies strengthened the external validity and robustness of these results, by mostly confirming the conclusions from the original studies (i.e., case studies in the upper section of each table in Sect. 4).

In this study, we have identified new optimal values for certain parameters, such as 0.8 in contrast to current 0.5 for Probability of Random Sampling. However, one limitation is that we have not yet looked into how these values would perform when combined. It is difficult to predict how various parameter combinations can interact due to the complexity of SBST and mature tools such as EVOMASTER. We need to conduct more studies to fill this important knowledge gap and see whether combining these parameters could have any unanticipated side-effects or emergent behaviors. Also, there is the need to study in more details how the search budget impacts parameter tuning. But, to be able to do it properly, studies will be needed to identify what are the common values for the search budgets selected by practitioners in industry that use SBSE tools.

This type of studies could also be beneficial in other mature SBSE tools such as EvoSuite and Pynguin.

Acknowledgment. This work is funded by the European Research Council (ERC) under the European Union's Horizon 2020 research and innovation programme (EAST project, grant agreement No. 864972).

References

1. EvoMaster. https://github.com/EMResearch/EvoMaster
2. Evomaster benchmark (emb). https://github.com/EMResearch/EMB Accessed 20 May 2022
3. Arcuri, A., Briand, L.: A Hitchhiker's guide to statistical tests for assessing randomized algorithms in software engineering. Softw. Test., Verification Reliab. (STVR) **24**(3), 219–250 (2014)
4. Arcuri, A., et al.: EMB: A curated corpus of web/enterprise applications and library support for software testing research. In: IEEE International Conference on Software Testing, Verification and Validation (ICST). IEEE (2023)
5. Arcuri, A.: Many Independent Objective (MIO) algorithm for test suite generation. In: International Symposium on Search Based Software Engineering (SSBSE), pp. 3–17 (2017)
6. Arcuri, A.: Test suite generation with the Many Independent Objective (MIO) algorithm. Inf. Softw. Technol. **104**, 195–206 (2018)
7. Arcuri, A., Fraser, G.: Parameter tuning or default values? an empirical investigation in search-based software engineering. Empirical Softw. Eng. (EMSE) **18**(3), 594–623 (2013)
8. Arcuri, A., Galeotti, J.P.: Enhancing search-based testing with testability transformations for existing APIs. ACM Trans. Softw. Eng. Methodol. (TOSEM) **31**(1), 1–34 (2021)
9. Arcuri, A., Galeotti, J.P., Marculescu, B., Zhang, M.: Evomaster: a search-based system test generation tool. J. Open Source Softw. **6**(57), 2153 (2021)

10. Črepinšek, M., Liu, S.H., Mernik, M.: Replication and comparison of computational experiments in applied evolutionary computing: common pitfalls and guidelines to avoid them. Appl. Soft Comput. **19**, 161–170 (2014)
11. Eiben, A.E., Smit, S.K.: Parameter tuning for configuring and analyzing evolutionary algorithms. Swarm Evol. Comput. **1**(1), 19–31 (2011)
12. Fraser, G., Arcuri, A.: EvoSuite: automatic test suite generation for object-oriented software. In: ACM Symposium on the Foundations of Software Engineering (FSE), pp. 416–419 (2011)
13. Freisleben, B., Härtfelder, M.: Optimization of genetic algorithms by genetic algorithms. In: Artificial Neural Nets and Genetic Algorithms: Proceedings of the International Conference in Innsbruck, Austria, 1993, pp. 392–399. Springer (1993)
14. Kim, M., Xin, Q., Sinha, S., Orso, A.: Automated test generation for rest apis: No time to rest yet. In: Proceedings of the 31st ACM SIGSOFT International Symposium on Software Testing and Analysis, p. 289–301. ISSTA 2022, Association for Computing Machinery, New York, NY, USA (2022). https://doi.org/10.1145/3533767.3534401
15. Lukasczyk, S., Fraser, G.: Pynguin: Automated unit test generation for python. In: Proceedings of the ACM/IEEE 44th International Conference on Software Engineering: Companion Proceedings, pp. 168–172 (2022)
16. Tawosi, V., Sarro, F., Petrozziello, A., Harman, M.: Multi-objective software effort estimation: a replication study. IEEE Trans. Software Eng. **48**(8), 3185–3205 (2021)
17. Zamani, S., Hemmati, H.: A cost-effective approach for hyper-parameter tuning in search-based test case generation. In: 2020 IEEE International Conference on Software Maintenance and Evolution (ICSME), pp. 418–429. IEEE (2020)
18. Zhang, M., Arcuri, A.: Adaptive hypermutation for search-based system test generation: a study on rest APIS with evomaster. ACM Trans. Softw. Eng. Methodol. (TOSEM) **31**(1), 1–52 (2021)
19. Zhang, M., Arcuri, A.: Enhancing resource-based test case generation for RESTful APIs with SQL handling. In: O'Reilly, U.-M., Devroey, X. (eds.) SSBSE 2021. LNCS, vol. 12914, pp. 103–117. Springer, Cham (2021). https://doi.org/10.1007/978-3-030-88106-1_8
20. Zhang, M., Arcuri, A.: Open problems in fuzzing restful apis: A comparison of tools. ACM Transactions on Software Engineering and Methodology (TOSEM) (2023). https://doi.org/10.1145/3597205
21. Zhang, M., Marculescu, B., Arcuri, A.: Resource-based test case generation for restful web services. In: Proceedings of the Genetic and Evolutionary Computation Conference, pp. 1426–1434 (2019)
22. Zhang, M., Marculescu, B., Arcuri, A.: Resource and dependency based test case generation for restful web services. Empir. Softw. Eng. **26**(4), 1–61 (2021)

Search-Based Optimisation of LLM Learning Shots for Story Point Estimation

Vali Tawosi[1]([⊠]) [ID], Salwa Alamir[1] [ID], and Xiaomo Liu[2] [ID]

[1] J.P.Morgan AI Research, London, UK
{vali.tawosi,salwa.alamir}@jpmorgan.com
[2] J.P.Morgan AI Research, New York, USA
xiaomo.liu@jpmorgan.com

Abstract. One of the ways Large Language Models (LLMs) are used to perform machine learning tasks is to provide them with a few examples before asking them to produce a prediction. This is a meta-learning process known as few-shot learning. In this paper, we use available Search-Based methods to optimise the number and combination of examples that can improve an LLM's estimation performance, when it is used to estimate story points for new agile tasks. Our preliminary results show that our SBSE technique improves the estimation performance of the LLM by 59.34% on average (in terms of mean absolute error of the estimation) over three datasets against a zero-shot setting.

Keywords: Search-Based Software Effort Estimation · Large Language Model · Few-shot Learning · Multi-objective Optimisation

1 Introduction

Several studies proposed AI-based approaches to estimate the effort required to complete a user story in agile software development. The state-of-the-art uses deep-learning methods, leveraging the semantic similarity of the current user story to the previously estimated ones. However, the estimation performance of these methods is still inferior to baselines [9], which incites further research to find more effective models. Recent advances with Large Language Models (LLMs) demonstrated several emergent abilities including Natural Language Understanding (NLU) at a higher level than that attained by smaller language models [5]. In light of these advances, we investigated the ability of such LLMs to estimate story points for software tasks.[1]

Problem: During these investigations, we realised that few-shot learning, in which the LLM is provided with a few sample tasks with their estimated story points, can affect the estimation accuracy of the LLM to better or worse, depending on the samples used. On the other hand, including many samples in the prompt is not feasible (because of the prompt length limitation issues), nor is efficient (because of the cost of a long prompt, amongst other reasons).

---

[1] User stories, software tasks, and issues are used interchangeably in this paper.

P. Arcaini et al. (Eds.): SSBSE 2023, LNCS 14415, pp. 123–129, 2024.
https://doi.org/10.1007/978-3-031-48796-5_9

Therefore, we investigated the idea of using SBSE techniques to optimise the shots (i.e., the set of tasks sampled from the training set) in order to improve the LLM's estimation accuracy. To this end, we employ an uncertainty-aware multi-objective software effort estimation method called CoGEE (Confidence Guided Effort Estimation) [10]. We apply our proposed approach to three previously used datasets of agile software tasks, to demonstrate how effective search-based optimisation of LLM learning shots is for story point estimation. To the best of our knowledge, this is the first study using an SBSE approach to optimise learning shots for an LLM to estimate software effort.

2   Proposed Approach

We adopt CoGEE, a bi-objective software development effort estimation algorithm [10], which is originally proposed to optimise regression-based effort estimation models by minimising (i) the Sum of Absolute Error (SAE) of predictions, and (ii) the Confidence Interval (CI) of the error distribution. Instead of a regression-based model, we use CoGEE to optimise the set of examples that help an LLM achieve better estimations in a few-shot learning scenario. Thus, we define and optimise for three objectives. Two are inherited from CoGEE (i.e., SAE and CI). The third, added in this study, minimises the number of examples provided to the LLM. It helps reduce the number of tokens per prompt, hence, reducing the cost of inference using an LLM [1], and avoiding prompt length limitation issues [5]. Below is how we calculate each of the three fitness values.

1) Sum of Absolute Errors (SAE) is the sum of the distances between the actual story point values from the estimated values: $SAE = \sum_{i=1}^{n} |a_i - e_i|$, where n is the number of user stories in the test set, a_i is the actual story point value, and e_i is the estimated value for the ith issue.

2) Confidence Interval (CI) is defined in Equation (1), where the fraction is the sample standard deviation of the distribution of the absolute errors with n being the size of the sample, and $\phi(p, dof)$ is the quantile function (Eq. 2) which returns a threshold value x below which random draws from the given cumulative distribution function would fall p percent of the times [4].

$$CI = \phi(p, dof) \times \frac{std(AbsoluteErrors)}{\sqrt{n}} \tag{1}$$

$$\phi(p, dof) = inf\{x \in \mathbb{R} : p \leq F(x, dof)\} \tag{2}$$

For a probability $0 < p < 1$, $F(x, dof)$ is the probability density function of a t-distribution function, which is a function of x and dof (i.e., degree of freedom) [3]. Confidence intervals are calculated so that this percentage is 95%. The degree of freedom, dof, depends on the number of parameters we are estimating. For an n sized sample, $dof = n - k$, where k is the number of parameters to be estimated (here $k = 1$).

3) Number of Shots (N) is the number of sample user stories from the training set provided to the LLM in a few-shot setting: $N = |E|$, where E is the set of shots. Note that E can be empty, leading to a zero-shot prompt.

2.1   Computational Search

We use a multi-objective genetic evolutionary algorithm for optimisation and implement it using `pymoo` library in Python. Below is the configuration we used.

Problem Representation. As we are looking for a (near)optimal subset of the training set to use as learning shots, it is natural to define the chromosome as the sequence of indexes from the training set, with each example index being a single gene. We allow for dynamic-length chromosomes with a maximum number of eight genes in the initial population.

Evolutionary Operators. A modified single-point crossover is used, which can produce zero-length offspring, as well as offspring with a length longer than eight. Specifically, we randomly select an independent breakpoint for each of the parents a and b and append the first block from parent a to the second block from parent b, and vice versa. Mutation uses three operations: (i) replace a gene with a new one (randomly sampled from the training set) with a 50% chance, (ii) remove a randomly selected gene with a 25% chance, and (iii) append a random new gene to the chromosome with a 25% chance. Both cross-over and mutation operations are controlled to avoid introducing duplicate genes into the chromosome. The mutation and crossover rates are set to 0.8 and 0.2, respectively.

Evolutionary Algorithm. We use NSGA-II [2], a popular multi-objective evolutionary algorithm for optimisation. We ran the optimisation with a population of 50 individuals for 20 generations. These numbers are lower than the usual configuration used for evolutionary algorithms. We justify this experimental design choice by the fact that evaluation of each individual is too expensive when it comes to multiple inferences with an LLM (note that for each individual the LLM has to estimate all the user stories in the test set). Nevertheless, we use small parameters to demonstrate the feasibility of the idea and call for extended research on the topic from the SBSE community.

2.2   Estimation Model (Large Language Model)

We use GPT-4 API from OpenAI to do the story point estimation. Specifically, we use the `test-gpt4` engine, with `temperature=0.0` to limit non-deterministic responses. Note that according to Ouyang et al. [6] this does not eliminate the risk of non-deterministic response, but minimises it. The rest of the parameters are set to their default values.

Prompting the LLM. A common challenge with LLMs is that the output is in the form of natural text. Therefore, to use its output in a pipeline (such as ours, where the estimation needs to be extracted from the LLM output to compute the fitness values), we need to design the prompt such that the required

```
input ← example_issues[ ], target_issue

prompt = "You are asked to estimate effort for the user story given in <>.
          Use {list of SP values used in the project} as estimated value."

if len(example_issues)>0:
    prompt += "A few example user stories from the same project with their estimated
               effort are given in the following:"
    for each example in example_issues:
        prompt += example[text] + ". " + example[story_points] + " Story Points."

prompt += "Estimate the following user story and generate the output as a single scalar
           number only, equal to the estimated story point value."
           <" + target_issue[text] + ">"

return prompt
```

Fig. 1. The prompt used with the LLM to estimate story points for a target issue, in a zero/few-shot learning (depending on the length of the example issues list).

post-processing is minimised. Hence, we used the prompt template provided in Fig. 1. The output usually is in the form of a scalar value, or a scalar value followed by 'story points' (or a similar text). We used regular expressions to extract the estimated value from the LLM output. It is worth mentioning that we only experimented with GPT-4 as initial experiments with other models with smaller number of parameters yielded much less deterministic output.

2.3   Dataset

We use three projects with Jira issues published in the TAWOS dataset [7]. The three projects are Appcelerator Studio (APSTUD), Apache Mesos (MESOS), and Spring XD (XD). A sample of issues from these projects is used in previous story point estimation studies [8]. We use the same sample and train-test splits in this study (refer to [8] for descriptive statistics), except that our test sets include only 30 first issues from the original test sets. We use a limited number of projects and issues in this paper to minimise the cost of running LLMs.

3   Preliminary Results

Figure 2 shows the Pareto front formed after 20 generations of CoGEE running. It is clear that non-dominated solutions are forming a Pareto optimal front, where shots-length (N) and their combination (i.e., the specific observations selected from the train set to achieve the best performance) have a significant effect on the estimation error of the model and its level of uncertainty. In the case of MESOS, zero-shot estimation produces a large error with a wide confidence interval. However, once this individual is discarded, the column-shaped Pareto front spreads more similar to the other two projects. Overall, for all three projects, an increase in the number of shots helps the LLM to estimate better (i.e., low SAE and/or low CI). The set of non-dominated solutions provides the user with different trade-offs. One can choose to use the set of examples that minimises the number of shots to an affordable level while keeping the error and its uncertainty under an acceptable level.

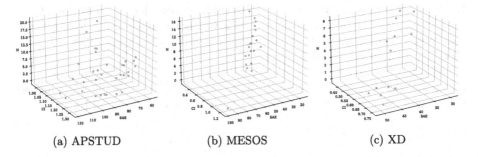

(a) APSTUD   (b) MESOS   (c) XD

Fig. 2. Pareto fronts achieved by our proposed approach for three projects.

To further present the effectiveness of the proposed method, we show in Table 1 the MAE (Mean Absolute Error, defined as $\frac{SAE}{n}$) achieved by the three sample individuals from the Pareto front, each with minimum (i.e., (near)optimal) value in one of the three objectives. We also provide MAE for three baseline methods including the Mean, Median, and Random Guessing baselines (see [8] for definitions). We observe that the LLM model with zero-shot prompting (i.e., using no samples from the previously estimated user stories) performs worse than Mean and Median baselines. In the case of MESOS, even Random Guessing performs better than the LLM with zero-shots. However, the individual with the lowest SAE outperforms all the other models.

Table 1. Mean absolute estimation error over the test set for sample individuals from the Pareto front achieved by CoGEE, and the baseline methods. Other objective values (i.e., N and CI) are in parenthesis. The best results are in bold.

Project	Pareto Individuals with			Baselines		
	Zero-shot (**N=0**)	best SAE	best CI	Mean	Median	Random
APSTUD	3.87 (CI=1.20)	**1.90** (N=9, CI=1.21)	2.77 (N=3, CI=**0.98**)	2.44	2.27	5.04
MESOS	1.87 (CI=0.66)	**0.47** (N=10, CI=0.29)	1.03 (N=7, CI=**0.23**)	1.16	1.10	1.77
XD	2.10 (CI=0.82)	**1.00** (N=6, CI=0.45)	1.43 (N=7, CI=**0.39**)	1.60	1.60	2.52

4   Conclusion

In this paper, we demonstrated promising results using SBSE techniques to improve the effectiveness of the GPT-4 model for story point estimation, via optimising the set of examples the LLM should be provided with in a few-shot learning setting. The same can be applied to tune LLMs for any downstream task that leverages LLMs in a few-shot setting. In this paper, we used story point estimation as an example of a common software engineering task for demonstration purposes. The same idea can be applied to any downstream task that leverages LLMs in a few-shot setting. Future work can also consider minimisation of the number of tokens used per prompt, which will not only optimise to use fewer user stories as examples but also will prefer shorter user stories. This will help save even more tokens in the prompt.

Although we experimented with a limited number of projects and issues in this study, the preliminary result attests to the feasibility of the idea and invites future work to extend the study using a larger dataset and more LLMs.

Disclaimer

This paper was prepared for informational purposes by the Artificial Intelligence Research group of JPMorgan Chase & Co and its affiliates ("JP Morgan"), and is not a product of the Research Department of JP Morgan. JP Morgan makes no representation and warranty whatsoever and disclaims all liability, for the completeness, accuracy or reliability of the information contained herein. This document is not intended as investment research or investment advice, or a recommendation, offer or solicitation for the purchase or sale of any security, financial instrument, financial product or service, or to be used in any way for evaluating the merits of participating in any transaction, and shall not constitute a solicitation under any jurisdiction or to any person, if such solicitation under such jurisdiction or to such person would be unlawful.

References

1. Chen, L., Zaharia, M., Zou, J.: FrugalGPT: How to use large language models while reducing cost and improving performance. arXiv preprint arXiv:2305.05176 (2023)
2. Deb, K., Pratap, A., Agarwal, S., Meyarivan, T.: A fast and elitist multiobjective genetic algorithm: NSGA-II. IEEE Trans. Evol. Comput. **6**(2), 182–197 (2002)
3. Grigelionis, B.: Student's t-distribution and related stochastic processes. Springer (2013)
4. Hill, G.W.: Algorithm 396: Student's t-quantiles. Commun. ACM **13**(10), 619–620 (1970)
5. OpenAI: GPT-4 technical report (2023)
6. Ouyang, S., Zhang, J.M., Harman, M., Wang, M.: LLM is like a box of chocolates: the non-determinism of ChatGPT in code generation. arXiv preprint arXiv:2308.02828 (2023)
7. Tawosi, V., Al-Subaihin, A., Moussa, R., Sarro, F.: A versatile dataset of agile open source software projects. In: Proceedings of the 19th International Conference on Mining Software Repositories, pp. 707–711 (2022)

8. Tawosi, V., Al-Subaihin, A., Sarro, F.: Investigating the effectiveness of clustering for story point estimation. In: 2022 IEEE International Conference on Software Analysis, Evolution and Reengineering (SANER), pp. 827–838. IEEE (2022)
9. Tawosi, V., Moussa, R., Sarro, F.: Agile effort estimation: have we solved the problem yet? insights from a replication study. IEEE Trans. Software Eng. **49**(4), 2677–2697 (2022)
10. Tawosi, V., Sarro, F., Petrozziello, A., Harman, M.: Multi-objective software effort estimation: a replication study. IEEE Trans. Softw. Eng. **48**(8), 3185–3205 (2021)

Challenge Track

StableYolo: Optimizing Image Generation for Large Language Models

Harel Berger[3] , Aidan Dakhama[1] , Zishuo Ding[4] ,
Karine Even-Mendoza[1] , David Kelly[1] , Hector Menendez[1(✉)] ,
Rebecca Moussa[2] , and Federica Sarro[2]

[1] King's College London, London, UK
{aidan.dakhama,karine.even_mendoza,david.a.kelly,
hector.menendez}@kcl.ac.uk
[2] University College London, London, UK
{r.moussa,f.sarro}@ucl.ac.uk
[3] Georgetown University, Washington, D.C, USA
[4] University of Waterloo, Waterloo, Canada
zishuo.ding@uwaterloo.ca

Abstract. AI-based image generation is bounded by system parameters and the way users define prompts. Both prompt engineering and AI tuning configuration are current open research challenges and they require a significant amount of manual effort to generate good quality images. We tackle this problem by applying evolutionary computation to Stable Diffusion, tuning both prompts and model parameters simultaneously. We guide our search process by using Yolo. Our experiments show that our system, dubbed StableYolo, significantly improves image quality (52% on average compared to the baseline), helps identify relevant words for prompts, reduces the number of GPU inference steps per image (from 100 to 45 on average), and keeps the length of the prompt short ($\approx$ 7 keywords).

Keywords: LLMS · SBSE · Image Generation · Stable Diffusion · Yolo

1 Introduction

Generative AI [4] has proven to be one of the advances of the decade, disrupting the way AI contributes to Arts. Large Language Models (LLMs), in combination with generative models, provide interfaces that greatly scale up content generation. The training of these systems normally consists of a massive training dataset with associated descriptions. The correct description –or prompt– would create the desired outcome almost exactly. However, the level of vagueness and ambiguity in the description can lead to unexpected results or errors.

Image generation is a good example of this specific problem. When generating images, generative models like DALL-E, Midjourney or Stable Diffusion recommend variations to the prompt to guarantee that the quality of the generated image is closer to expectations [9]. For example, if the user aims to create a

P. Arcaini et al. (Eds.): SSBSE 2023, LNCS 14415, pp. 133–139, 2024.
https://doi.org/10.1007/978-3-031-48796-5_10

(a) Elephant, before and after   (b) Zebra, before and after

Fig. 1. Before-and-after snapshots of optimization with StableYolo of two images: an elephant and a zebra.

photorealistic image, it is recommended to include words like *"professional photoshoot, 8k resolution, photorealistic masterpiece"* or *"natural lighting"*. However, it is not clear which words obtain the best results. Parameters of the algorithm, such as the number of steps used to generate an image, the initial random seed or the classifier-free guidance scale, significantly affect the outcome, as well.

The objective is to create images under the specific condition of photorealistic images.

To this end, we propose a framework, StableYolo, which aims to improve the quality of automatic image generation for photo-realistic images by leveraging the power of multi-objective search coupled with vision. The search process aims to improve different parameters of an image generation system (i.e., Stable Diffusion) according to the outcome of the chosen visualization system (i.e., Yolo). In this work, we use Stable Diffusion [2] and Yolo, respectively, but the framework can be extended to work with other systems. Our results show that StableYolo significantly improves the quality of the generated images and helps direct prompts effectively across various contexts (Fig. 1). StableYolo provides a 52% increase in quality compared to the baseline results.

Contributions. The main contributions of this work are:

(1) Creating the first system combining search and vision for image generation;
(2) Testing this system on 42 different objects that can be obtained with image generation and detected by our vision system; and
(3) Obtaining significant improvements and prompt recommendations for the generation process of photo-realistic images.

2   Proposed Approach

Given a user-provided prompt of a photo-realistic image to a generative AI system, StableYolo attempts to improve image quality by finding an optimal combination of both, the prompt and the model's parameters. It uses a search-based process to identify an optimal combination, using Yolo's confidence estimates as the fitness function.

StableYolo uses a Genetic Algorithm (GA) for the search process, where each individual is a dictionary object with values taken from StableDiffusion's documentation [11]. These include: (1) *Number of iterations*: the number of iterations needed for the AI to go through the image (range [1,100]); (2) *Classifier-free guidance scale (CFG)*: a parameter that controls the prompt's influence on the resulting image (range [1,20]); (3) *Positive prompt*: enables the prompt to describe the images and their details; (4) *Negative prompt*: a sequence of keywords to be avoided during the image generation process; (5) *Seed*: the generation seed for randomization; and (6) *Guidance rescale*: prevents over-exposure by re-scaling the guidance factor (range [0,1]). Positive prompt: In this work, we pass to the prompt, words that aim to produce more realistic images, according to different images extracted from the Photo-realistic Prompts documentation [10]; e.g., 'photograph', 'digital', 'color', 'Ultra Real' and 'award winning'. Negative prompt: We select references that might reduce the realistic component of the image; e.g., 'illustration', 'painting', 'drawing' and 'art'.

Utilizing GA, StableYolo optimizes both the LLM's parameters and the prompts based on the encoding of each potential individual. We start with a population of a set of individuals initialized with randomly selected parameters. Next, we evaluate the individuals using the fitness function. The fitter the individuals, the higher the chance they have of being chosen during the Tournament Selection process, after which the pair of individuals would undergo the crossover and mutation operators.

The crossover operator creates a pair of new offsprings by exchanging the attributes among the selected parents. On the other hand, the mutation operator (if applied) changes the parameters of an offpsring by uniformly assigning them new values within a given range. This results in the creation of a new population after each iteration of the algorithm. A stopping criterion is required to end the algorithm which is usually indicated by a number of generations specified by the user.

StableYolo aims to maximize its objective function through the following steps: (i) StableYolo creates positive and negative prompts and sets the parameters of Stable Diffusion to create four images per prompt; (ii) Yolo evaluates the images by identifying objects within it. These objects have an identification confidence that StableYolo uses to evaluate image quality; and (iii) StableYolo then calculates the fitness as the average quality of individual objects and images. This results in a different search objective based on the quality of each object. To avoid a multi-dimensional Pareto front, whose dimensions are unknown, the fitness calculates the object's quality average obtained with Yolo.

3   Experimental Setup and Results

In this section, we describe our research questions, experimental setup and results.

RQ. We aim to answer the following research questions:

- **RQ1** To what extent can we improve the quality of an image generation system?

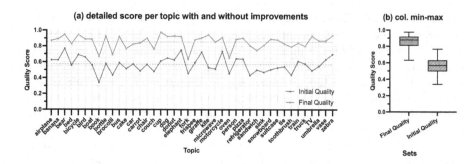

Fig. 2. RQ1: Quality Score Comparison: StableYolo (orange) vs. Non-Optimized (blue) Image Generation. StableYolo always produces better images on our dataset.

- **RQ2** What is the average prompt length to achieve maximum quality?
- **RQ3** What is the keyword frequency associated with quality images?

In order to provide a wide set of elements to evaluate StableYolo, we used 42 different categories of objects, animals and people that Yolo can recognize, (e.g., person, elephant, zebra, dog, boat, and TV among others). For RQ2, we consider a 1–2 word prompt as *small*, 3–6 words as *medium* and 7+ words as *large*.

Experimental Setup. For the GA, the settings were as follows; the population size was 25, the number of generations was set to 50, the mutation rate and crossover were both set to 0.2, and the tournament selection value was set to 5. Even given the small population size, we find the algorithm produces good results (Fig. 2a). The experiments were repeated 4 times. All experiments were conducted on a workstation running Ubuntu 20.04 LTS with 36 CPU cores, 256 GB RAM and an NVIDIA Titan V GPU with 12 GB memory.

Results. Figure 2 shows the results based on Yolo's quality assessment, ranked with a score from 0 to 1, where 1 is best. Figure 2a shows the quality score with and without improvements, grouped by topic. The orange line represents the quality score per topic after applying StableYolo, while the blue line denotes the baseline before improvement (e.g., the topic baseline score is 0.558). The blue and orange dotted lines represent the mean quality score before and after improvement, respectively. Figure 2b presents the quality score across all topics, where the orange boxplot shows the results with improvements, and the blue one shows them with no improvements. Figure 2a shows improvement on all 42 prompts, with the orange line scores always being above the blue line scores. The initial prompt quality average is 0.567 with a standard deviation (SD) of 0.096, while the average score after optimization is 0.854 with an SD of 0.0836. This gives an average improvement of 52% in the quality scores after optimization. As the final quality scores fail the normality test, we applied the Wilcoxon test under the null hypothesis that both results follow the same distribution. The resulting p-value for the test is $4.55 \cdot 10^{-13}$, clearly rejecting the null hypothesis,

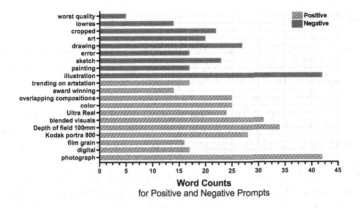

Fig. 3. RQ3: Positive and negative prompt terms counting for the best individuals.

and showing a statistically significant difference between both sets of results. The optimized set demonstrates a significant increase in the quality of the generated images.

Parameters and Prompts. The average *optimal* value for the guidance scale is 9.65 ± 3.99 in the range $[0,20]$ while the rescale value is 0.56 ± 0.29 on average. The number of inference steps to 45.3 ± 30.29 on average, in the range $[0,100]$. The positive prompt length on average is 6.5 ± 1.66 and the negative one is 4.45 ± 1.09. At the end of the optimization process, the most relevant keywords were found to be 'photograph' and 'Depth of field 100 mm' for the positive prompt, and 'illustration' and 'drawing' for the negative one (Fig. 3). The memory cost to the GPU was 9 GB, with each prompt optimization taking approximately 2 h to execute. On average, the GA takes 45.05 ± 10.01 iterations to converge. StableYolo can scale through multiple GPUs linearly for both the generation and the visualization process.

4 Related Work

Generative AI systems have been used to perform the task of image generation for many years [1,5,7,8]. Progress in this domain has resulted in incremental adjustments or entirely novel architectures, including but not limited to generator regularization [8], additional memory gate incorporation [12], use of dynamic thresholding [9], and fusion of neural architecture search with generative adversarial networks [6]. To the best of our knowledge, our work is the first to leverage the power of MOEAs to improve prompts and model parameters simultaneously. A comprehensive survey on other uses of LLMs can be found in Fan et al.'s work [3].

5   Conclusions

We introduce StableYolo, an innovative framework that enhances the fidelity of photo-realistic image generation by means of an iterative online optimization procedure applied to the initial textual prompt. StableYolo combines the text-to-image approach of Stable Diffusion v2 for image generation making use of the image-to-text mechanism of Yolo v8 for caption generation. An iterative process based on multi-objective search is adopted, utilizing affirmative and opposing prompts until convergence is attained. Opportunities for further enhancement persist, most notably the current iteration of StableYolo is constrained to classes identified by Yolo. Widening the spectrum of recognizable classes may enhance the diversity and analytical scope of generated images. Nonetheless, StableYolo exhibits a remarkable enhancement in the quality of image generation. In terms of generality, the StableYolo can easily be extended to other image generation models like DALL-E or Midjourney and different visualization systems apart from Yolo, for instance captioning systems, this will allow more objects and contexts to be addressed.

Acknowledgments. Authors are listed in alphabetical order. This work was supported by the ERC grant no. 741278 (EPIC), the UKRI TAS Hub grant no. EP/V00784X/1 and EP/V026801/2.

Data Availability Statement. StableYolo is publicly available at https://github.com/SOLAR-group/StableYolo.

References

1. Avrahami, O., Lischinski, D., Fried, O.: Blended diffusion for text-driven editing of natural images. In: IEEE/CVF CVPR, pp. 18208–18218 (2022)
2. Chefer, H., Alaluf, Y., Vinker, Y., Wolf, L., Cohen-Or, D.: Attend-and-excite: attention-based semantic guidance for text-to-image diffusion models. ACM Trans. Graph. (TOG) **42**(4), 1–10 (2023)
3. Fan, A., et al.: Large language models for software engineering: survey and open problems (2023)
4. Jo, A.: The promise and peril of generative AI. Nature **614**(1), 214–216 (2023)
5. Kang, M., et al.: Scaling up GANs for text-to-image synthesis. In: IEEE/CVF CVPR, pp. 10124–10134 (2023)
6. Li, W., Wen, S., Shi, K., Yang, Y., Huang, T.: Neural architecture search with a lightweight transformer for text-to-image synthesis. IEEE Trans. Netw. Sci. Eng. **9**(3), 1567–1576 (2022)
7. Li, W., et al.: Object-driven text-to-image synthesis via adversarial training. In: IEEE/CVF CVPR, pp. 12174–12182 (2019)
8. Mao, Q., Lee, H.Y., Tseng, H.Y., Ma, S., Yang, M.H.: Mode seeking generative adversarial networks for diverse image synthesis. In: IEEE/CVF CVPR, pp. 1429–1437 (2019)
9. Saharia, C., et al.: Photorealistic text-to-image diffusion models with deep language understanding. Adv. Neural. Inf. Process. Syst. **35**, 36479–36494 (2022)

10. Stable Diffusion Photorealistic Prompts. https://prompthero.com/stable-diffusion-photorealistic-prompts
11. The Stable Diffusion documentation. https://huggingface.co/docs/diffusers/api/pipelines/stable_diffusion/text2img
12. Zhu, M., Pan, P., Chen, W., Yang, Y.: DM-GAN: dynamic memory generative adversarial networks for text-to-image synthesis. In: IEEE/CVF CVPR, pp. 5802–5810 (2019)

Improving the Readability of Generated Tests Using GPT-4 and ChatGPT Code Interpreter

Gregory Gay[✉][ID]

Chalmers and University of Gothenburg, Gothenburg, Sweden
greg@greggay.com

Abstract. A major challenge in automated test generation is the *readability* of generated tests. Emerging large language models (LLMs) excel at language analysis and transformation tasks. We propose that improving test readability is such a task and explore the capabilities of the GPT-4 LLM in improving readability of tests generated by the Pynguin search-based generation framework. Our initial results are promising. However, there are remaining research and technical challenges.

Keywords: Automated Test Generation · Search-Based Test Generation · Readability · Large Language Models · Generative AI

1 Introduction

Software testing is a crucially important, yet labor-intensive, stage in the software development lifecycle. Automation could partially relieve the burden of test creation. Search-based test generation—the use of optimization algorithms to produce tests [2,4]—is both efficient and effective at fault-detection [2].

However, *humans must work with generated tests* to interpret and debug program behavior. Therefore, a major challenge is the *readability* of generated tests. Generated tests are often difficult to understand—e.g., lacking documentation, incorporating uninterpretable actions, or checking trivial assertions [7]. Partial solutions have been proposed, e.g., synthesizing informative test names or documentation [3,6]. However, comprehensive solutions do not yet exist.

Large language models (LLMs), machine learning models trained on massive corpora of text—including natural language and source code—are an emerging technology with great potential for *language analysis and transformation tasks* such as translation, summarization, and decision support [5]. We propose that improving generated test readability can be viewed as a similar task—the transformation of a test into a form with identical semantic meaning, but presented in a manner easier for human testers to interpret.

In this study, we explore the capabilities of LLMs to improve generated test readability[1]. In particular, we apply the state-of-the-art GPT-4 LLM [5], through the ChatGPT interface with the Code Interpreter plug-in, to Python unit test suites generated by the Pynguin framework [4].

---

[1] LLMs can generate tests, which have been found to be more readable than alternative approaches [8]. We instead focus on improving readability of already-extant tests.

P. Arcaini et al. (Eds.): SSBSE 2023, LNCS 14415, pp. 140–146, 2024.
https://doi.org/10.1007/978-3-031-48796-5_11

2   Background and Related Work

Search-Based Unit Test Generation: Test creation can be viewed as a optimization problem where, given a limited time budget, we seek tests that best meet testing goals [2]. Metaheuristic optimization algorithms sample possible test inputs to identify those that maximize or minimize fitness functions representing those goals. In this study, we focus on generation of unit tests targeting individual modules within broader systems [2, 4].

Factors Affecting Readability: Through a mapping study, Winkler et al. identified readability factors [7] including meaningful test and identifier names, enforcement of a predictable test structure, avoidance of too many or meaningless assertions, avoidance of too many dependencies and interdependent tests, understandable input values, test documentation (summaries and in-line comments), and other language properties such as consistent identifier styles. Our approach targets all of these factors, except for dependencies and test data, as those should be targeted during generation rather than refactoring.

Automated Readability Improvement: Approaches have been proposed to address the factors above. For example, test documentation has been generated using deep learning models [6] and natural language processing and code summarization techniques [3]. Our approach is the first to apply a general LLM, GPT-4, to improving readability of pre-generated tests. An advantage of a general LLM is that it can target many readability factors simultaneously. However, it could be outperformed in individual aspects by targeted tools. In future work, we will compare LLM performance to targeted solutions.

3   Approach

Our approach transforms already-generated tests as part of a series of prompts to GPT-4, a state-of-the-art LLM that has shown human-competitive performance on certain language tasks [5]. Prompts are applied manually through the ChatGPT interface[2] to take advantage of the Code Interpreter plug-in[3]—a ChatGPT plug-in that enables file uploads and execution, as well as enhanced analysis capabilities, of Python code. We target `pytest`-formatted tests generated by Pynguin [4]. However, this approach should be applicable to tests generated by other frameworks, e.g., [2], or created by humans. An example of a transformed test case is shown in Fig. 1.

Enhancements to Readability: We identified potential readability enhancements to readability by examining past literature. In particular, we were influenced by Winkler et al. [7]. We also prompted GPT-4 for a definition of test readability, and drew on its suggestions. We make the following transformations:

- **Use Meaningful Test and Variable Names:** Rather than generic names like `int_0`, we apply names related to the test or variable usage context.

---

[2] https://chat.openai.com/.

[3] https://openai.com/blog/chatgpt-plugins#code-interpreter.

```
# BEFORE TRANSFORMATION
def test_case_38():
    str_0 = "X"
    bool_0 = module_0.is_palindrome(str_0)
    assert bool_0 is True
    assert (
        module_0.URLS_RAW_STRING == "([a-z-]+://)([a-z_\\d-]+:[a-z_\\d-]+@)?(www\\.)?" +
        "((?<!\\.)[a-z\\d]+[a-z\\d.-]+\\.[a-z]{2,6}|\\d{1,3}\\.\\d{1,3}\\.\\d{1,3}\\.\\" +
        "d{1,3}|localhost)(:\\d{2,})?(/[a-z\\d_%+-]*)*(\\.[a-z\\d_%+-]+)*" +
        "(\\?[a-z\\d_+%-=]*)?(#\\S*)?" )
    assert (
        module_0.EMAILS_RAW_STRING == "[a-zA-Z\\d._\\+\\-'`!%#$&*/=\\?\\^\\{\\}\\|~\\\\]+" +
        "@[a-z\\d-]+\\.?[a-z\\d-]+\\.[a-z]{2,4}" )
    assert len(module_0.CREDIT_CARDS) == 6
    assert len(module_0.PRETTIFY_RE) == 8

# AFTER TRANSFORMATION
def test_single_character_palindrome():
    # Test to check the is_palindrome function in the module for single character strings.
    # Setup: Define a test string with a single character
    test_string = "X"
    # Execution: Check if the string is a palindrome
    is_palindrome = module_0.is_palindrome(test_string)
    # Assertion: The string is a single character, so the function should return True
    assert is_palindrome is True
```

Fig. 1. Example of a readability transformation for a test for the `validation` module in the `python-string-utils` project.

- **Define Variables for Constants:** Rather than using hard-coded values, we define constants at the beginning of each test with descriptive names.
- **Separate Test Steps into Setup, Execution, and Assertion Phases**
- **Remove Unnecessary or Redundant Assertions**
- **Code Formatting Following the PEP 8 Style Guide**[4]
- **Test Documentation:** Comments are added to explain the purpose of the test, actions taken, and code coverage achieved by the test case.

Prompt Structure: We apply the following prompts, in sequence[5]:

- *If a single module is imported by the generated test suite:* I will provide a Python module, then a series of unit tests targeting that module. First, here is the Python module. [`module-under-test`]
- *If the imported modules are in multiple files (M):*
  - I will provide *M* Python modules, then a series of unit tests targeting those modules. Here is the first Python module. [`module-under-test`]
  - *For each additional module:* Here is the next Python module. [`module`]
- I will now provide each unit test individually. After making the requested changes to each, incorporate each into a single test suite. The test suite should have the following import statements: {`import statements`}

---

[4] https://peps.python.org/pep-0008/.

[5] Square brackets ("[") indicate a file upload, while curly brackets ("{") indicate text that should be added directly to the prompt.

- *For each test case:* I have written the following pytest test case for the previously uploaded Python file: {`test code`} Make the following changes to the test case, in the order they are listed. Use the resulting modified test case following a change to make the subsequent change. The changes are, in order: add constants inside of the test case, separate setup, execution, and assertion, remove unnecessary assertions, add a meaningful test name, use meaningful variable names, format the code according to PEP 8. After making these changes, add comments to explain the purpose of the test, actions taken, and code coverage achieved by the modified test case. Add the final test case to the test suite.
- I have finished creating the test suite. Provide the test suite as a file.

Research and Technical Challenges: We developed the prompts iteratively. During this process, we encountered multiple challenges. Some we were able to partially or completely overcome, while others remain as future work.

- **Non-Determinism:** Different sessions can yield tests with potentially significant differences in readability, interpretation of the original test, and judgement on how to apply transformations (e.g., which assertions are unnecessary)[6]. We limit the scope of non-determinism by explicitly describing transformations, but this challenge remains unsolved.
- **Potential Semantic Changes to Test Cases:** The model interprets the semantic meaning of a test case. It then can change the test according to its inferences. In our observations, we saw the model remove method calls, assign calls to different objects, and even add method calls.
  Initially, we also experimented with removing redundant test steps. However, this yielded tests that, in some cases, were very different from the originals. Therefore, we removed this transformation. For the remaining transformations, we added clear descriptions and an explicit order. This limited the scope for changing semantic meaning. Still, some sessions yield larger reinterpretations of tests than others. Under the current prompt structure, code coverage seems to remain the same and the same outcomes are achieved. However, there is still potential for the semantic meaning to change.
- **Transformation Order:** The order that transformations are applied can affect results. For example, if comments are added first, they may reference elements that are removed or changed later. We account for this by applying an explicit transformation order.
- **Manual Application:** Prompts are applied manually, which can be very time consuming. Rather than applying transformations to all tests, this process could be used selectively for difficult tests.
- **Text Limits:** We initially uploaded the test suite and made transformations to all tests with a single prompt. However, GPT-4 can only process a finite quantity of text in a single prompt. We transitioned to performing one prompt per test and providing the test within the prompt rather than as part of

---

[6] A speculated, but currently unconfirmed, reason for performance variance is that OpenAI is deploying sub-models of GPT-4 with decreased computational cost [1].

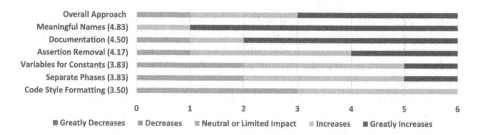

Fig. 2. Perceived impact of individual and overall readability transformations.

a file upload. Some issues are still encountered with long individual tests (e.g., over 100 lines of code). We would like to explore suite-wide readability transformations (e.g., extraction of helper functions and grouping related test cases). However, such transformations are hindered by this limitation.

- **Prompt Limits:** OpenAI restricts the number of prompts in a single session[7]. If a suite contains too many tests, multiple sessions may be needed.
- **Code Interpreter Limitations:** The Code Interpreter plug-in currently only supports Python. The same transformations can be attempted on tests for other languages, but the results may be less effective. Code Interpreter also can only execute a single Python module without complex dependencies, so it cannot execute `pytest` suites currently.
- **Differences Between Screen and File Output:** The transformed tests output to the screen do not always match the versions in the file produced at the end of the session, e.g., comments may be missing.

4 Preliminary Evaluation

We make a replication package available for our study[8]. We developed and tested our approach using three case examples: a `queue`, the module `validation` from the `python-string-utils` project, and the module `sessions` from `httpie`. The latter two were selected at random from complex modules previously tested with Pynguin [4]. Generated tests were retrieved from the Pynguin documentation[9] (for `queue`) and replication package [4].

For `queue`, we used all eight tests. For the other examples, we selected 10 tests that captured a range of sizes and functionalities tested. For each test suite, we performed two transformation trials. After transformation, we manually ensured that the semantic meaning was intact. We also executed the modified suite to ensure unchanged execution results.

Three tests were broken: (1) a variable was removed but still referenced, (2) two variables had values swapped, (3) the contents of a dictionary were

---

[7] We encountered limits of 25 in a two hour period and 50 in a three hour period.
[8] https://doi.org/10.5281/zenodo.8296610.
[9] https://pynguin.readthedocs.io/.

changed—resulting in a mismatch between result and assertion—and a method call was removed that threw an exception. Due to assertion removal, two additional tests passed when they were marked as "expected failures". **Overall, 51/56 tests (91%) were successfully transformed.**

To assess the readability improvement, each of the six transformed test suites was sent to a professional software developer (average of five years of testing experience). Only a small evaluation—six test suites, six developers—was conducted at this time to gain initial feedback. Each was asked to compare the original and transformed tests and assess the overall approach and the impact of each individual transformation. The survey is included in the replication package.

The results are illustrated in Fig. 2. Overall, all-but-one respondent indicated improvement in readability. Of the individual transformations, meaningful names and documentation were perceived to have the greatest impact, followed by assertion removal, variables for constants, and separation of phases. Style formatting only had a limited impact. One respondent positively noted that—after transformation—the tests could survive code review.

However, the transformations "improved a horrible test suite"—as stated by one respondent. Respondents explained that the original tests tested too many behaviors simultaneously and lacked clear rationale for the assertions included[10]. One respondents indicated that they would still need to make improvements manually—although the transformations made that improvement possible. The potential for readability transformation seems to be limited by the quality of the original tests. Respondents suggested that there would be value in applying these transformations to human-written tests.

5   Conclusions

Our results indicate that LLMs are a promising method of improving generated test readability. However, there are also significant research and technical challenges. In future work, we will further develop these initial ideas, explore automation, and conduct a full evaluation.

Acknowledgements. Vetenskapsrådet Grant 2019-05275.

References

1. Chen, L., Zaharia, M., Zou, J.: How is ChatGPT's behavior changing over time? (2023). arXiv preprint arXiv:2307.09009
2. Fontes, A., Gay, G., de Oliveira Neto, F.G., Feldt, R.: Automated support for unit test generation. In: Romero, J.R., Medina-Bulo, I., Chicano, F. (eds.) Optimising the Software Development Process with Artificial Intelligence, pp. 179–219. Springer, Singapore (2023). https://doi.org/10.1007/978-981-19-9948-2_7

---

[10] One respondent mistrusted the assertion removal, as it was not clear why some assertions were present in the first place.

3. Li, B., Vendome, C., Linares-Vásquez, M., Poshyvanyk, D., Kraft, N.A.: Automatically documenting unit test cases. In: 2016 IEEE International Conference on Software Testing, Verification and Validation (ICST), pp. 341–352 (2016)
4. Lukasczyk, S., Kroiß, F., Fraser, G.: An empirical study of automated unit test generation for python. Empir. Softw. Eng. **28**(2), 36 (2023)
5. OpenAI. GPT-4 technical report (2023). arXiv preprint arXiv:2303.08774
6. Roy, D., et al.: DeepTC-enhancer: improving the readability of automatically generated tests. In: Proceedings of the 35th IEEE/ACM International Conference on Automated Software Engineering, ASE 2020, New York, NY, USA, pp. 287–298. Association for Computing Machinery (2021)
7. Winkler, D., Urbanke, P., Ramler, R.: What do we know about readability of test code? - a systematic mapping study. In: 2022 IEEE International Conference on Software Analysis, Evolution and Reengineering (SANER), pp. 1167–1174 (2022)
8. Yuan, Z., et al.: No more manual tests? Evaluating and improving chatGPT for unit test generation (2023). arXiv preprint arXiv:2305.04207

Evaluating Explanations for Software Patches Generated by Large Language Models

Dominik Sobania[1(✉)] [iD], Alina Geiger[1] [iD], James Callan[2] [iD],
Alexander Brownlee[3] [iD], Carol Hanna[2] [iD], Rebecca Moussa[2] [iD],
Mar Zamorano López[2] [iD], Justyna Petke[2] [iD], and Federica Sarro[2] [iD]

[1] Johannes Gutenberg University Mainz, Mainz, Germany
{dsobania,geiger}@uni-mainz.de
[2] University College London, London, UK
{james.callan.19,carol.hanna.21,r.moussa,maria.lopez.20,
j.petke,f.sarro}@ucl.ac.uk
[3] University of Stirling, Stirling, UK
alexander.brownlee@stir.ac.uk

Abstract. Large language models (LLMs) have recently been integrated in a variety of applications including software engineering tasks. In this work, we study the use of LLMs to enhance the explainability of software patches. In particular, we evaluate the performance of GPT 3.5 in explaining patches generated by the search-based automated program repair system ARJA-e for 30 bugs from the popular Defects4J benchmark. We also investigate the performance achieved when explaining the corresponding patches written by software developers. We find that on average 84% of the LLM explanations for machine-generated patches were correct and 54% were complete for the studied categories in at least 1 out of 3 runs. Furthermore, we find that the LLM generates more accurate explanations for machine-generated patches than for human-written ones.

Keywords: Large Language Models · Software Patches · AI Explainability · Program Repair · Genetic Improvement

1 Introduction

Generative AI tools, especially large language models (LLMs), have recently been used for a variety of general application scenarios [5]. Moreover, applications like ChatGPT are known to an even broader public. In addition to these general applications, LLMs are often used for software development tasks. Recent work studies, for example, their usage for automated code generation [2], bug fixing [11] and explaining source code [1].

Genetic improvement (GI) [10] uses search-based strategies to find patches that improve existing software. GI can improve a software's functional (i.e., fix

P. Arcaini et al. (Eds.): SSBSE 2023, LNCS 14415, pp. 147–152, 2024.
https://doi.org/10.1007/978-3-031-48796-5_12

bugs) or non-functional properties (e.g., runtime). Despite the successful application of GI in various application domains [10], GI has not yet seen a wider uptake in industry. One of the limitations of current tools is the lack of explanations of the generated patches. Thus it is not surprising, that the use of automatic explanations has already been discussed [7] and investigated [6]. However, the quality of the generated patch explanations has not yet been studied in detail.

Therefore, this work presents an empirical study investigating the quality of LLM-generated explanations of the patches obtained when applying GI. For comparison, we examine how well LLMs can explain human-written software patches. Specifically, we use the API of the gpt-3.5-turbo-16k LLM model by OpenAI to generate explanations for software patches, automatically generated by one of the most well-known GI tools, namely ARJA-e [12], to fix 30 bugs extracted from the popular Defects4J benchmark [4]. We also consider corresponding human-written patches to fix the same bugs, in order to assess the quality of LLM-generated explanations for patches generated automatically by GI tooling vs. those applied manually by the developers. Each generated explanation was evaluated by three independent reviewers.

We find that, on average across the studied categories, 84% of the explanations for machine-generated patches were correct and 54% were complete in at least 1 out of 3 runs. We observe a low level of complexity in the explanations.

Given the positive results achieved herein, in the future, it would be interesting to extend the current investigation and include other GI tools, LLM models, and benchmarks. We made the source code along with the relevant scripts and all of the LLM's patch explanations available online.[1]

To the best of our knowledge this is the first work investigating the effectiveness of LLMs for generating explanations for software patches. A comprehensive survey on the use of LLMs in Software Engineering can be found in the work by Fan et al. [3].

2   Experimental Design

In this section, we explain in detail how we generated and evaluated the explanations for the considered software patches.

2.1   Generation of Software Patch Explanations

To analyse and compare explanations of an LLM for human-written and machine-generated patches, we considered bugs from three projects: Chart, Lang, and Math, included in the well-known Defects4J benchmark [4] and used the API of the gpt-3.5-turbo-16k LLM model by OpenAI for the explanations. In total, we used 30 randomly sampled bugs under the condition that all changes are made in one file and the length of a file has a maximum of 1500 lines after removing comments, since the used LLM has an upper limit for the length of

---

[1] https://github.com/SOLAR-group/ExplanationsForSoftwarePatches.

requests. We took the human-written patches from Defects4J[2] and the machine-generated patches (one patch per bug) from the ARJA-e repository.[3]

In the given code, lines starting with an "o" indicate
unchanged lines, lines starting with a "+" indicate added
lines, and lines starting with a "−" indicate removed lines.
Please explain only the modifications made using the
provided template:

Condition: Under what circumstances or conditions was the
change necessary?
Consequence: What are the potential impacts or effects of
this change?
Position: Where in the codebase was the change implemented?
Cause: What was the motivation for this change? Why was the
previous implementation insufficient or problematic?
Change: How was the code or behavior being altered to address
the identified condition or problem?

The code:

```
− import java.io.Serializable;
o import java.util.Collections;
+ import java.util.List;
```

Fig. 1. The prompt we used for requests to the LLM with 3 example code lines. Line breaks were added and relevant keywords are printed in **bold** font for better display.

The prompt we used to issue a request to the LLM is shown with some example code lines in Fig. 1 and consists of three parts. In the first part, we explain how we represent the changes introduced by a patch. In the second part, we force the LLM to describe the main characteristics of a software patch as identified by Liang et al. [8]. The third part consists of the source code of the whole file where the patch was applied and each line is marked with the symbols indicating the introduced changes.

Overall, we performed 3 runs for each manually and automatically generated patch for each of the 30 bugs resulting in a total of 180 explanations. For the requests to the LLM, we set the temperature $t = 0.8$, as used by Chen et al. [2].

2.2 Evaluation of the Software Patch Explanations

To evaluate the explanations of the considered patches, we carried out manual assessment. Specifically, we provided each of our 9 reviewers with a set of 10

---

[2] https://github.com/rjust/defects4j.
[3] https://github.com/yyxhdy/arja/tree/arja-e.

bugs with their corresponding patches. This means that each of these sets was evaluated by 3 independent reviewers. Furthermore, we anonymized whether it was a human-written or machine-generated patch during the evaluation process.

In order to ensure consistent evaluation, we used the following applicable content-based categories for evaluation of explainable AI as recommended by Nauta et al. [9]:

- **Correctness:** Is the explanation accurate with regards to the provided patch?
- **Completeness:** Does the explanation of the patch describe the changes in the patch in full?
- **Complexity:** Does the explanation for the patch have unnecessary complexity?
- **Continuity:** Does the model give similar explanations for the same patch over all 3 runs?

Table 1. Results of the manual validation of the LLM-generated explanations for the machine-generated and human-written patches for 30 bugs. At least 1 run refers to the case that in at least 1 out of 3 runs, the reviewers evaluated the categories positively. 3 out of 3 refers to the case where the evaluation was positive for all runs. For Complexity results are reported for a negative evaluation. Best results are marked in **bold** font.

Patch generated by:		At least 1 run		3 out of 3 runs	
		Machine	Human	Machine	Human
Correctness	Condition	**24**	21	**12**	7
	Consequence	**25**	22	**11**	7
	Position	29	29	**22**	21
	Cause	**25**	21	**9**	6
	Change	**23**	22	**9**	6
Completeness	Condition	13	13	**3**	2
	Consequence	**16**	14	**5**	4
	Position	16	**19**	7	7
	Cause	**17**	14	**4**	3
	Change	**19**	18	**6**	3
Complexity	Condition	**5**	7	**0**	1
	Consequence	**5**	7	**0**	1
	Position	4	**3**	0	0
	Cause	**5**	9	**0**	1
	Change	**6**	14	**1**	3
Continuity	Condition	–	–	10	10
	Consequence	–	–	**11**	6
	Position	–	–	**17**	12
	Cause	–	–	9	9
	Change	–	–	**11**	8

For each considered patch and each category (see Fig. 1), reviewers checked whether the explanations given by the LLM are correct. After that, we used a majority vote in order to get the final result. Furthermore, we calculated the inter-rate agreement.

3   Results

Table 1 shows the results of our evaluation for both the machine-generated and the human-written patches. Since we performed 3 runs per patch (API calls to retrieve a patch explanation), we report the sum of correct patch explanations for the case where only 1 run per patch was correct and for the case where all 3 runs provided a correct patch explanation. Best results are printed in **bold** font. Note that for the results in the Complexity category lower values are better.

We see that in most cases, best results are achieved for the machine-generated patches. On average across all categories, explanations for machine-generated patches are correct in 84% of the cases and complete in 54% of the cases in at least 1 out of 3 runs. For human patches, explanations were on average 76.67% correct and 52% complete (in 1 out of 3 runs). It is thus noticeable that the results for Correctness are quite high, but for Completeness we observe significantly lower results. Although descriptions are often formally correct, important details are sometimes missing. On a positive note, the complexity of the patch explanations is generally very low.

Moreover, we calculated the inter-rate agreement between the reviewers by analysing how often all three reviewers agreed in their ratings of the explanations. We found that the inter-rate agreement between the reviewers was 84.27%.

4   Threats to Validity

It is worth mentioning, that we collected the LLM explanations via the API for the `gpt-3.5-turbo-16k` model. Since this is a proprietary model offered by OpenAI, future responses may differ from those in our experiments.

Additionally, the evaluation of the given explanations was done manually and therefore reflects the subjective opinion of the reviewers. To counteract this, each patch was evaluated by three reviewers and the final result was determined by a majority vote. Further, we reported the inter-rate agreement.

Moreover, the patches examined were all correct with respect to the existing software tests, but this does not necessarily mean that they are correct in general. However, this does not pose a threat to our evaluation, as we have investigated how well LLMs can explain the changes made.

5   Conclusions and Future Work

In this paper, we evaluated the quality of explanations generated by an LLM for software patches. Furthermore, we studied whether the quality of LLM explanations differs for machine-generated and human-written patches. We found that, on average across the studied categories, 84% of the LLM explanations for machine-generated patches were correct and 54% were complete in at least 1 out of 3 runs. Our analysis shows that the explanations for machine-generated patches were overall better than the explanations for human-written patches.

In future work, we intend to expand our study to include more benchmark problems and patches generated by other GI tools, in addition to analysing LLM-generated explanations for patches improving non-functional software properties.

Acknowledgements. This work was supported by the UKRI EPSRC grant no. EP/P023991/1 and the ERC advanced fellowship grant no. 741278.

References

1. Chen, E., Huang, R., Chen, H.S., Tseng, Y.H., Li, L.Y.: GPTutor: a ChatGPT-powered programming tool for code explanation. arXiv preprint arXiv:2305.01863 (2023)
2. Chen, M., et al.: Evaluating large language models trained on code. arXiv preprint arXiv:2107.03374 (2021)
3. Fan, A., et al.: Large language models for software engineering: survey and open problems (2023)
4. Just, R., Jalali, D., Ernst, M.D.: Defects4J: a database of existing faults to enable controlled testing studies for Java programs. In: Proceedings of the 2014 International Symposium on Software Testing and Analysis, pp. 437–440. ISSTA 2014, Association for Computing Machinery, New York, NY, USA (2014)
5. Kaddour, J., Harris, J., Mozes, M., Bradley, H., Raileanu, R., McHardy, R.: Challenges and applications of large language models. arXiv preprint arXiv:2307.10169 (2023)
6. Kang, S., Chen, B., Yoo, S., Lou, J.G.: Explainable automated debugging via large language model-driven scientific debugging. arXiv preprint arXiv:2304.02195 (2023)
7. Krauss, O.: Exploring the use of natural language processing techniques for enhancing genetic improvement. In: 2023 IEEE/ACM International Workshop on Genetic Improvement (GI), pp. 21–22. IEEE (2023)
8. Liang, J., Hou, Y., Zhou, S., Chen, J., Xiong, Y., Huang, G.: How to explain a patch: an empirical study of patch explanations in open source projects. In: 2019 IEEE 30th International Symposium on Software Reliability Engineering (ISSRE), pp. 58–69. IEEE (2019)
9. Nauta, M., et al.: From anecdotal evidence to quantitative evaluation methods: a systematic review on evaluating explainable AI. ACM Comput. Surv. **55**(13s), 1–42 (2023)
10. Petke, J., Haraldsson, S.O., Harman, M., Langdon, W.B., White, D.R., Woodward, J.R.: Genetic improvement of software: a comprehensive survey. IEEE Trans. Evol. Comput. **22**(3), 415–432 (2017)
11. Sobania, D., Briesch, M., Hanna, C., Petke, J.: An analysis of the automatic bug fixing performance of ChatGPT. In: 2023 IEEE/ACM International Workshop on Automated Program Repair (APR), pp. 23–30. IEEE Computer Society (2023)
12. Yuan, Y., Banzhaf, W.: Toward better evolutionary program repair: an integrated approach. ACM Trans. Softw. Eng. Methodol. (TOSEM) **29**(1), 1–53 (2020)

Enhancing Genetic Improvement Mutations Using Large Language Models

Alexander E. I. Brownlee[1]([✉])(iD), James Callan[2](iD), Karine Even-Mendoza[3](iD),
Alina Geiger[4](iD), Carol Hanna[2](iD), Justyna Petke[2](iD), Federica Sarro[2](iD),
and Dominik Sobania[4](iD)

[1] University of Stirling, Stirling, UK
`alexander.brownlee@stir.ac.uk`
[2] University College London, London, UK
[3] King's College London, London, UK
[4] Johannes Gutenberg University Mainz, Mainz, Germany

Abstract. Large language models (LLMs) have been successfully applied to software engineering tasks, including program repair. However, their application in search-based techniques such as Genetic Improvement (GI) is still largely unexplored. In this paper, we evaluate the use of LLMs as mutation operators for GI to improve the search process. We expand the *Gin* Java GI toolkit to call OpenAI's API to generate edits for the JCodec tool. We randomly sample the space of edits using 5 different edit types. We find that the number of patches passing unit tests is up to 75% higher with LLM-based edits than with standard Insert edits. Further, we observe that the patches found with LLMs are generally less diverse compared to standard edits. We ran GI with local search to find runtime improvements. Although many improving patches are found by LLM-enhanced GI, the best improving patch was found by standard GI.

Keywords: Large language models · Genetic Improvement

1 Introduction

As software systems grow larger and more complex, significant manual effort is required to maintain them [2]. To reduce developer effort in software maintenance and optimization tasks, automated paradigms are essential. Genetic Improvement (GI) [15] applies search-based techniques to improve non-functional properties of existing software such as execution time as well as functional properties like repairing bugs. Although GI has had success in industry [12,13], it remains limited by the set of mutation operators it employs in the search [14].

Large Language Models (LLMs) have a wide range of applications as they are able to process textual queries without additional training for the particular task at hand. LLMs have been pre-trained on millions of code repositories spanning many different programming languages [5]. Their use for software engineering tasks has had great success [9], showing promise also for program repair [17,19].

P. Arcaini et al. (Eds.): SSBSE 2023, LNCS 14415, pp. 153–159, 2024.
https://doi.org/10.1007/978-3-031-48796-5_13

Kang and Yoo [10] have suggested that there is untapped potential in using
LLMs to enhance GI. GI uses the same mutation operators for different optimization tasks. These operators are hand-crafted prior to starting the search
and thus result in a limited search space. We hypothesize that augmenting LLM
patch suggestions as an additional mutation operator will enrich the search space
and result in more successful variants.

In this paper, we conduct several experiments to explore whether using LLMs
as a mutation operator in GI can improve the efficiency and efficacy of the search.
Our results show that the LLM-generated patches have compilation rates of
51.32% and 53.54% for random search and local search, respectively (with the
MEDIUM prompt category). Previously LLMs (using an LLM model as-is) were
shown to produce code that compiled roughly 40% of the time [16,18]. We find
that randomly sampled LLM-based edits compiled and passed unit tests more
often compared to standard GI edits. We observe that the number of patches
passing unit tests is up to 75% higher for LLM-based edits than GI INSERT edits.
However, we observe that patches found with LLMs are less diverse. For local
search, the best improvement is achieved using standard GI STATEMENT edits,
followed by LLM-based edits. These findings demonstrate the potential of LLMs
as mutation operators and highlight the need for further research in this area.
To the best of our knowledge this is the first work investigating the use of LLMs
for enhancing GI mutations. We refer the reader to the survey by Fan et al. [6]
for other uses of LLMs in Software Engineering .

2   Experimental Setup

To analyze the use of LLMs as a mutation operator in GI, we used the GPT
3.5 Turbo model by OpenAI and the GI toolbox Gin [3]. We experimented with
two types of search implemented within Gin: random search and local search.
Requests to the LLM using the OpenAI API were via the Langchain4J library,
with a temperature of 0.7. The target project for improvement in our experiments
was the popular JCodec [7] project which is written in Java. 'Hot' methods to
be targeted by the edits were identified using Gin's profiler tool by repeating the
profiling 20 times and taking the union of the resulting set.

For the random sampling experiments, we set up the runs with statement-
level edits (copy/delete/replace/swap from [14] and insert break/continue/return
from [4]) and LLM edits, generating 1000 of each type at random. A timeout of
10000 milliseconds was used for each unit test to catch infinite loops introduced
by edits; exceeding the timeout counts as a test failure. For local search, experiments were set up similarly. There were 10 repeat runs (one for each of the top
10 hot methods) but the runs were limited to 100 evaluations resulting in 1000
evaluations in total, matching the random search. In practice this was 99 edits
per run as the first was used to time the original unpatched code.

We experimented with three different prompts for sending requests to the
LLM for both types of search: a SIMPLE prompt, a MEDIUM prompt, and a
DETAILED prompt. With all three prompts, our implementation requests five dif-
ferent variations of the code at hand. The SIMPLE prompt only requests the code

---

Give me 5 different Java implementations of this method body:
` ` `

<code>
` ` `

This code belongs to project <projectname>.
Wrap all code in curly braces, if it is not already.
Do not include any method or class declarations.
label all code as java.

Fig. 1. The MEDIUM prompt for LLM requests, with line breaks added for readability.

without any additional information. The MEDIUM prompt provides more information about the code provided and the requirements, as shown in Fig. 1. Specifically, we provide the LLM with the programming language used, the project that the code belongs to, as well as formatting instructions. The DETAILED prompt extends the MEDIUM prompt with an example of a useful change. This example was taken from results obtained by Brownlee et al. [4]. The patch is a successful instance of the INSERT edit applied to the jCodec project (i.e., an edit that compiled, passed the unit tests and offered a speedup over the original code). We use the same example for all the DETAILED prompt requests used in our experiments; this is because LLMs are capable of inductive reasoning where the user presents specific information, and the LLM can use that input to generate more general statements, further improved in GPT-4 [8].

LLM edits are applied by selecting a block statement at random in a target 'hot' method. This block's content is <code> in the prompt. The first code block in the LLM response is identified. Gin uses JavaParser (https://javaparser.org) internally to represent target source files, so we attempt to parse the LLM suggestion with JavaParser, and replace the original block with the LLM suggestion.

3   Results

The first experiment compares standard GI mutations, namely INSERT and STATEMENT edits, with LLM edits using differently detailed prompts (SIMPLE, MEDIUM, and DETAILED) using Random Sampling. Table 1 shows results for all patches as well as for unique patches only. We report how many patches were successfully parsed by JavaParser (named as Valid), how many compiled, and how many passed all unit tests (named as Passed). We excluded patches syntactically equivalent to the original software. Best results are in **bold**.

We see that although substantially more valid patches were found with the standard INSERT and STATEMENT edits, more passing patches could be found by using the LLM-generated edits. In particular, for the MEDIUM, and DETAILED prompts 292 and 230 patches passed the unit tests, respectively. For the INSERT and STATEMENT edits only 166 and 91 passed the unit tests, respectively. Anecdotally, the hot methods with lowest/highest patch pass rates differed for each operator: understanding this variation will be interesting for future investigation.

Table 1. Results of our Random Sampling experiment. We exclude patches syntactically equivalent to the original software in this table. For all and unique patches we report: how many patches passed JavaParser, compiled, and passed all unit tests.

EditCategory	Unique				All			
	Patches	Valid	Compiled	Passed	Patches	Valid	Compiled	Passed
STATEMENT	896	**819**	199	80	967	**869**	227	91
INSERT	785	785	**284**	**161**	860	860	295	166
SIMPLE	193	0	0	0	1000	0	0	0
MEDIUM	324	260	183	154	645	463	**331**	**292**
DETAILED	332	268	126	110	606	456	250	230

Table 2. Local Search results. We exclude all empty patches. We report how many patches compiled, passed all unit tests, and how many led to improvements in runtime. We report best improvement found and median improvement among improving patches.

EditCategory	Patches	Compiled	Passed	ImpFound	BestImp(ms)	Median(ms)
STATEMENT	990	213	105	71	**508.0**	137.0
INSERT	948	414	264	136	313.0	81.0
SIMPLE	990	2	2	2	176.0	**137.5**
MEDIUM	990	**530**	520	164	395.0	75.5
DETAILED	990	379	369	**196**	316.0	95.0

It is also notable that LLM patches are less diverse: over 50% more unique patches were found by standard mutation operators than the LLM using MEDIUM, and DETAILED prompts. With the SIMPLE prompt, however, not a single patch passed the unit tests, since the suggested edits often could not be parsed. Thus detailed prompts are necessary to force LLM to generate usable outputs.

We investigated further the differences between MEDIUM and DETAILED prompts to understand the reduction in performance with DETAILED (in the unique patches sets) as MEDIUM had a higher number of compiled and passed patches. In both prompt levels, the generated response was the same for 42 cases (out of the total unique valid cases). However, DETAILED tended to generate longer responses with an average of 363 characters, whereas MEDIUM had an average of 304 characters. We manually examined several DETAILED prompt responses, in which we identified some including variables from other files, potentially offering a significant expansion of the set of code variants GI can explore.

The second experiment expands our analysis, comparing the performance of the standard and LLM edits with Local Search. Table 2 shows the results of the Local Search experiment. We report the number of compiling and passing patches as well as the number of patches were runtime improvements were found. Furthermore, we report the median and best improvement in milliseconds (ms). In the table, we excluded all empty patches. As before, best results are in **bold**.

Again, we see that more patches passing the unit tests could be found with the LLM using the MEDIUM, and DETAILED prompts. In addition, more improvements could be found by using the LLM with these prompts. Specifically, with MEDIUM and DETAILED, we found 164 and 196 improvements, respectively, while we only found 136 with INSERT and 71 with STATEMENT. The best improvement could be found with 508 ms with the STATEMENT edit. The best improvement found using LLMs (using the MEDIUM prompt) was only able to improve the runtime by 395 ms. We also examined a series of edits in Local Search results to gain insights into the distinctions between MEDIUM and DETAILED prompts due to the low compilation rate of DETAILED prompt's responses. In the example, a sequence of edits aimed to inline a call to function CLIP. The DETAILED prompt tried to incorporate the call almost immediately within a few edits, likely leading to invalid code. On the other hand, the MEDIUM prompt made less radical changes, gradually refining the code. It began by replacing the ternary operator expression with an if-then-else statement and system function calls before eventually attempting to inline the CLIP function call.

4 Conclusions and Future Work

Genetic improvement of software is highly dependent on the mutation operators it utilizes in the search process. To diversify the operators and enrich the search space further, we incorporated a Large Language Model (LLM) as an operator.

Limitations. To generalise, future work should consider projects besides our target, jCodec. Our experiments used an API giving us no control over the responses generated by the LLM or any way of modifying or optimizing them. Though we did not observe changes in behaviour during our experiments, OpenAI may change the model at any time, so future work should consider local models. We experimented with only three prompt types for LLM requests and within this limited number of prompts found a variation in the results. Finally, our implementation for parsing the responses from the LLMs was relatively simplistic. However, this would only mean that our reported results are pessimistic and an even larger improvement might be achieved by the LLM-based operator.

Summary. We found that, although more valid and diverse patches were found with standard edits using Random Sampling, more patches passing the unit tests were found with LLM-based edits. For example, with the LLM edit using the MEDIUM prompt, we found over 75% more patches passing the unit tests than with the classic INSERT edit. In our Local Search experiment, we found the best improvement with the STATEMENT edit (508 ms). The best LLM-based improvement was found with the MEDIUM prompt (395 ms). Thus there is potential in exploring approaches combining both LLM and 'classic' GI edits.

Our experiments revealed that the prompts used for LLM requests greatly affect the results. Thus, in future work, we hope to experiment more with prompt engineering. It might also be helpful to mix prompts: e.g., starting with MEDIUM then switching to DETAILED to make larger edits that break out of local minima. Further, the possibility of combining LLM edits with others such as standard copy/delete/replace/swap or PAR templates [11] could be interesting. Finally, we hope to conduct more extensive experimentation on additional test programs.

Acknowledgements. This work was supported by the UKRI EPSRC grant no. EP/P023991/1 and the ERC advanced fellowship grant no. 741278.

Data Availability Statement. The code, LLMs prompt and experimental infrastructure, data from the evaluation, and results are available as open source at [1]. The code is also under the 'llm' branch of github.com/gintool/gin (commit 9fe9bdf; branched from master commit 2359f57 pending full integration with Gin).

References

1. Artifact of Enhancing Genetic Improvement Mutations Using Large Language Models. Zenodo (2023). https://doi.org/10.5281/zenodo.8304433
2. Böhme, M., Soremekun, E.O., Chattopadhyay, S., Ugherughe, E., Zeller, A.: Where is the bug and how is it fixed? an experiment with practitioners. In: Proceedings of ACM Symposium on the Foundations of Software Engineering, pp. 117–128 (2017)
3. Brownlee, A.E., Petke, J., Alexander, B., Barr, E.T., Wagner, M., White, D.R.: Gin: genetic improvement research made easy. In: GECCO, pp. 985–993 (2019)
4. Brownlee, A.E., Petke, J., Rasburn, A.F.: Injecting shortcuts for faster running Java code. In: IEEE CEC 2020, pp. 1–8 (2020)
5. Chen, M., et al.: Evaluating large language models trained on code. arXiv preprint arXiv:2107.03374 (2021)
6. Fan, A., et al.: Large language models for software engineering: survey and open problems (2023)
7. Github - jcodec/jcodec: Jcodec main repo. https://github.com/jcodec/jcodec
8. Han, S.J., Ransom, K.J., Perfors, A., Kemp, C.: Inductive reasoning in humans and large language models. Cogn. Syst. Res. **83**, 101155 (2023)
9. Hou, X., et al.: Large language models for software engineering: a systematic literature review. arXiv:2308.10620 (2023)
10. Kang, S., Yoo, S.: Towards objective-tailored genetic improvement through large language models. arXiv:2304.09386 (2023)
11. Kim, D., Nam, J., Song, J., Kim, S.: Automatic patch generation learned from human-written patches (2013). http://logging.apache.org/log4j/
12. Kirbas, S., et al.: On the introduction of automatic program repair in bloomberg. IEEE Softw. **38**(4), 43–51 (2021)
13. Marginean, A., et al.: Sapfix: automated end-to-end repair at scale. In: ICSE-SEIP, pp. 269–278 (2019)
14. Petke, J., Alexander, B., Barr, E.T., Brownlee, A.E., Wagner, M., White, D.R.: Program transformation landscapes for automated program modification using Gin. Empir. Softw. Eng. **28**(4), 1–41 (2023)
15. Petke, J., Haraldsson, S.O., Harman, M., Langdon, W.B., White, D.R., Woodward, J.R.: Genetic improvement of software: a comprehensive survey. IEEE Trans. Evol. Comput. **22**, 415–432 (2018)

16. Siddiq, M.L., Santos, J., Tanvir, R.H., Ulfat, N., Rifat, F.A., Lopes, V.C.: Exploring the effectiveness of large language models in generating unit tests. arXiv preprint arXiv:2305.00418 (2023)
17. Sobania, D., Briesch, M., Hanna, C., Petke, J.: An analysis of the automatic bug fixing performance of chatGPT. In: 2023 IEEE/ACM International Workshop on Automated Program Repair (APR), pp. 23–30. IEEE Computer Society (2023)
18. Xia, C.S., Paltenghi, M., Tian, J.L., Pradel, M., Zhang, L.: Universal fuzzing via large language models. arXiv preprint arXiv:2308.04748 (2023)
19. Xia, C.S., Zhang, L.: Keep the conversation going: fixing 162 out of 337 bugs for $0.42 each using chatgpt. arXiv preprint arXiv:2304.00385 (2023)

SearchGEM5: Towards Reliable Gem5 with Search Based Software Testing and Large Language Models

Aidan Dakhama[1](✉)(iD), Karine Even-Mendoza[1](✉)(iD), W.B. Langdon[2](✉)(iD), Hector Menendez[1](✉)(iD), and Justyna Petke[2](✉)(iD)

[1] King's College London, London, UK
{aidan.dakhama,karine.even_mendoza,hector.menendez}@kcl.ac.uk
[2] University College London, London, UK
{w.langdon,j.petke}@ucl.ac.uk

Abstract. We introduce a novel automated testing technique that combines LLM and search-based fuzzing. We use ChatGPT to parameterise C programs. We compile the resultant code snippets, and feed compilable ones to `SearchGEM5`, our extension to `AFL++` fuzzer with customised new mutation operators. We run thus created 4005 binaries through our system under test, `gem5`, increasing its existing test coverage by more than 1000 lines. We discover 244 instances where `gem5` simulation of the binary differs from the binary's expected behaviour.

Keywords: AI · LLM · SBSE · SBFT · genetic improvement of tests

1 Introduction

Testing plays a key role in software's lifecycle. Today test generation is often expensive, tedious and labor-intensive. Instead, we propose to automate software testing by combining large language models (LLMs) and search-based techniques and demonstrate this on `gem5`.

Creating a test suite for `gem5` is challenging. `gem5` simulates software execution on different architectures, either processor micro-architectures or system-level. `gem5` is a large piece of code (1.34 million lines of code, LOC). Considering that the set of test inputs for `gem5` is a combination of both the architecture simulation and the program that runs within that simulation, the space of possible inputs for testing is exponentially large.

We propose a novel way of testing `gem5`. First, starting from a mix-collection of (1) industry-standard C compiler test suites and (2) tutorial programs, Chat-GPT (GPT 3.5) [14] automatically creates a set of parameterized C programs with information on how to execute it. The *information* is a valid value of arguments and their data types, upon which the parameterized C program terminates normally. *Arguments* are the real values passed to the program. By compiling the LLM-generated parameterized C programs, we construct a corpus of test inputs. A *test input* is a **binary** and its **information**. Second, we extend `AFL++`, a coverage-based fuzzer [9,18]. To generate new test inputs, we have introduced

P. Arcaini et al. (Eds.): SSBSE 2023, LNCS 14415, pp. 160–166, 2024.
https://doi.org/10.1007/978-3-031-48796-5_14

custom mutators. These can modify (i) a binary using bit-flips. (ii) its arguments with their data types (e.g., mutating 0:INT32 to 55:INT32).

To check whether our generated test inputs lead to errors in gem5, we use feedback from AFL++ (crash testing) and the resultant binary run on the given architecture as an *automatic test oracle*: if gem5 produces the same result, we deem the test run as successful. We treat it as a potential bug otherwise. We generated 4005 unique test inputs, 244 of which caused gem5 to produce behaviour different to the one observed when the binary was run outside of gem5.

2   SearchGEM5

A single test input for gem5 is composed of a binary file (--binary) and its arguments (--options). Consequently, to test gem5, we need a set of binaries. These binaries can be generated in two ways: 1) Compiling programs, which yield the desired binaries; 2) Alternatively, we can create binaries by mutating an existing binary. We first select a set of example programs and use a Large Language Model (LLM) to create variants that extract internal parameters as program arguments. We compile them. Subsequently, we diversify them using AFL++ and our custom mutators.

1. **Test Input** We use LLM to generate a set of C programs suitable for testing gem5. We use a BASH script to amend minor errors.
2. **Coverage-Guided Mutation-Based Fuzz Testing** using AFL++ [9,18].
3. **Differential Testing** Per test case, we compare the result from gem5 to the actual test execution.

Creating a Corpus of Programs. We create a corpus of parameterized test inputs. To execute a single test in gem5, we need: the program binary that gem5 simulates; its arguments; and their types (e.g. 32-bit int). We generate the binary by compiling programs obtained from LLM. We also prompt LLM for a file containing the program's arguments and their types.

Training LLM to Generate Test Inputs. We have three prompts to train it: 1) a simple prompt that describes the task using a small C code and a free text description; 2) a prompt that gives an example of a good response; 3) a prompt that gives an example of a wrong response with a short explanation of what is not valid. Then we automatically construct a prompt with many programs from a single source (e.g., a single git repository):

```
"I will give you a set of N programs from source X, can you generate
a pair per program with an input sample and its type information for the
second program? These are the programs: (name: code, name: code,...)".
```

The LLM returns pairs of programs, consisting of the original C program and its parameterized counterpart, plus, for each argument, an example of a valid argument (input value) and its type (e.g., 5 INT32). (The original program is for sanity checks and types are needed by SearchGEM5 when it mutates an input.)

The sources of programs used with LLM are: c-testsuite, the LLVM test suite and C Examples. The programs that have no arguments or fail to compile are invalid. We try up to three times to automatically fix them, either using a BASH script for known problems (e.g., missing includes) or by asking the LLM again.

Fuzzing. We use AFL++ fork [9] of the American Fuzzy Lop (AFL) fuzzer [18]. AFL++ operates by taking an initial set of files each of which is an input to the System Under Test (SUT) and instrumenting the SUT to measure test coverage. Whilst running, AFL++ uses code coverage to guide its search towards previously untested code. The next section describes our extension of AFL++ for gem5, with its complex test inputs, using a coverage-guided mutational approach.

Custom AFL++ Mutation Operators. We have extended AFL++ by reimplementing the mutation operators and part of the mutation strategy though we still make use of AFL++ coverage selection criteria. This enables the selection of specific test input from the corpus and mutation of its binary file, arguments or their types, based on the test coverage data collected by AFL++ for each test input.

We have introduced two mutation operators of a test input for gem5: 1) bit-flip operator to edit a program's compiled binary file and 2) an operator to edit the value of its arguments. We do not mutate gem5 itself. Operator (2) uses type information so that the arguments remain valid.

We have implemented the extension to AFL++ in a new tool, SearchGEM5. SearchGEM5 evaluates new test inputs in the form of binary name, arguments list, types. SearchGEM5 then uses this information to carry our mutation operators either directly on the compiled binaries or to their arguments.

Experimental Setup. The corpus of C programs was created using ChatGPT (August 3, 2023) GPT-3.5-turbo. The compiler was GCC-11, except for coverage measurements done with gcov-9 due to gem5's requirements. The Python script chosen is an example file provided by the SSBSE Challenge Track 2023 organisers, in particular, hello-custom-binary.py. SearchGEM5 uses AFL++ as the search engine, using its default parameters.

We ran our experiments on a single virtual machine with 8 virtual CPU Cores and 72 GB RAM, running Ubuntu 20.04.2 LTS x86_64. The host had a single AMD EPYC 7313P CPU (single socket, 3.0 GHz, 16 cores, 2 threads per CPU).

3 Results

We evaluated SearchGEM5 on its test generation capabilities, coverage, bug finding and efforts required to reproduce the results. We provide further details about the discovered bugs at [2].

Test Generation. To assess the reliability of LLMs as a source of test cases for gem5 when given the prescribed test framework, we aim to evaluate: **(RQ1)** to what extent can GPT-3.5-turbo effectively generate parameterized C programs for gem5 that adhere to the specified requirements (see Sect. 2).

Beyond the basic prompt, we presented GPT-3.5-turbo extra examples: 1) pairs of a valid C program and a valid input for it and 2) pairs of a valid C program but with an invalid input. We ran GPT-3.5-turbo for 25 h, often waiting due to usage limits. With GPT-4 and no subscription limits, results could be obtained within minutes. We generated **1869 C parameterized files:** 1086 compiled ok with GCC-11 -O3, forming a valid set of LLM-generated test programs for AFL++. AFL++ used 744 out of 1086 GPT-3.5-turbo test inputs whilst searching for new tests (AFL++ ignored 342 test inputs, usually because of invalid arguments). During 10 days run, AFL++ generated further **2136** unique mutated test inputs. *In total,* SearchGEM5 generated **4005** unique tests, with 3222 of them becoming binaries.

Test Coverage. Our objective is to evaluate the gap between LLM-generated test inputs and the overall coverage achieved by our hybrid approach, which combines LLMs with AFL++ search for additional coverage leveraging our novel mutation operators. **(RQ2)** What is the coverage of LLM- and AFL++-generated test inputs? Can AFL++ improve the basic coverage achieved by LLM-generated ones in gem5?

For coverage measurements, we used 1086 and 2136 distinct binaries generated using LLM and AFL++, respectively. We built gem5 with g++ 9.4 -O1 and gcov, adding gcov instrumentation overheads. We measured a smaller part of the gem5 codebase, i.e. that relevant only to X86. We used the gcov-based tool gfauto[10] to generate the coverage results in a human-readable format for 3380 files in the gem5 codebase (including header and system header files). The LLM-generated test inputs achieved a total of 39,143 lines of coverage on the gem5 codebase. While our AFL++ covered 40,337 lines, an extra 1,194 lines (inclusive).

Bug Finding in gem5. Our primary objective here is to estimate the effectiveness of our approach in uncovering bugs within gem5. That is, **(RQ3)** how effective is our approach at finding bugs in gem5?

We have found panic crashes, assertion violations, crashes, hangs and missimulation bugs in gem5 summarized in Table 1. We have investigated and classified all the crashes, identifying two different types of assertion violations and 10 different panic crashes in the gem5 codebase. Although the hangs may be caused by several different issues, they are grouped together in Table 1 (none of them are associated with pending inputs or lack of resources).

For example, a test input on line #14 of Table 1 was generated by GPT-3.5-turbo. It was incorrectly simulated by gem5 (running without simulating the operating system as well as the program, SE mode), resulting in a different output than the native X86 run. During the simulation with gem5, with an invalid input, the program terminated wrongly with an exit code 0. However the same combination of program and bad input led to the program, on reaching line 11 when run on a native X86 being terminated with a segmentation

Table 1. List of errors in `gem5` found with `SearchGEM5`-generated test inputs. Mutation operations: **B** = Binary bit-flip; **C** = Constants bit-flip of arguments; **B/C** = B and/or C; **B (C optional)** = B with or without C; **ANY** = LLM-generated or B/C. #**Input**: distinct test inputs of the same bug.

#	Error Kind	Operations	#inputs	Details
1	Panic error	B	1	File exec-ns.cc.inc, line 17, "attempt to execute unimplemented instruction 'femm' (...)".
2	Panic error	B/C	52	File sim/faults.cc, line 60, "panic condition !FullSystem occurred: fault (General-Protection) detected (...)".
3	Panic error	B	4	File base/loader/elf_object.cc, line 129, "gelf_getphdr failed for segment 0 (...)".
4	Panic error	B	3	File base/loader/memory_image.hh, line 70, "panic condition offset + size >ifd->len() occurred (...)".
5	Panic error	B	1	File cpu/simple/timing.cc, line 953, "panic condition pkt->isError() occurred: Data access (...)".
6	Panic error	B (C optional)	26	File arch/x86/faults.cc, line 131, "Unrecognized/invalid instruction executed (...)".
7	Panic error	B	1	File arch/x86/faults.cc, line 164, "Tried to execute unmapped address (...)".
8	Panic error	B (C optional)	14	File arch/x86/faults.cc, line 166, "Tried to execute unmapped address (...)".
9	Panic error	B/C	61	File arch/x86/faults.cc, line 166, "Tried to read unmapped address (...)".
10	Panic error	B/C	12	File arch/x86/faults.cc, line 166, "Tried to write unmapped address (...)".
11	Crash(assert fail)	B	2	File base/loader/elf_object.cc, line 80, "virtual gem5::loader::ObjectFile*gem5::loader::ElfObjectFormat (...)".
12	Crash(assert fail)	B	1	File base/loader/elf_object.cc, line 311, "void gem5::loader::ElfObject::determineOpSys(): Assertion (...)".
13	Hangs	B/C	6	gem5hangs with a timeout of 500 s on small programs.
14	Mis-simulation	ANY	56	Invalid program is simulated as valid a program.
15	Mis-simulation	B	1	Variable's value is random in X86 but fixed in simulation.
16	Crash	C	1	X86 terminates normally but the simulation failed to parse input arguments (UnicodeDecodeError).
17	Mis-simulation	C	2	X86 and simulation had different outputs.

fault (LLM-generated program executed as `./00172.c.o 0`; available at [2]). It appears that the address space of `gem5` might mask these kinds of pointer errors, similarly to what happens with virtualization for obfuscations [15], where invalid addresses that normally belong to the operating system are part of the process address space.

Portability. `AFL++` has been applied to various targets [1,12,16,17] and hence a different target SUT should be easy. Our custom `AFL++` mutator can be re-used since we are doing target-independent bit-level mutations.

`GPT-3.5-turbo` has been trained on a wide range of code from many programming languages, such as Python and Java. By adjusting the LLM prompt and program examples to use the desired language, our method can easily be adapted to the generation of test inputs in other programming languages [5,8].

4 Conclusions

Finding bugs in complex simulation systems like gem5 [4] requires new combinations of search-based strategies (like fuzzing) and LLMs like ChatGPT to provide extensive test cases by re-purposing and improving existing benchmarks of test programs. Although the initial complexity can be discouraging because preparing the simulation system for feedback-based fuzzing tools, like AFL++ [18], requires the instrumentation of the whole system, it allows us to automatically discover new errors, which need not be the catastrophic faults, such as segmentation errors, which fuzz testing usually demands, but can be a simple but automatically recognized difference in output, which is easily detected by an internal oracle (see Sect. 3) [13]. In tandem with differential testing, we showed that it allows masked errors discovery. Our approach uses AFL++ in an unconventional way, replacing test input fuzzing with a more sophisticated input format as discussed in Sect. 2, an idea which was adopted by various domains such as compiler testing [1,3] or network protocol analysis to manipulate network protocols for fuzzing [16]. In terms of testing gem5, while there are efforts in verifying its architectural compliance [7] and the integrity of its code, gem5 testing or verification approaches [6] that can go deeper into its internals, such as SearchGEM5, are essential to validate its many possible options. The portability discussion and Table 1, which quantifies instances of test inputs per bug, offer partial insights on bug reproducibility limitations stemming from non-determinism in random testing and LLMs (Sect. 3). We defer further analysis to future research.

Acknowledgments. Authors are listed in alphabetical order. This work was supported by the UKRI EPSRC grant no. EP/P023991/1 and the UKRI TAS Hub grant no. EP/V00784X/1 and EP/V026801/2.

Data Availability Statement. SearchGEM5, the LLMs prompt and the experimental infrastructure, data, and results are freely available via [2,11].

References

1. AFL compiler fuzzer. https://github.com/agroce/afl-compiler-fuzzer
2. Artifact of SearchGEM5. Zenodo (2023). https://doi.org/10.5281/zenodo.8316685
3. Aschermann, C., Frassetto, T., Holz, T., Jauernig, P., Sadeghi, A.R., Teuchert, D.: NAUTILUS: fishing for deep bugs with grammars. In: NDSS (2019)
4. Binkert, N., et al.: The gem5 simulator. ACM SIGARCH Comput. Archit. News **39**(2), 1–7 (2011)
5. Biswas, S.: Role of ChatGPT in computer programming: ChatGPT in computer programming. Mesopotamian J. Comput. Sci. **2023**, 8–16 (2023)
6. Bossuet, L., Grosso, V., Lara-Nino, C.A.: Emulating side channel attacks on gem5: lessons learned. In: EuroS&PW, pp. 287–295. IEEE (2023)
7. Bruns, N., Herdt, V., Große, D., Drechsler, R.: Toward RISC-V CSR compliance testing. IEEE Embed. Syst. Lett. **13**(4), 202–205 (2021)

8. Destefanis, G., Bartolucci, S., Ortu, M.: A preliminary analysis on the code generation capabilities of GPT-3.5 and Bard AI models for java functions (2023)
9. Fioraldi, A., et al.: AFL++ : Combining incremental steps of fuzzing research. In: USENIX Workshop at WOOT 20. USENIX Association (2020)
10. Git repository of gfauto. https://github.com/google/graphicsfuzz.git
11. Git repository of searchGEM5. https://github.com/karineek/SearchGEM5/
12. Kersten, R., Luckow, K., Păsăreanu, C.S.: POSTER: AFL-based fuzzing for java with kelinci. In: SIGSAC, pp. 2511–2513. CCS 2017. ACM (2017)
13. Langdon, W.B., Yoo, S., Harman, M.: Inferring automatic test oracles. In: SBST, pp. 5–6. Buenos Aires, Argentina (2017)
14. Lund, B.D., Wang, T.: Chatting about ChatGPT: how may AI and GPT impact academia and libraries? Library Hi Tech News **40**(3), 26–29 (2023)
15. Menéndez, H.D., Suárez-Tangil, G.: ObfSec: measuring the security of obfuscations from a testing perspective. Expert Syst. Appl. **210**, 118298 (2022)
16. Pham, V.T., Böhme, M., Roychoudhury, A.: AFLNET: a greybox fuzzer for network protocols. In: ICST, pp. 460–465 (2020)
17. AFL's' fork for fuzzing pure Python. https://github.com/jwilk/python-afl
18. Zalewski, M.: Technical "whitepaper" for afl-fuzz. Accessed 21 Apr 2023. http://lcamtuf.coredump.cx/afl/technical_details.txt

Author Index

A
Alamir, Salwa   123
Arcuri, Andrea   52, 108
Arrieta, Aitor   84
Auer, Michael   3

B
Berger, Harel   133
Brownlee, Alexander   147
Brownlee, Alexander E. I.   153

C
Callan, James   147, 153
Chan, Kenneth H.   19
Cheng, Betty H. C.   19

D
Dakhama, Aidan   133, 160
Ding, Zishuo   133

E
Even-Mendoza, Karine   133, 153, 160

F
Fraser, Gordon   3

G
Gay, Gregory   35, 67, 140
Geiger, Alina   147, 153
Golmohammadi, Amid   108

H
Hanna, Carol   147, 153

I
Illarramendi, Miren   84

K
Kelly, David   133

L
Langdon, W.B.   160
Liu, Xiaomo   123
López, Mar Zamorano   147
Lyu, Haozhou   35, 67

M
Menendez, Hector   133, 160
Moussa, Rebecca   133, 147

P
Panichella, Annibale   101
Petke, Justyna   147, 153, 160
Pusl, Michael   3

S
Sakamoto, Maiko   35, 67
Sarro, Federica   133, 147, 153
Seran, Susruthan   52
Sobania, Dominik   147, 153

T
Tawosi, Vali   123

V
van Dinten, Imara   101

Z
Zaidman, Andy   101
Zhang, Man   52, 108

P. Arcaini et al. (Eds.): SSBSE 2023, LNCS 14415, p. 167, 2024.
https://doi.org/10.1007/978-3-031-48796-5

Printed in the United States
by Baker & Taylor Publisher Services